ERCATORS PROJECTION,

Three Voyages *with* the Tracks *of the* Ships *under his command.*

Joseph Banks'
FLORILEGIUM

Thames & Hudson

Joseph Banks'
FLORILEGIUM

Botanical Treasures from Cook's First Voyage

With texts by Mel Gooding, commentaries
on the plates by David Mabberley, and
an afterword by Joe Studholme

WITH 181 ILLUSTRATIONS

To Chris Humphries (1947–2009)

Mel Gooding is an art historian, writer and curator. He has taught at Edinburgh and Wimbledon Schools of Art, among others, and contributes regularly to the art press.

Professor David Mabberley has served as Executive Director of the Royal Botanic Gardens and Domain Trust in Sydney. He is an Emeritus Fellow at Wadham College, Oxford, Adjunct Professor at Macquarie University, Sydney, and Professor Extraordinary at the University of Leiden, The Netherlands.

Joe Studholme co-founded Editions Alecto and undertook the printing of Banks' Florilegium from the original copper plates between 1980 and 1990.

On the cover: (front) Detail of *Passiflora aurantia*, see Pl. 93, p. 196; (back) Joseph Banks' library stamp.

Endpapers: Map from *An Historical Account of the Voyages of Captain James Cook, to the Southern and Northern Hemispheres* by William Mavor (London, J. Harris, 1805). The track of *Endeavour* shown on the original map has been highlighted here in red.

Half-title: An unfinished engraving of *Acacia humifusa* by Frederick Nodder, based on his own watercolour drawing dated 1781, derived from Parkinson's surviving pencil drawing (BF 94; Diment et al., 1984: A2/106).

Title page: Ipomoea aquatica, see Pl. 145, p. 290.

First published in the United Kingdom in 2017 by Thames & Hudson Ltd, 181A High Holborn, London WC1V 7QX

This compact edition first published in 2019

Joseph Banks' Florilegium © 2017 and 2019 Thames & Hudson Ltd, London

'The Making of Banks' Florilegium' © 2017 and 2019 Mel Gooding Introduction and Commentaries on the Plates © 2017 and 2019 David Mabberley 'The Modern Printing of the Florilegium' © 2017 and 2019 Joe Studholme

Reproductions from *Banks' Florilegium* © 2017 Editions Alecto Ltd and the Trustees of the Natural History Museum

Designed by Karin Fremer

British Library Cataloguing-in-Publication Data A catalogue record for this book is available from the British Library

ISBN 978-0-500-02287-0

Printed and bound in China by C & C Offset Printing Co. Ltd

To find out about all our publications, please visit **www.thamesandhudson.com**. There you can subscribe to our e-newsletter, browse or download our current catalogue, and buy any titles that are in print.

CONTENTS

The Voyage of *Endeavour* 1768–1771

MEL GOODING

> It being the Design of the *Royal Society*, for the better attaining the End of
> their Institution to study *Nature* rather than *Books*, and from the Observations,
> made of the *Phenomena* and effects she presents, to compose such a History
> of Her, as may hereafter serve to build a Solid and Useful Philosophy upon…
>
> 'Directions for Seamen, bound for far voyages'
Royal Society *Philosophical Transactions* I, 1665/6

PLYMOUTH, 25 AUGUST 1768: 'After having waited in this place ten days, the ship, and every thing belonging to me, being all that time in perfect readyness to sail at a moments warning, we at last got a fair wind, and this day at 3 O'Clock in the even weigd anchor, and set sail, all in excellent health and spirits perfectly prepard (in Mind at least) to undergo with Chearfullness any fatigues or dangers that may occur in our intended Voyage.'[1] Thus begins the *Endeavour* journal of the young Joseph Banks (1743–1820). It is the man himself: quick and direct to the point, the language vigorously idiosyncratic and careless of stylistic finesse, yet precise, energetic and high-spirited, and animated by a generous optimism. Banks was 25 years old, in possession of an extensive inherited estate in his native Lincolnshire and a considerable fortune. Already a seasoned and intrepid traveller and a highly motivated natural historian, he was, above all, an experienced and passionate botanist.

Included among 'every thing belonging' to him was an impressive quantity of specialized equipment and the reference materials necessary for his scientific purposes. Both study and fieldwork had provided Banks with a sound understanding of what was required for such a venture. 'No people ever went to sea better fitted out for the purpose of Natural History, nor more elegantly', wrote the distinguished English botanist and marine naturalist John Ellis (*c.* 1710–1776) to the great Swedish botanist and taxonomer

Carl Linnaeus (1707–1778).[2] 'They have got a fine library of Natural History; they have all sorts of machines for catching and preserving insects; all kinds of nets, trawls, drags and hooks for coral fishing.… All this is owing to you and your writings.' In addition, of course, they had guns, and before long the captain and crew of *Endeavour* had grown accustomed to the loud reports on the upper deck that announced the death and collection of another avian specimen from the skies above the ship.

The 'fine library' of around 40 volumes that Banks took with him included, crucially, the *Systema Naturae* and *Species Plantarum* of Linnaeus himself, as well as recent volumes on South Seas exploration and discovery by the French polymath Charles de Brosses (1709–1777) and the great traveller and cartographer Alexander Dalrymple (1737–1808), who were both proponents of the existence of a great unknown Southern Continent. Also on board was everything needed for the accurate recording in drawings and paintings of botanical, marine and ornithological species, for the objective rendering of hitherto unknown topographies, and for the portrayal of the native peoples the explorers expected to encounter on the voyage, and of their dwellings and artefacts. Without question, Banks' previous natural history voyage, to Newfoundland and Labrador in 1766, had prepared him well for his highly ordered and efficient planning for *Endeavour*'s scientific programme.

The equipping of the bark *Endeavour*, a converted collier from Whitby – to which Banks contributed a prodigious sum of around ten thousand pounds – became a model for all such future voyages of scientific discovery. The Royal Society provided an array of gleaming astronomical instruments, the

Mezzotint print after the portrait of Joseph Banks by Benjamin West, painted 1771. Fresh from the Endeavour *voyage, he wears a Māori cloak of flax fringed with dog hair, and is surrounded by items he collected, including a drawing of New Zealand flax.*

best available, for the use of the ship's captain, Lieutenant James Cook (1728–1779), and his appointed astronomer, Charles Green (1735–1771), a diligent assistant observer of some years standing at the Royal Observatory at Greenwich. The equipment was essential for the fulfilment of the expedition's primary commission from both the Royal Society and the Admiralty: to sail to King George's Island, soon after known as Tahiti, and there observe and record the rare occurrence of the Transit of Venus across the face of the Sun,[3] expected on 3 June 1769.

On board *Endeavour*, Banks headed a remarkable, if small, team of highly skilled professionals. His momentous journey round the world stands in sharp contrast to those of his contemporaries of a similar age and background wealth who undertook the Grand Tour in Europe. As Benjamin West's 1771 portrait celebrating Banks' triumphant return, and Joshua Reynolds' vigorously direct portrayal begun in the same year, both so clearly indicate, he was no mere connoisseur preening with the gloss of continental sophistication. In the former, Banks the adventurer steps forward in a Māori cloak of woven flax, surrounded by Tahitian and Polynesian ceremonial objects and working tools, with a botanical album at his feet open at a drawing of the flax plant itself (*Phormium tenax*). In the latter, Banks, man of action and scholar, dynamically turns to the spectator, fist clenched over his working papers, on one of which is scrawled '*cras ingens iterabimus aequor*': 'tomorrow we will sail once more the vast ocean'. The truly grand tour around the globe on which Banks had knowingly embarked was both arduous and hazardous, and for all his good-natured love of life, sex, food, drink and adventure, his total professional dedication was to the increase and improvement of scientific knowledge and the scope of natural philosophy.

To these ends, and with the requirements of accurate recording and eventual publication always in mind, he had recruited (again at his own cost) two excellent young artists, Sydney Parkinson (1745–1771) and Alexander Buchan (d. 1769). Parkinson, a young Scot from Edinburgh, was a fine and dedicated botanical draughtsman and painter, whom Banks had met at 'The Vineyard', the Hammersmith nursery of his friend, the highly respected botanist and plantsman James Lee (1715–1795). Banks immediately employed Parkinson to paint the specimens (plants, fish and birds) he had collected on his previous voyage, to Newfoundland and Labrador. Alexander Buchan was also from Edinburgh, and had possibly met Parkinson at the design school set up there (officially encouraged, the first of its kind in Scotland) by the French artist William Delacour (1700–1767). Little is known of Buchan, save that he was regarded as a skilled depicter of landscapes and people. He was, however, also

a chronic epileptic, and was to die of a seizure soon after *Endeavour* reached Tahiti, with little achieved except some drawings of the Tierra del Fuegans, their huts and artefacts, and a handful of insect and marine invertebrate studies.

Chief among Banks' party, and his close collaborator ever after, was the distinguished and assiduous Swedish naturalist and taxonomist Dr Daniel Solander (1733–1782), who had studied under Linnaeus before becoming his esteemed colleague and editor of his work, in the years when Uppsala was the epicentre of the revolution in botany and taxonomy. Solander had arrived in London in 1760 to catalogue, according to the Linnaean system, the natural history collections at the recently opened British Museum, and was soon elected to the prestigious Royal Society. He had also already assisted Banks in the cataloguing of the diverse materials from his previous expedition, and at a dinner early in 1768 he immediately and impulsively volunteered to go with his botanical friend on the projected voyage to the South Seas.

With the amiable Solander came his invaluable secretary and factotum, Herman Spöring (1733–1771), a precise Finn

Sydney Parkinson, here in a possible self-portrait, was one of two artists who accompanied Banks on the Endeavour *voyage. His principal task was to record the plants collected by Banks and Solander. He produced almost 1,500 works before he died at sea aged only 25.*

Dr Daniel Solander, a favourite pupil of Carl Linnaeus, was an indispensable member of Banks' team on board Endeavour. *He enthusiastically collected botanical specimens, and then dried, recorded and named them throughout the voyage. Society portraitist Johan Zoffany painted him here in c. 1776.*

of exceptional talents, which included botanical and topographical drawing, as well as clock- and instrument-making. It was Spöring who ably took care of the precious scientific instruments on board *Endeavour*, and who, after the death of Buchan, undertook the drawing of some of the coastal profiles that complemented Cook's cartography. He died, as did so many others, including Parkinson, on the Indian Ocean journey back from Batavia (now Jakarta) to Cape Town, and was remembered by Banks as a 'grave, thinking man'.

None of the party could have anticipated the magnitude and diversity of the eventual achievements – cartographical, scientific and ethnological – of the voyage. Banks himself was aware at the outset, as was Cook, that *Endeavour* was bound for a longer and more speculative journey than the initial sailing to Tahiti, and with a different purpose. For Cook carried with him sealed orders from the Admiralty that instructed him, after the observation of the Transit of Venus on Tahiti, to put again to sea on an exploratory quest of considerable geopolitical significance: 'Whereas there is reason to imagine that a Continent or Land of great extent may be found…. You are to proceed to the Southward in order to make discovery [and take British ownership] of the Continent abovementioned.' There was, of course, no such continent, at least as they imagined it – the fabled

Terra Australis Incognita – in that direction. In the event, Cook was to persevere in this effort southward for about 2,780 kilometres (1,500 miles) over 20 degrees of latitude and three weeks of hard sailing, until at latitude 40 degrees south, and in increasingly bad weather, he doubled back and finally set a course westward towards New Zealand. Cook had satisfied himself that the 'unknown continent' did not exist.

With respect to the scientific purposes of the voyage, work began on board *Endeavour* almost immediately after setting sail, with lively and enthusiastic observations of things great and very small. On the evening of the second day at sea, Banks (notwithstanding chronic seasickness) reported on a school of porpoises; two days later he and Solander examined 'a very minute sea insect' (an aquatic springtail) taken in a cask, and gathered several jellyfish 'whose different motions of swimming amus'd us very much'; on 4 September 1768 they netted a number of salps (translucent invertebrates related to sea squirts):

> shining in the water with very beautifull Colours; but another insect which we took today was possest of more beautiful Colouring than any thing in nature I have ever seen, hardly excepting gemms. He is of a new genus [Banks was correct in this supposition] … this which we called *opalinum* shone in the water with all the splendor and variety of colours that we observe in a real opal; he livd in the Glass of salt water in which he was put for examination several hours; darting about with great agility, and at every motion shewing an almost infinite variety of changeable colours.

They were surprised that evening to see crabs in great number, swimming 'as if the surface of the water and not the bottom was their Proper station'; they correctly identified the creatures as those named by Linnaeus '*cancer depurator*' (later *Liocarcinus depurator*). The two naturalists 'went to bed well contented with the Produce of the day'.

The first landfall was at Funchal, Madeira, on 13 September 1768. Sydney Parkinson was moved to write lyrically in his journal that the country was 'cultivated to the very tops of the mountains; and, being covered with vines, citrons, oranges, and many other fine fruit-trees, it appears like one wide, extended, beautiful, garden.'[4] Banks and Solander went ashore, where they were welcomed to stay at the home of the British consul, and immediately set about the first serious botanizing of the voyage. Thomas Heberden (1703–1769), the island physician, was an able naturalist, and greatly assisted them with information and written records of his own investigations. Of over 200 specimens they collected, many were already known and named, and of 21 hitherto unknown plants painted by Parkinson, only 11 were eventually to be engraved for publication.[5] In nice examples of original nomenclature, the pretty, low-growing creeper Madeira moneywort was named *Sibthorpia peregrina* (Pl. 3, p. 26), after Banks' famously inactive professor of botany at Oxford, Humphrey Sibthorp (1713–1797), and the helpful Heberden was commemorated by *Heberdenia bahamensis* (Pl. 2, p. 24), the subject of a beautiful completed drawing by Parkinson (in which it is named as *Heberdenia excelsa*).

Five days after arrival, *Endeavour*, now loaded with casks of Madeira wine[6] and clean water, and fresh meat and vegetables, sailed southwest out of Funchal and headed across the South Atlantic for Brazil. An eagerly anticipated landfall was made on 13 November at the spectacular port city of Rio de Janeiro. However, the crew, the marines and Banks' 'gentlemen' were forbidden to land by the Portuguese governor, who doubted that their modest bark was a *bona fide* Royal Navy vessel. No one but the captain

was allowed to go ashore, and then only under supervision and in order to purchase supplies. This proved to be irksome to the upright and punctilious Cook, who wanted work done on the ship, and infuriating to the naturalists, tantalized by the extraordinary botanical richness and lushness of the vegetation clearly visible around the city and on the steep hills above it. But clandestine and highly risky forays ashore yielded a rewarding number of specimens, as did the plenteous greenery fetched aboard for the livestock. Parkinson was able to make many drawings of the abundant fish in the harbour, and he was also directed to draw nearly 40 of the plant specimens, 23 of which were later to be engraved for publication. On 5 December, as they awaited a fair wind, the exasperated Banks wrote of the governor in his journal: 'many curses were this day expended on his excellence'.

There followed the most arduous passage on the outward voyage. *Endeavour* sailed due southwest, standing well off the east coast of South America. The further south they travelled, the colder it became, and all on board were issued with naval

While confined on board Endeavour *in Rio de Janeiro harbour, Parkinson sketched these dolphins and fish. Later in the voyage, he produced a huge number of annotated sketches of fresh plant specimens, which had to be recorded swiftly before they wilted in the tropical or sub-tropical conditions (see p. 301).*

winter gear, or donned their own. Cook was a phlegmatic, determined voyager, personally courageous, but never fool-hardy: he had a job to do, one that in itself was full of dangers, but he was averse to any subsidiary and unnecessary risk, and held the lives of all his seamen, at every level, as sacrosanct. His strictest discipline, enforced by judicious but not excessive (by contemporary standards) use of the lash, was reserved for matters concerning any threat to the safety and wellbeing of those on board (or, where appropriate, on shore) and for the observance of measures designed to promote health. He was a pioneer of antiscorbutic dietary regimes, and he insisted on the aeration and fumigation of the lower decks, and on the continuous and rigorous cleaning of all quarters. As a consequence, though a few suffered slightly from scurvy, none died of it on the voyage.

Cook's first objective was to reach Tahiti in time to prepare thoroughly for the Transit of Venus. In spite of entreaties from Banks, who was keen to be the first to botanize on the islands, he therefore refused to land on the Falklands, and continued to beat south and southwest to Tierra del Fuego, the archipelago that forms the southernmost tip of the continent. It was hereabouts he would seek to land to take on fresh water and firewood, before undertaking the difficult and dangerous rounding of Cape Horn and embarking on the long haul across the South Pacific towards Tahiti.

Something of the irrepressible enthusiasm that drove Banks, Solander and their party can be felt in journal entries made on their arrival at that bleak location, in the bitter cold of Antarctic winds, snow and hail. On 12 January 1769, the 'land of fires' first came into sight. Banks' journal recounts:

> When we were nearest in we could plainly discover with our glasses spots in which the colour of white and yellow were predominant which we judg'd to be flowers, the white were in large clusters almost every where, the yellow in small spots or patches on the side of a hill coverd with a beautifull verdure; the trees could now be distinguishd very plainly and seemd to be 30 or 40 feet high with flat bushy tops, their trunks in many places were bare and resembled rocks a good deal till the glasses cleard up the deception.

Two days later, Cook, although unable to anchor inshore, patiently allowed a preliminary botanical sortie, described by Banks: 'we found ourselves the third time drove out, wind SSW, Short sea and ship pitching most violently. The Captn stood into a bay just without Cape St Vincent and while the ship plyd off and on Dr Solander and myself went ashore in the boat and found many plants, about 100, tho

A WOMAN *of the Island of* TERRA DEL FUEGO.

Alexander Buchan's task as artist on the voyage was to record the landscapes and people, though he was not able to achieve much before his death from epilepsy on Tahiti. While in Tierra del Fuego he made several drawings of the inhabitants, taking care to depict their clothing, ornaments, hairstyles and habitations.

we were not ashore above 4 hours; of these I may say every one was new and intirely different from what either of us had before seen.' Parkinson reported: 'Mr. Banks and Dr. Solander collected a great number of plants, shot several birds, and returned to the ship much pleased with their adventure.' The indulgent Cook's laconic response suggests a certain seamanlike scepticism: 'At 9 they return'd on board bringing with them several Plants Flowers, etc. most of them unknown in Europe and in that alone consisted their whole Value.'

Cook finally anchored in the inappropriately named Bay of Good Success, where Banks and Solander immediately undertook an extended foray inland to gather specimens with a party of 'gentlemen' (including Green the astronomer), seamen and servants. At nightfall, foul weather trapped them on the hills above the shore, and during the second night two of Banks' servants, drunk and sadly incapable on ill-gotten rum, froze to death in the snow. Their way back to the shore was down a steep hillside through tangled underbrush of stunted southern beech (see Pl. 13,

Endeavour *anchored at the Bay of Good Success, Tierra del Fuego, on 15 January 1769. Alexander Buchan's painting, fresh and direct, shows the crew collecting clean water in casks and attempting to converse with the local inhabitants. A botanical expedition into the hills by Banks and others ended in the death of two servants; Buchan suffered a seizure but survived.*

p. 46; identified incorrectly by Solander as a birch – 'Betula antarctica'). Solander, cold and exhausted by the effort, lay down and fell asleep. He would certainly have perished had Banks not ordered a fire to be lit and then heaved and carried his comatose friend to it through the snow. Earlier in the day Buchan had suffered a seizure, but recovered just enough to survive the rigours of the unlucky expedition. It was a terrifying experience: 'expos'd', in Banks' words, 'to the most penetrating cold I ever felt as well as continual snow'. Parkinson painted 70 of the 148 specimens of the spare flora of Tierra del Fuego that were collected, including the troublesome beech, and the engravings made from them provide some of the most subtle and minimally elegant images in the whole of the Florilegium that would be created after Banks' return from the voyage.

The bark *Endeavour*, now held in affectionate admiration by all aboard for its stolid fitness for deep sea service, continued southwest to Cape Horn before, after nine days, taking a course 45 degrees to northwest for Tahiti and Cook's appointment with Venus. It would take 12 more weeks, and throughout that period, as in each of the successive long legs of the voyage, Banks, Solander, Parkinson and Spöring would be working in the great cabin. Parkinson had learned to deal deftly with the constant sea swell, the lift and fall of the boat, and would spend his hours immersed in the task of painting the specimens placed before him. In his journal, Banks later (3 October 1769) described a part of the scene in that cabin, summoning up the conversational camaraderie and infinite optimism of their project:

> Now do I wish that our freinds in England could by the assistance of some magical spying glass take a peep at our situation: Dr Solander setts at the Cabbin table describing, myself at my Bureau Journalizing, between us hangs a large bunch of sea weed, upon the table lays the wood and barnacles; they would see that notwithstanding our different occupations our lips move very often, and without being conjurors might guess that we were talking about what we should see upon the land which there is now no doubt we shall see very soon.

At last, on 13 April 1769, *Endeavour* anchored in the beautiful Matavai Bay on the northeast coast of Tahiti. It was the third European vessel in as many years to do so. In June 1767, HMS *Dolphin*, under Lieutenant Samuel Wallis (1728–1795), had spent 40 days there and formed friendly relations with the local people, whose easygoing sexual mores were much appreciated by his crew. After ten days on the island in April of the following year, the explorer Louis-Antoine de Bougainville (1729–1811), in the course of the first French circumnavigation of the globe, claimed it for France as *Nouvelle-Cythère*, after one mythical birthplace of Venus-Aphrodite. (Cook was unaware of Bougainville's visit until he reached Batavia in October 1770.) An extensive literature exists concerning the extraordinary adventures – anthropological, social, amatory, astronomical, botanical and cartographical – of *Endeavour*'s crew, and of its indefatigably curious scientific and artistic passengers, on the paradisiacal island.[7] Cook's approach to the behaviour of those in his charge was humanely intelligent. Although he was tolerant in respect of friendly relations of any kind with the indigenous islanders, he paid proper regard to their dignity; his first rule for all concerned was clear: 'To endeavour by every fair means to cultivate a friendship with the Natives and to treat them with all imaginable humanity.'

In preparation for the observation of the Transit, Cook, with characteristic foresight, created an onshore stockade, which proved wise in view of the Tahitians' lack of European scruples with regard to the ownership of valued materials, most notably iron and other metals. Banks noted with uncensorious objectivity 'that great and small cheifs and common men all are firmly of opinion that if they can once get possession of any thing it immediately becomes their own'. During the three months of the expedition's stay in Tahiti there were many occurrences of items, more or less valuable, being appropriated, including one night when Banks, in bed with a Tahitian lady of high rank, awoke to find his breeches gone, never to be returned. The iron nails kept in abundance by the ship's carpenter became a significant currency in trading for foodstuffs, livestock, goods and services, including sexual; towards the end of their time on the island unscrupulous seamen were not above stealing, at risk of the lash, even the nails that held the bark together.

Sydney Parkinson's drawing of Matavai Bay, Tahiti, from One Tree Hill, which Endeavour *reached on 13 April 1769. Cook set up camp here at Fort Venus in order to take observations of the Transit of Venus across the Sun. While the astronomers prepared for this event, Banks was occupied in trading for food for the crew and learning about the lives and customs of the people of the island.*

The most momentous incident in this respect was the near disastrous theft on the night of 2 May of the irreplaceable astronomical quadrant supplied by the Royal Society, a heavy and intricate instrument without which the effective observation of the Transit would be impossible. Impulsive and naturally brave, Banks set off at dawn, accompanied by the astronomer Green, in pursuit of the thief. He dashed several miles into the island in intense heat before, with the aid of a close Tahitian friend, he caught up with the miscreant and recovered the instrument, returning it to the fort. In this as in so much else, Banks showed himself to be a man of considerable resolution and fortitude. He had no great personal interest in matters astronomical, and when on 2 and 3 June he accompanied the officer John Gore and the ship's surgeon William Monkhouse to the nearby island of Moorea, where they were to make an alternative observation of the Transit (a necessary precaution in the event of cloudy weather at Fort Venus), he spent his time trading for food (a task which he had made especially his own during the Tahiti sojourn) and happily gathering plants.

While on Tahiti, Banks also busily pursued matters diplomatic and ethnological – components of an avidly immersive observation of the life and customs of the islanders. His easy tact, and the close and generous relations he quickly established with the Tahitians, earned him their affection and respect, enhanced no doubt by his strenuous efforts to understand their language and learn about their traditions – with which, when appropriate, he happily joined in. With Banks otherwise occupied, the primary botanical task of collection had mostly fallen to the phlegmatic Solander, as well as to Spöring and Parkinson, who, after Buchan's tragic death from an epileptic seizure, were now entrusted with the additional burden of making topographical and ethnographic drawings.

The observations of the Transit completed, on 13 July Cook set sail, determined to investigate the other islands of the group he had named the Society Islands. On 14 August, as *Endeavour* at last headed into the southern Pacific in what turned out to be the fruitless search for the great unknown Southern Continent, Banks began in his journal his extraordinary 'Description of the Manners and Customs of the South Seas Islands'. As he explained: 'The account I shall give of them is taken cheifly from Otahite where I was well acquainted with their most interior policy, as I found them to be a people so free from deceit that I trusted myself among them almost as freely as I could do in my own countrey, sleeping continualy in their houses in the woods with not so much as a single companion.' He means, of course, a European companion. His 'Customs' is remarkable for its empathetic, non-judgmental curiosity, its empirical exactitude, the humane objectivity of its descriptions of social behaviour, and its close records of custom and ritual, and of the technologies and usages of material culture. This astonishing account, at over 21,000 words, is a pioneering work of ethnography, a minor anthropological masterpiece of the Enlightenment.

Diagram of the observation of the Transit of Venus on 3 June 1769, by Cook (above) and the astronomer Charles Green (below), published in the Royal Society's journal, Philosophical Transactions.

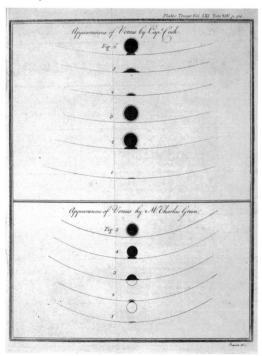

While Banks was writing his 'Customs' there was plenty of work to occupy the other inhabitants of the cramped great cabin. Solander and Spöring, with Banks always in attendance, were concerned to document and classify the hundreds of specimens collected during their four-month stay in the Society Islands. Parkinson, working as quickly and diligently as conditions allowed, completed paintings of no fewer than 114 of the specimens in order to catch them before their colours faded. In Tahiti and the Islands, Parkinson's Quaker principles constrained his conduct amid the general licence, but he had nevertheless seen, like his companions, a vision of other possibilities of human existence, other ways of being and knowing. It is difficult not to feel that the fullness and lushness, the lyrical richness of the 89 plates later engraved from his paintings of the islands' flora, reflects not only the natural abundance he witnessed there, but also recollects something of the plenitude of that experience.

Cook was a highly skilled navigator and map-maker – this is his map of New Zealand 'or the Islands of Aeheinomouwe and Tovypoenammu', produced after several months' sailing around the islands, charting everything in detail. He established that there were two main islands, with a strait between them (named after him), and was the first to record the coastline accurately.

Over the seven weeks of the long, late summer voyage, south and then across the western reaches of the South Pacific, the first (if necessarily incomplete) taxonomy of South Seas flora was created. Banks described the rigour of the process by which the detailed records of their collected botanical materials were delineated and collated. Sitting across the table from Parkinson, Banks and Solander would indicate the significant features of each specimen: and then '[we] hurriedly made descriptions of all the natural history objects while they were still fresh.… When a long journey from land had exhausted fresh things, we finished each description and added the synonyms to the books we had.

These completed accounts were immediately entered by a secretary [Spöring] in the books in the form of a flora of each of the lands we visited.' At the heart of this concentrated taxonomical effort, and of crucial importance to its projected eventual publication, was the steadily accumulating body of scientifically accomplished and aesthetically beautiful paintings and drawings. And yet these intrepid mariner-naturalists could have had no premonition of the even greater botanical riches that lay ahead.

The first landfall on the east coast of the North Island of New Zealand occurred early in October 1769. A period beset with hazard and occasionally confusion followed. Unlike

Two portraits of 'a New Zeland Man', in pen and wash, by Sydney Parkinson. Parkinson was evidently fascinated by their facial markings, and also recorded in detail their ornaments, including the hei tiki *worn around the neck of the man on the left. Not all the encounters between the indigenous population and the Europeans were friendly. The man on the right is 'Otegoowgoow' (Te Kuukuu), who had been involved in a conflict between some Māori and members of the crew of* Endeavour *in which he was wounded in the leg by musket shot.*

the Society Islanders, the Māori were fierce and war-like, suspicious of the strangers who had arrived so suddenly and mysteriously among them, and often violently aggressive. It was a traditional practice among certain of their peoples, it transpired, to eat the flesh of their vanquished enemies. In addition, there were discomfiting moments offshore. On 5 December Banks reported laconically:

> We were all happy in our breeze and fine clear moon-light; myself went down to bed and sat upon my cott undressing myself when I felt the ship strike upon a rock, before I could get upon my leggs she struck again. I ran upon deck but before I could get there the danger was over; fortunately the rock was to wind ward of us so she went off without the least damage and we got into the proper channel, where the officers who had examind the bay declard there to be no hidden dangers – much to our satisfaction as the almost certainty of being eat as soon as you come ashore adds not a little to the terrors of shipwreck.

Cook spent several months circumnavigating the two main islands, establishing for the first time that there was a strait between them, to which he gave his own name. Charting the coast with his characteristic exactitude, despite the frequent difficulties that prevented him from sailing close inshore, Cook created the first serviceable map of the country. Assisting him, Parkinson proved himself also capable of drawing spatially sophisticated coastal topographies – so-called 'profiles' – that were to prove invaluable navigational aids to future seamen. He had by now established himself as a gifted artist of people and places as well as plants, and in New Zealand he made studies of the complex facial tattoos and hairstyles of the Māori, of their carved weaponry and patterned domestic objects, and skilfully depicted their boats and dwelling places.

As was their custom and compulsion, wherever and whenever possible, Banks and Solander put ashore to botanize, often in situations where the local warriors had offered frightening displays of aggression. On the first landfall, some of the ship's crew found themselves quickly surrounded by apparently hostile natives, and an altercation resulted in a Māori fatality, much to the chagrin of Cook, who was present. Even so, the pair collected assiduously as and when they were allowed by Cook to go ashore (a mere 44 days in five months), and they returned to England with a remarkable collection of over 360 specimens, as well as many drawings and paintings by Parkinson, of which 182 were to be engraved for the intended Florilegium. The distinctive characteristics of the New Zealand flora, and a number of native fern species (there are 22 in the Florilegium, for instance Pl. 55, p. 127), are well represented by the selection Banks and Solander made for the great publication.

Even this unprecedented collection, however, was to be surpassed by the astonishing scale and diversity of the plant life they were to discover on the next stage of their journey, a series of landfalls on the eastern seaboard of Australia (then known, and for some time thereafter, as New Holland, so named by Abel Tasman in 1644). This – the first European discovery of eastern Australia – was a major achievement of Cook's circumnavigation on *Endeavour*, and a key stage in the establishment of the existence of New Holland as an island continent. It was also to be the last and most extensive botanical exploration of the voyage, and began on 28 April 1770 in the great natural bay soon after appropriately named by Cook, as he explained: 'The great quantity of New Plants etc. Mr Banks and Dr Solander collected in this place occasioned my giveing it the name of Botany Bay.' It was a location and a name that would be forever associated with Banks, and with the penal settlement of Australia that he later advocated.

In the week spent here, Banks and Solander botanized with great energy and with such success that after only four days Banks had to take special measures to protect the specimens, recording on 3 May 1770:

> Our collection of Plants was now grown so immensely large that it was necessary that some extrordinary care should be taken of them least they should spoil in the books. I therefore devoted this day to that business and carried all the drying paper, near 200 Quires of which the larger part was full, ashore and spreading them upon a sail in the sun kept them in this manner exposd the whole day, often turning them and sometimes turning the Quires in which were plants inside out. By this means they came on board at night in very good condition.

The expedition spent nine days (28 April to 6 May 1770) in what Cook was to name Botany Bay in recognition of the vast collection of plant specimens Banks and Solander brought back on board for Parkinson to record as quickly as possible. It was their first landfall in Australia, and this is Cook's own chart of the great natural bay.

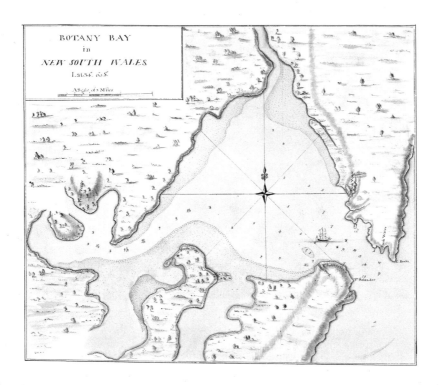

In the course of charting the eastern coast of Australia, Endeavour *ran aground on the Great Barrier Reef. The vessel was badly damaged, and there was a real danger it would be lost, along with the lives of everyone on board as well as Banks' entire collection of specimens. Fortunately, after great effort, the ship was beached for repairs at what was named Endeavour River, where Parkinson made this drawing in June 1770.*

The groups of local people they encountered had shown themselves at once curious but also suspicious and timid of the clothed white strangers with their loud guns. The landing parties were happy to penetrate inland, Banks noting insouciantly: 'Myself in the woods botanizing as usual, now quite void of fear as our neighbours have turnd out such rank cowards.' On the last day their efforts were redoubled: 'As tomorrow was fixd for our sailing Dr Solander and myself were employd the whole day in collecting specimens of as many things as we possibly could to be examind at sea.' Banks, as usual, also shot as many birds as he could manage, for both his records and the ship's table. Parkinson made sketches and drawings of the people and their dwellings, of such animals as they saw, and of the coastal landscapes – the invaluable first visual records of the new found land. Above all, he was occupied in painting the numerous previously unknown plants brought on board during that momentous landfall.

Cook now continued to sail north, charting the coast and naming landmarks as he went. On the night of 9 June 1770, catastrophe struck. *Endeavour* stuck fast on a coral shoal of the Great Barrier Reef, unknown until then to Cook and his seamen, and was badly holed below water. Jettisoning heavy items, such as cannons and water barrels, towing the anchor behind in the bark's pinnace, and continually pumping water from the hold, seamen and gentlemen worked side by side to keep the ship afloat. After several perilous days, *Endeavour* was beached on the sheltered banks of a river estuary named from then on for the vessel that had started life as a modest Whitby collier. Every mortal on board, as well as the precious cargo of natural specimens, drawings, paintings, charts and journals, had been for those hectic days fatally endangered, and the extraordinary outcome of the epic voyage – material and intellectual – might have been utterly lost to history.

As it was, the botanical specimens, kept for safety in a bread hold deep in the stern, were accidentally immersed in seawater. Banks and Solander carried them ashore to be dried; most, wrote Cook, 'were, by [their] indefatigable care and attention restored to a state of preservation'. For seven weeks the blacksmith and carpenters worked on the keel's timbers, and eventually rendered the bark seaworthy once more. Time enough for a bonanza of botanizing. When the relieved and happy company sailed from the sanctuary of Endeavour River, Banks and Solander had the satisfaction of having amassed an astounding collection of botanical specimens from a continent hitherto unknown to science, which would form the solid basis of any subsequent attempt to classify the flora of Australia. From Parkinson's almost 700 drawings no fewer than 337 plates of Australian specimens were engraved for the intended Florilegium.

There still remained a hazardous journey home. Cook was anxious to chart the coast further and to find a passage westwards through what was surmised to be the Torres Strait between New Holland and New Guinea. Having successfully navigated a tortuous course through the Great Reef, on 16 August, as fierce oceanic winds inexorably drove them back, *Endeavour* was in dire danger of running aground once more. All aboard feared the end, but good fortune swept them through what Cook aptly and no doubt gratefully named Providential Channel. Banks' immediate ruminations evince a heroic fatalism: 'The fear of Death is Bitter: the prospect we now had before us of saving our lives tho at the expence of every thing we had made my heart set much lighter on its throne, and I suppose there were none but what felt the same sensations.'

Cook claimed the entire coast for the British Crown on 22 August 1770. On that date *Endeavour* had cleared the tip of Queensland and was bound for Batavia (now Jakarta) in Java, where she arrived on 10 October. Here the bark was refitted and re-provisioned for the voyage home by way of the Indian Ocean and Cape Town. However, the three months ashore in the unhealthy miasmas of a filthy and disease-ridden town of stinking rivers and stagnant canals were to prove fatal to the vigorously fit crew and gentlemen of *Endeavour*. Banks went down with malarial fever; Cook was ill also; Solander was sick to the point of death but was nursed back to relative health with great care by Banks. Parkinson took on the task of botanizing: with some help he gathered around 150 specimens of the luxuriant flora of Java, and painted 43, of which 30 were to be engraved for the Florilegium. This was to be the last harvest. When the bark set out to sea in late December, it was a ship of the dying and the near-dead. All suffered terribly; Spöring, Green the astronomer, and the high-minded and industrious artistic hero of the voyage, Sydney Parkinson, all died of dysentery, the 'bloody flux', which also ravaged, but finally spared, Banks and Solander.

On 12 July 1771, *Endeavour* moored off Deal on the south coast of England. Joseph Banks, already widely celebrated among the cognoscenti, returned to London to a general fame more luminous than that of James Cook. There had been other naturalists on voyages of discovery before this, but none with so exacting and industrious a programme of collection, identification and classification, and none had ever returned with such an inordinate wealth of materials: botanical and other natural specimens, expertly recorded and classified, ethnographic objects, and above all, an unprecedented number of drawings, sketches and paintings. But Banks' hopes of another voyage with Cook were to be dashed, his overweening and vain demands for accommodating his party and equipment displeasing the Admiralty. And the much-anticipated publication of his great Florilegium of newly discovered plants was to be postponed for more than 200 years.

1. Quotations from Banks, unless otherwise cited, are from the text file prepared in 2005 from the manuscript of *The Endeavour Journal of Sir Joseph Banks, 1768–1771*, held at the State Library of New South Wales, a Project Gutenberg of Australia eBook. Cook is quoted from *Captain Cook's Journal During the First Voyage Round the World*, a Project Gutenberg eBook; the original is held at the National Library of Australia, Canberra. The standard printed editions of both Cook's and Banks' journals are those edited by J. C. Beaglehole: Beaglehole, 1955–69 and Beaglehole, 1963.
2. Quoted in O'Brian, 1987.
3. The Transit of Venus is a predictable astronomical phenomenon that occurs twice within eight years, after gaps of 121.5 and 105.5 years. Its importance to the Royal Society, and to the Admiralty, was that an accurate record of the Transit (when the planet Venus visibly traverses the surface of the Sun) would facilitate the calculation of the Earth's distance from the Sun, and this in turn would make calculations of longitude, essential to navigation, more accurate. Conditions were good for Cook and Green at Point Venus, and at the two other locations they chose for observations. An optical interference, known as the 'black drop effect', compromised the accuracy of the records, however, and led to discrepancies between the three observations. Cook's findings were presented to the Royal Society on 21 November 1771.
4. Quotations here from Parkinson are from a copy of the 1773 edition of *A Journal of a Voyage to the South Seas*, held in the Library of the Ohio State University and digitized by Google Books.
5. The definitive source for information regarding the drawings, paintings and engravings of the *Endeavour* voyage is Diment et al., 1984 and 1987. The indispensable Introduction, enlarged and updated, became the Introduction to the *Catalogue of Banks' Florilegium* (London, Alecto Historical Editions/British Museum (Natural History) 1990).
6. Madeira wine, fortified with grape spirit, derives its distinctive quality from heating, over time, either by natural temperatures or by artificial means. It improves on long sea journeys during which it may pass through high temperatures. It does not, moreover, quickly deteriorate after being opened. This made it a favoured beverage for long sea journeys, 'far voyages', and made Madeira an essential port of call for vessels striking south.
7. Notable titles of general interest on the islands of the South Pacific, their discovery at this time, and its momentous consequences include: Smith, 1960; Moorehead, 1966; Adams, 1986; Gascoigne, 1994; Chambers et al., 2016.

The Plates

DAVID MABBERLEY

Joseph Banks' botanical curiosity was evident at an early age. He was fortunate to reach maturity during the lifetime of Carl Linnaeus, the most influential botanist of the Enlightenment and principal proponent of binomial nomenclature, the system of naming organisms that persists to this day. Daniel Solander, Linnaeus' favourite pupil, was by disposition and temperament perhaps most comfortable working in the library and herbarium, but – under Banks' instruction – he became a useful field botanist during the *Endeavour* voyage. Together, Banks and Solander were a formidable combination and indefatigable collectors of plant material wherever opportunity arose.

Under their watchful eye, it then fell to Sydney Parkinson to paint specimens selected by the pair as worthy of recording for future intended publication. Because of the ever-increasing volume of new plants found by Banks and Solander and passed to him for drawing, however, Parkinson could complete hardly any from the later stages of the voyage, so the engravings of many of the illustrations here are from the finished portraits worked up from Parkinson's sketches and colour notes. To achieve this, on his return to London, Banks employed five painters and eighteen engravers (see pp. 298–300).

In 1772 the Keeper of the Ashmolean Museum, Oxford, the Revd William Sheffield, wrote to Gilbert White, describing Banks' collection at New Burlington Street (see also p. 302). After mentioning the remarkable number and variety of botanical specimens, he described the drawings: '987 plants drawn and coloured by Parkinson; and 1300 or 1400 more drawn with each of them a flower, a leaf, and a portion of the stalk, coloured by the same hand…and what is more extraordinary still, all the new genera and species contained in this vast collection are accurately described, the descriptions fairly transcribed and fit to be put to the press.'

Until now, only a handful of Parkinson's drawings and watercolours made during the *Endeavour* voyage, and those completed in London from his unfinished field sketches, have been published in a way accessible to the general public. The aim here is to provide a representative selection of the very best of the engravings of those works, now all housed in the Natural History Museum in London, especially those depicting economically or ecologically significant species. The illustrations of the plants are arranged chronologically by landfall from Madeira to Java.

It is worth noting here that Banks' original commission of these engravings was driven by his sense of scientific responsibility. Banks never published his discoveries in his lifetime. Had he done so, many of the plants drawn in his *Florilegium* would be the type specimens for numerous species recognized today, and his and Solander's work would be more readily appreciated. This book, and the publication of the engravings themselves (see pp. 306–11), will, we hope, belatedly restore Banks' and Solander's reputation. As it is, Parkinson's work represents a window into the Georgian fascination with scientific collecting and the exotic, Sir Joseph Banks being perhaps its supreme advocate.

The fact that Parkinson's work was in effect unpublished might suggest that it had no role in the advance of science, but this is not entirely so. Although the plates for Madeira, South America, Polynesia and Indonesia have been of limited scientific consequence, those relating to Australia and New Zealand cannot be so summarily dismissed. In Banks' lifetime some of the engravings were run off and distributed. A set reached Linnaeus and thence James Edward Smith (1759–1828), founding President of the Linnean Society of London, who published two of Parkinson's drawings in his *Exotic botany* (1805). See also how the plate from Parkinson's drawing of *Knightia excelsa* (Pl. 52, p. 120) was used in 1810.

Soon after *Endeavour*'s return, Stanfield Parkinson quarrelled with Banks over the rights to his brother Sydney's journal, which he then published, amid considerable controversy. Following that publication in 1773, a number of plant names in it were, and are still, attributed to Sydney Parkinson. Notable is *Spondias dulcis* Parkinson (Pl. 20, p. 58),* but also *Sitodium altile* Parkinson, today's *Artocarpus altilis* (Parkinson) Fosb., the breadfruit, which was to figure prominently in Pacific history, not least the famous mutiny on HMS *Bounty* (commanded by Captain Bligh), again a direct result of Banks' interest in Pacific plants.

NOTES ON THE COMMENTARIES

My commentaries on the plates may be read as captions, image by image, but also as a continuous narrative. This reduces unnecessary repetition, and, in general, related plants are grouped together within the section devoted to each landfall.

Each entry is headed by the scientific and common name, and the botanical family to which the plant belongs. Following traditional practice, I have maintained the older of the permitted family names for several families, including Compositae, Cruciferae and others, rather than the later alternatives for them, Asteraceae, Brassicaceae and so on. Both the traditional and the later names are legal under the International Code of Nomenclature for Algae, Fungi and Plants. Modern technical names for plants are made up of at least two parts, both italicized: an initial *generic* name (e.g. *Pinus* – pine), and a second *specific* epithet (e.g. *edulis* – edible). As *species* (abbreviated as spp.; singular: *species*) are arranged in *genera* (singular: *genus*), the double name for a species is a *binomial*. Genera are arranged in *families* (e.g. Pinaceae). Usually, the first published name for a genus or a species is the correct one (such names are said to have *priority*). Generic names have an initial capital letter, specific ones a lower case one, even when commemorating people or places. Traditionally, generic names were based on Greek words, generally brought into Latin form, while species epithets were based on Latin words (in discussions of derivation of the Latin epithet, the masculine singular form is used). However, epithets can be derived from any root whatsoever.

A third epithet is added where recognizable races, *sub-species* (subsp.) or *varieties* (var.), have been named. Such *trinomials* in botany have the linking element 'subsp.' or 'var.'. In technical works, the binomial is followed by an authority, an abbreviated version of the name of the person who coined the name, for example, 'L.' (for Linnaeus). If the species is moved to a different genus, that person's name is

A herbarium sheet with an original specimen of Banksia dentata *at the Natural History Museum, London. This and other specimens from the* Endeavour *voyage are kept in the present-day herbarium of the museum's Botany Department; some of the cabinets are possibly Joseph Banks' own, made for his house in Soho Square.*

put in parentheses and, in botany, followed by the authority that made the move, for example, '(L.) Sm.' (for J. E. Smith). This is given beneath each commentary; also indicated is the place of publication of the binomial. The name of the artist and engraver of each plate are also listed, together with the Alecto Historical Editions *Banks' Florilegium* number (BF), and a reference to the catalogue by Judith Diment and co-authors (Diment et al., 1984 and 1987).

DIMENSIONS OF THE REPRODUCTIONS

All the plants in the *Florilegium* except one (not included in this selection) were depicted life-size. The original copper plates are almost all the same size, *c.* 18 × 12 inches (457 × 305 mm). The prints reproduced here are taken from one of the two sets of the Alecto Historical Editions *Banks' Florilegium* in the Natural History Museum, London, where they were photographed. Here the portrait plates are reproduced at approximately two thirds of their original size.

---

* The other names published were the screwpine genus, *Pandanus* Parkinson (and *P. tectorius* Parkinson), though these were really Solander's manuscript names without attribution to Solander himself, as was his *Aniotum fagiferum* (which Sydney Parkinson's brother Stanfield, or his ghost-writer, William Kenrick, seems to have mistranscribed, because Solander's manuscript name was 'Amotum fagiferum'), today's *Inocarpus fagifer* (Parkinson) Fosb. (Pl. 25, p. 68).

I.

CLETHRA ARBOREA
folhado, Clethraceae

The first collections of the *Endeavour* voyage were made from 13 to 18 September 1768 on Madeira, which the Portuguese had colonized around 1420–25. The most remarkable vegetation there is still the *laurisilva*, with four dominant tree species of Lauraceae, a relic of the subtropical evergreen forests typical of the Mediterranean Tertiary.[1] Once forming 60 per cent of the vegetation cover of the island, it is now reduced to some 16 per cent.

Clethra arborea was Solander's manuscript name for this small *laurisilva* tree or shrub with fragrant flowers – hence its English name, 'lily-of-the-valley tree'. It was officially named later from material collected by Francis Masson (1741–1805), Kew Gardens' first collector, sent to Madeira by Banks in 1784. The tree is found up to 600 m (1,970 ft) high on the island, as well as in the Azores,[2] but because it is superficially similar to *C. sumatrana* of eastern Sumatra it was formerly considered by some to have been introduced from Asia by Europeans,[3] a theory now discredited. The foliage has been used as fodder for stock animals.

Clethra (from the Greek *klethra*, for the unrelated alder) comprises up to about 60 species native in Asia and America;[4] *arboreus* indicates this species is a tree.

Clethra arborea Aiton, *Hortus Kewensis* 2: 73 (1789)

Copper plate by Gerard Sibelius, based on Parkinson's 1768 watercolour;
BF 394; Diment et al., 1987: M8

1. Press and Short, 1994, p. 3
2. Press and Short, 1994, p. 248
3. Huxley, 1992, 1, p. 655
4. Mabberley, 2014, p. 195 and 4th ed., 2017

HEBERDENIA BAHAMENSIS
Primulaceae

Growing up to 15 m (50 ft) tall in the *laurisilva*, this tree is now becoming rare in Madeira, although it is also found in the Canary Islands.[1] Its ripe fruit is purplish-black and is probably dispersed by birds.

It is the only species in the genus,[2] which was named by Banks and Solander to commemorate Dr Thomas Heberden (1703–1769),[3] who greatly assisted them in Madeira, in particular with his knowledge of the trees there, but also, as Solander wrote:

> He procured us access into a nunnery, and when they heard that Mr Banks and myself belonged to the Royal Society, they immediately took us for men of supernatural knowledge, and desired us to walk into their garden, and shew where they might dig for water; they wanted to know by what signs they should be able to foretel [sic] tempests, rains, and thunder and lightning. The answers and explanations of all of this would have taken us several days; but our captain would not stay for the gratification of the nuns.[4]

Solander's name, *Heberdenia excelsa*, was not published until 1841, but the tree was first described as *Anguillaria bahamensis* in 1788 by Josef Gaertner (1732–1791), a German physician and botanist who was given access to Banks' collections when writing his *De Fructibus*, an important treatise on fruits and seeds. Indeed, he copied, with acknowledgment, Solander's description for his new genus, but why he renamed it '*bahamensis*' is unclear, as no link with the Bahamas is evident. Despite this error, the species name cannot now be changed as it was the first validly published for this tree and temporal priority is a central tenet in scientific plant nomenclature.

Heberdenia bahamensis (Gaertn.) Sprague in *Journal of Botany, British and Foreign* 61: 241 (1923)

Copper plate by Daniel Mackenzie, based on Parkinson's 1768 watercolour; BF 395; Diment et al., 1987: M9

1. Press and Short, 1994, pp. 250–51

2. Mabberley, 2014, p. 393

3. Beaglehole, 1963, 1, p. 160

4. Beaglehole, 1963, 2, p. 310

3.
SIBTHORPIA PEREGRINA
hera terrestre, Plantaginaceae

A far-creeping hairy perennial herb, *Sibthorpia peregrina* is restricted to the Madeira group of islands, although it is also now naturalized near Sintra in metropolitan Portugal. It is common in woodlands, on shady banks and in other damp places,[1] and is in cultivation elsewhere, having been introduced into England in 1771.[2]

Solander's manuscript name for it was 'Meadia repens', perhaps after Richard Mead (1673–1754), a London doctor and patron of science, but the plant is not generically distinct from *Sibthorpia.* That name commemorates Humphrey Sibthorp (1713–1797), professor of botany at Oxford, who was notable for giving just one lecture in his career. He did, however, provide the introduction that led to Banks appointing the Cambridge botanist Israel Lyons (1739–1775) to deliver lectures on botany at Oxford.[3] The specific epithet *peregrinus* means exotic, foreign or wandering.

The genus comprises some five species native to tropical and South America, and the African mountains; two are native to Europe – *Sibthorpia europaea* being the Cornish moneywort found in England.[4]

Sibthorpia peregrina L., *Species Plantarum* 2: 631 (1753)

Copper plate by Gerard Sibelius, based on Parkinson's 1768 watercolour;
BF 398; Diment et al., 1987: M13

1. Press and Short, 1994, p. 315

2. Chittenden, 1951, 4, p. 1951

3. Beaglehole, 1963, 1, p. 6

4. Mabberley, 2014, p. 794

4.
PERESKIA GRANDIFOLIA
rose cactus, Cactaceae

During *Endeavour*'s stay in Rio de Janeiro from 13 November to 7 December 1768, Banks and Solander, along with all except Cook, were not officially permitted by the Portuguese governor to go ashore and therefore could not collect plants. Solander wrote: 'Our few botanical Collections have been made by clandestinely hiring people; and we have got them on board under the name of Greens for our Table.'[1] He was clearly flummoxed by this tree, giving it the name 'Clusia dodecapetala', as if it belonged to the completely unrelated Guttiferae [Clusiaceae]. When it was named some 50 years later, the year before Banks' death, material growing at Kew Gardens was used as the basis for the description.

Pereskia grandifolia, which grows up to 10 m (33 ft) tall, is restricted to coastal forests on the acidic and nutrient-poor sandy soils of the *restingas* of northeastern Brazil. It has edible leaves to over 20 cm (8 in.) long and clusters of up to 90 spines to 6 cm (2½ in.) long, perhaps deterrents to long-extinct megafauna. The flowers superficially resemble those of roses, hence the common name.

Rose cactus belongs to the genus *Pereskia*, which most closely resembles the ancestral cacti, and comprises some 17 species of trees, shrubs and climbers native to the Caribbean and northeastern South America.[2] They are often used as grafting stocks for other cacti, while *P. aculeata*, Barbados gooseberry, is cultivated for its edible fruits and leaves, but is invasive in southern Africa and northeastern Australia. The generic name *Pereskia* commemorates Nicolas-Claude Fabri de Peiresc (1580–1637), a French astronomer, antiquarian and patron of science; *grandifolius* refers to the large size of the leaves.

Pereskia grandifolia Haw., *Supplementarum Plantarum Succulentarum*: 85 (1819)

Copper plate by Gerard Sibelius based on Parkinson's 1769 watercolour; BF 338; Diment et al., 1987: B1

1. Duyker and Tingbrand, 1995, p. 279

2. B. E. Leuenberger, *Pereskia* (Cactaceae), *Memoirs of the New York Botanical Garden* 41, 1986, pp. 111–18; Mabberley, 2014, p. 647

5·

STIGMAPHYLLON CILIATUM
orchid vine, Malpighiaceae

A rampant climber growing to 8 m (26 ft) tall, the orchid vine, also known as golden vine and butterfly vine, is native from Belize to Uruguay along beaches, rivers and roadsides, even in mangrove.[1] Originally described from plants collected in Brazil, it is now naturalized in Barbados and is becoming so in coastal Queensland, Australia, where it is potentially a serious invasive species. Its flowers are short-lived, but it is widely cultivated.

The genus *Stigmaphyllon* (meaning with a leaflike stigma) comprises some 120 species of lianes in the western Pacific and tropical America.[2] Solander's manuscript name, 'Banisteria ciliata', led to the adoption of the specific epithet *ciliatus*, alluding to the fringed leaf margins of the ovate to cordate (heart-shaped) leaves; *Banisteria* formerly included species now transferred to *Banisteriopsis*, a genus famous for *B. caapi*, the source of the hallucinogenic *ayahuasca* important in South American ritual.

Stigmaphyllon ciliatum (Lam.) A. Juss. in A. St-Hil., *Flora Brasiliae Meridionalis* 3: 49 (1833)

Copper plate by Gabriel Smith, based on Parkinson's 1768 watercolour; BF 341; Diment et al., 1987: B5

1. C. Anderson, 'Monograph of Stigmaphyllon (Malpighiaceae)', *Systematic Botany Monographs* 51, 1997
2. Mabberley, 2014, p. 823, and 4th ed., 2017

6.
TETRAPTERYS PHLOMOIDES
Malpighiaceae

This scrambling liane is restricted to Brazil, especially Matto Grosso, and neighbouring parts of Peru. It often has conspicuous insect galls caused by the fly *Schizomyia maricaensis*.[1]

Tetrapterys (meaning four-winged, referring to the fruits) is a tropical American genus of perhaps 90 species.[2] Hallucinogenic chemicals in the bark are comparable with *ayahuasca* from *Banisteriopsis caapi*, and some species are of local medicinal importance. The specific epithet means 'like *Phlomis*', referring to an Old World genus of labiates, some of which are grown in gardens.

Tetrapterys phlomoides (Spreng.) Nied. in Engl., *Das Pflanzenreich* IV, 141 (Heft 92): 208 (1928)

Copper plate by Charles White, based on Parkinson's 1769 watercolour (his field drawing in pencil also survives); BF 342; Diment et al., 1987: B6/7

1. L. Iendrike de Sousa and V. C. Maia, 'A new species of *Schizomyia* (Diptera, Cecidomyiidae, Asphondyliini) associated with *Tetrapterys phlomoides* (Malpighiaceae)', *Iheringia* (*Série Zoologia*) 97, 2007, pp. 311–13

2. Mabberley, 2014, p. 850

7.
SERJANIA FERRUGINEA
Sapindaceae

Native to the coastal Brazilian rain forest, this vigorous liane is notable for its branches, which are triangular in cross-section. Its large fruits are produced so profusely as to cover the foliage. Grown as an ornamental (often as *Serjania cuspidata*) on pergolas or fences in warm countries, it was introduced from Rio de Janeiro to England in 1823 by John Forbes (1798–1823), a collector for the Horticultural Society of London who was on his way to Mozambique, where he tragically died.

Serjania, named after Father Philippe Serjeant, a seventeenth-century French friar and botanist, comprises perhaps 230 species native in warmer parts of the Americas.[1] They are all lianes with 'watch-spring' tendrils, formed from the lowermost sterile branches of the inflorescences, and three-winged fruits. Some provide local cordage and fish poisons (they contain saponins). The specific name *ferrugineus* refers to the rusty-brown hairs on the foliage.

Serjania ferruginea (Lindl.) Mabb., *Mabberley's Plant-book* ed. 4: 1102 (2017)

Copper plate by Gerard Sibelius, based on Parkinson's 1768 watercolour; BF 343; Diment et al., 1987: B8

1. Mabberley, 2014, p. 791

BRAZIL, RIO DE JANEIRO, 13 NOVEMBER–7 DECEMBER 1768

8.

BOUGAINVILLEA SPECTABILIS
Nyctaginaceae

Bougainvilleas are some of the most commonly grown of all tropical climbers. There are 16 species native in tropical America, usually with thorns that aid climbing. The flowers, often pollinated by hummingbirds, are held in threes inside the persistent, coloured bracts, each group resembling a single flower.[1] Most often seen are cultivars of *Bougainvillea × buttiana*, a hybrid between *B. glabra* of Brazil and *B. peruviensis* from Colombia to Peru; 'double' forms have each flower replaced by a short shoot with variable numbers of coloured bracts.

Bougainvillea spectabilis is so named because it has the largest bracts (5–6 cm/2–2½ in. long) of any cultivated species; it was introduced into cultivation in England in 1829, and there are now several named cultivars. Native to the Atlantic coast of Brazil and growing up to 12 m (40 ft) tall, its stems and leaves are densely hairy. It is deciduous when grown in seasonal climates and is largely pollinated by Lepidoptera (butterflies and moths) seeking nectar. Extracts from the plant have been shown to have significant antibacterial and antiviral properties.[2]

Bougainvillea commemorates Louis-Antoine de Bougainville (1729–1811), mathematician, scientist and author, who sailed around the world in 1766–69 and visited Tahiti not long before Cook arrived there.

Bougainvillea spectabilis Willd., *Species Plantarum* 2: 348 (1799)

Copper plate by Gabriel Smith, based on Parkinson's 1768 watercolour; BF 355; Diment et al., 1987: B24

1. Mabberley, 1998, p. 120, 2014, p. 116 and 4th ed., 2017

2. R. Balasaraswathi et al., 'An antiviral protein from *Bougainvillea spectabilis* roots; purification and characterization', *Phytochemistry* 47, 1998, pp. 1561–65; A. Umamaheswari et al., '*In vitro* antibacterial activity of *Bougainvillea spectabilis* leaves extracts', *Advances in Biological Research* 2, 2008, pp. 1–5

9.
EPIDENDRUM SECUNDUM
crucifix orchid, Orchidaceae

One of the 'reed-stem' epidendrums, this tropical American orchid can grow on rocks and is also completely terrestrial; today it is often found in disturbed areas such as roadsides. Widely cultivated, it was introduced in England in 1798. It has stems to 1 m (3 ft) tall and produces white to pink or orange flowers all year round; these are pollinated by hummingbirds and several species of daytime-flying moths and butterflies.[1]

As a result of anthropogenic disturbance of the environment, this orchid now grows with the previously separated *Epidendrum fulgens*, and, where they share the same pollinators, natural hybrids arise. Deliberate crosses with the scarcely different *E. ibaguense* made by John Seden (1840–1921) at Veitch's Chelsea nursery in London first flowered in 1888 and are the 'scarlet orchids' commonly seen today. *E. × obrienianum*, for example, has now become naturalized in Hawaii.[2]

Although the name has long been used for almost any epiphytic orchid (see *Cattleya forbesii*, Pl. 10, p. 40),[3] *Epidendrum* – from Greek *epi-*, upon, and *dendron*, tree, as most species are epiphytes (growing on other plants) – comprises perhaps 1,500 species of tropical America, occurring north to Florida (seven), many of them in cultivation;[3] *secundus* means having organs turned towards one side only.

Epidendrum secundum Jacq., *Enumeratio Systematica Plantarum*: 29 (1760)

Copper plate by Gabriel Smith, based on Parkinson's 1768 watercolour; BF 356; Diment et al., 1987: B25

1. E. R. Pansarin and M. C. Amaral, 'Reproductive biology and pollination mechanisms of *Epidendrum secundum* (Orchidaceae). Floral variation: a consequence of natural hybridization?', *Plant Biology* 10, 2008, pp. 211–19

2. Mabberley, 1998, p. 132

3. Mabberley, 2014, p. 309 and 4th ed., 2017

10.

CATTLEYA FORBESII
Orchidaceae

When Banks and Solander found this Brazilian orchid, Solander named it 'Epidendrum bifolium' because of the paired leaves on the top of the pseudobulb. It was introduced into cultivation from Rio de Janeiro in 1823 by the tragic John Forbes (see *Serjania ferruginea*, Pl. 7, p. 34).

Cattleya commemorates Banks' friend William Cattley (1788–1835), a rich businessman with a large garden at Barnet, then in Hertfordshire and now part of London. He grew a wide range of plants there, both outside and under glass, and also built up a collection of botanical drawings, among which were many that he had commissioned of his new plants. When he needed an editor for the publication of these illustrations, what was to become *Collectanea Botanica* (1821), Banks suggested John Lindley (1799–1865), who would later become secretary of the Horticultural Society of London but at that time was a young assistant in Banks' library and herbarium. Lindley took on the project and obligingly gave the name *Cattleya* to one of Cattley's most spectacular orchids.

Cattleya (including *Sophronitis*) comprises 112 species native in tropical America.[1] They are usually epiphytes, with one to three thick leaves per pseudobulb, and they have been much hybridized; the familiar ones used in buttonholes and bouquets are derived from large-flowered species with one leaf.

Cattleya forbesii Lindl., *Collectanea Botanica*: sub t. 37 (1826)

Copper plate by Gabriel Smith, based on Parkinson's 1768 watercolour;
BF 358; Diment et al., 1987: B27

1. Mabberley, 2014, p. 161 and 4th ed., 2017

II.

BOMAREA EDULIS
salsilla, Alstroemeriaceae

After *Endeavour* left Rio de Janeiro, Banks collected this edible plant on the island of Raza, in the harbour of Santa Cruz, on 7 December 1768.[1] Solander's manuscript name for it was 'Alstroemeria salsilla', using the vernacular name for the specific epithet. In 1808 it was formally named *Alstroemeria edulis*, but it differs from the familiar garden *Alstroemeria* – named after Baron Claus Alstroemer (1736–1794), a friend of Linnaeus – in its climbing habit, presence of tubers as well as many other features.

Widespread in the West Indies, as well as Central and South America, salsilla scrambles to some 3 m (10 ft) and is grown for its root tubers, which are edible when cooked.

Bomarea, commemorating Jacques-Christophe Valmont de Bomare (1731–1807), French patron of science and author, comprises 107 species found in tropical America north to Mexico. They usually have twining stems and tubers at the root-tips, while their spectacular flowers are often conspicuous along roadsides and at forest edges; the red ones are pollinated by hummingbirds. Many are cultivated in other countries as ornamental climbers.[2]

Bomarea edulis (Tussac) Herb., *Amaryllidaceae*: 111 (1837)

Copper plate by Van Drazowa, based on Parkinson's 1768 watercolour;
BF 359; Diment et al., 1987: B29

1. Beaglehole, 1963, 1, p. 195
2. Mabberley, 2014, p. 112 and 4th ed., 2017

12.

RIBES MAGELLANICUM
Grossulariaceae

This deciduous shrubby currant, native to southern Chile and Argentina, was collected by Banks and Solander in Tierra del Fuego in January 1769, when Solander
gave it the manuscript name 'Ribes antarcticum'. Its ripe fruits are purple and can
be eaten fresh or used in preserves, and its potential as a commercial crop is being
investigated.[1] The species was described not long before, from material collected by
Philibert Commerçon (or Commerson; 1727–1773) in the Magellan Strait, during
Bougainville's voyage (see Pl. 8, p. 36). Commerçon's botanical assistant (and lover),
Jeanne Baret (1740–1807), who accompanied him disguised as a man, was the first
woman to circumnavigate the globe.

The genus *Ribes* comprises some 160 species of low shrubs, often armed with spines.[2]
They are found throughout the northern hemisphere, and also south to Tierra del
Fuego. Many are cultivated as 'currants', though that name derives from the city of
Corinth, and correctly refers to grapes, notably in the form of the dried currants
used today in cake-making. Another confusion arises from the generic name *Ribes*,
which was originally an Arabic name for a kind of sorrel.[3]

Most familiar is *Ribes nigrum*, the blackcurrant, from Eurasia, though modern
blackcurrants are hybrids involving American species. Its fruit is stewed or made
into jam or a liqueur (cassis) or soft drinks, and has a reputation for antioxidants
and higher levels of vitamin C than in citrus fruits. The redcurrant, *Ribes rubrum*,
is also from Eurasia, but many commercial redcurrants are hybrids with other
European species.

Ribes magellanicum Poir., *Encyclopédie Méthodique. Botanique* suppl. 2: 856
(1812)

Copper plate by Charles White, based on Parkinson's 1769 watercolour;
BF 686; Diment et al., 1987: TF18

1. M. E. Arena, et al., 'Growth and fruiting of *Ribes magellanicum* in
   Tierra del Fuego, Argentina', *New Zealand Journal of Crop
   and Horticultural Science* 35, 2007, pp. 61–66

2. Mabberley, 2014, p. 741

3. *Oxford English Dictionary*: ribes

13.
NOTHOFAGUS BETULOIDES
guindo, Fagaceae

Guindo is an evergreen tree which can grow to 25 m (80 ft) tall or more, though sometimes is merely a shrub of 2 m (6½ ft).[1] Found up to 500 m (1,640 ft) high in southern Argentina and Chile from 40 degrees southwards, it is a dominant tree on poorer soils, to which it is adapted, whereas *N. pumilio* dominates on better ones.

Banks noted that among the few tree species he found in Tierra del Fuego, guindo was valued for its timber;[2] its pinkish, hard wood is now used for construction and furniture. Solander's manuscript name was 'Betula antarctica', as he considered it to be a kind of birch (Betulaceae). It was correctly assigned to Fagaceae when first formally described in 1827 and named *Fagus betuloides*, the specific name referring to the resemblance to birches.

Guindo was introduced into cultivation in England by 1830.[3] Fuegian material has been successfully cultivated as far north as the Faroe Islands.

The genus *Nothofagus* (from the Greek *nothos*, false, and *fagus*, the Latin name for beech) comprises 34 species of these 'southern beeches'. They are found in temperate South America, New Zealand, Australia and New Guinea, with fossils from Antarctica dating from the Pliocene. Several are important timber trees.[4]

Nothofagus betuloides (Mirb.) Oerst. in *Kongelige Danske Videnskabernes Selskabs Skrifter*, s. 5, 9: 354 (1871)

Copper plate by Gerard Sibelius, based on Parkinson's 1769 watercolour; BF 727; Diment et al., 1987: TF66

1. Moore, 1983, p. 82
2. Beaglehole, 1963, 1, p. 226
3. Chittenden, 1951, 2, p. 1380
4. Mabberley, 2014, p. 588

14.

OSMORHIZA BERTEROI
Umbelliferae

Among the plants Banks and Solander collected in Tierra del Fuego was this short-lived aromatic perennial. It reaches 1 m (3 ft) in height in deciduous *Nothofagus* forest and on moist, shaded cliffs.[1] The floral heads comprise 4–120 florets, the central ones having only stamens. The root is eaten by indigenous people in both North and South America, and is also of local medicinal significance.

Together with just a handful of other plant species, it has a bipolar distribution,[2] flowering in late spring in the United States, and October to December, the southern spring, in Chile, which it is considered to have reached by long-distance dispersal from the north about a million years ago.[3]

Osmorhiza (Greek *osme*, scent or smell; *rhiza*, root) is a genus of ten species of the Americas and eastern Asia;[4] *berteroi* commemorates Carlo Luigi Giuseppe Bertero (1789–1831), an Italian physicist, doctor and naturalist, who collected in Chile the specimen ('type specimen') on which the original description was based.

Osmorhiza berteroi DC., *Prodromus Systematis Naturalis Regni Vegetabilis* 4: 232 (1830)

Copper plate by William Tringham, based on Parkinson's 1769 watercolour; BF 698; Diment et al., 1987: TF31

1. Moore, 1983, p. 178

2. Mabberley, 2014, p. 614

3. J. Wen and S. M. Ickert-Bond, 'Evolution of the Madrean-Tethyan disjunctions and the North and South American amphitropical disjunctions in plants', *Journal of Systematics and Evolution* 47, 2009, pp. 331–48

4. P. P. Lowry and A. G. Jones, 'Systematics of *Osmorhiza* Raf. (Apiaceae: Apioideae)', *Annals of the Missouri Botanical Garden* 71, 1984, pp. 1128–71

15.
CODONORCHIS LESSONII
white dog orchid, Orchidaceae

The white dog orchid is a terrestrial herb native to southern Argentina and Chile, as well as to the Falkland Islands (Malvinas), where it grows in *Nothofagus* forest and also, rarely, in grassland among rocks.[1]

Codonorchis (from the Greek *kodon*, bell, and *orchis*, a classical Greek name from the word for testicles, which the asymmetric paired tubers of certain orchids allegedly resemble) comprises two or three South American species;[2] *lessonii* commemorates the collector René Primevère Lesson (1794–1849), a French surgeon-naturalist, who served on Louis Isidore Duperrey's round-the-world voyage on *La Coquille* in 1822–25.

Codonorchis lessonii (d'Urv.) Lindl., *The Genera and Species of Orchidaceous Plants*: 411 (1840)
Copper plate by Gabriel Smith, based on Parkinson's 1769 watercolour; BF 730; Diment et al., 1987: TF69
1. Moore, 1983, p. 349
2. Mabberley, 2014, p. 200

16.
CALTHA APPENDICULATA
Ranunculaceae

Found in the Falklands Islands (Malvinas) and southern Andes[1] in wet places up to around 2,000 m (6,500 ft), this is a creeping semi-succulent plant. It is dioecious, that is, the male and female flowers grow on different plants, the males having aborted ovaries, the females aborted stamens (staminodes); the flowers are faintly scented.

The leaves appear to have leafy outgrowths from near the midrib, hence Solander's manuscript name 'Caltha paradoxa'. These outgrowths are equivalent to the basal lobes of the leaves typical of north temperate *Caltha* species.

Caltha (in classical Latin a yellow flower, possibly *Calendula officinalis*, marigold, Compositae) is a genus comprising some 12 species in temperate regions,[2] the most familiar being *C. palustris*, the marsh marigold or king-cup of wet habitats in northern regions; *appendiculatus* means with small appendages, referring to the leaves. They produce a volatile toxin, protoanemonin, which is an irritant to skin and mucous membranes.

Caltha appendiculata Pers., *Synopsis Plantarum* 2: 107 (1806)
Copper plate by Daniel Mackenzie, based on Parkinson's 1769
watercolour; BF 675; Diment et al., 1987: TF3
1. Moore, 1983, p. 68
2. Mabberley, 2014, p. 140

17.
GUNNERA MAGELLANICA
Gunneraceae

This dioecious creeping plant, which roots at the nodes, is found in moist, sheltered places in southern South America and the Andes of Ecuador and Peru.[1] The first published description was based on a specimen collected by Philibert Commerçon on Bougainville's voyage (see *Ribes magellanicum*, Pl. 12, p. 44). It is grown in gardens as a carpet-forming perennial, having been introduced into cultivation in Britain around 1879.[2]

Gunnera, commemorating the Norwegian botanist-bishop Johan Ernst Gunnerus (1718–1773), comprises some 60 species of the southern hemisphere including the tropics. They range from gigantic pachycaul (with a thick stem or trunk) perennial herbs to small creeping herbs, and even tiny annuals such as *G. herteri* from Brazil and Uruguay.[3] Most familiar in gardens are the statuesque *G. manicata* from southern Brazil and *G. tinctoria* from Chile, grown for their gigantic bristly leaves, up to 3 m (10 ft) across in what are perhaps hybrids between them. They are now becoming invasive in Britain, Ireland, the Azores and New Zealand.

Gunnera magellanica Lam., *Encyclopédie Méthodique. Botanique.* 3: 61 (1789)
Copper plate by Daniel Mackenzie, based on Parkinson's 1769
watercolour; BF 690; Diment et al., 1987: TF24
1. Moore, 1983, p. 149
2. Chittenden, 1951, 2, p. 937
3. Mabberley, 2014, p. 380 and 4th ed., 2017

18.

BERBERIS ILICIFOLIA
chelia, Berberidaceae

Chelia is a shrub up to 4 m (13 ft) tall, found to 40 degrees south in *Nothofagus* woods of Argentina and Chile, often with *Ribes magellanicum* (Pl. 12, p. 44).[1] Its orange-yellow flowers appear August to December; its wood was used to make bows.[2] Although it was named 'Berberis sempervirens' by Solander in manuscript, it was described with a different name by the Swedish naturalist Anders Sparrman (1748–1820) from material collected in 1774 on Cook's second voyage, also in Tierra del Fuego. The specific name refers to the holly-like leaves; though *Ilex* today is used for holly, it actually derives from the Latin name for the holm oak, *Quercus ilex*.

Berberis is the Latinized form of the Arabic word for barberry, the fruit of *B. vulgaris*. It is a genus (including *Mahonia*) of some 500 species of Eurasia, reaching south to tropical mountains as well as to southern South America.[3] Many are grown as ornamentals, especially *B.* × *hortensis* (*Mahonia* × *media*), a winter-flowering shrub familiar in northern gardens; others yield useful fruits as well as dyes and medicinal preparations from the bark and wood. Several species are hosts to stem-rusts of cereals, as was recognized by Banks as early as 1805 but not accepted until the 1860s.

Berberis ilicifolia L.f., *Supplementum plantarum*: 210 (1782)

Copper plate by Daniel Mackenzie, based on Parkinson's 1769 watercolour; BF 676; Diment et al., 1987: TF5

1. Moore, 1983, p. 142

2. L. R. Landrum, 'Revision of *Berberis* (Berberidaceae) in Chile and adjacent southern Argentina', *Annals of the Missouri Botanical Garden* 86, 1999, 793–834

3. Mabberley, 2014, p. 100 and 4th ed., 2017

19.

MARSIPPOSPERMUM GRANDIFLORUM
Juncaceae

This rush is a wind-pollinated perennial growing to 30 cm (1 ft) high or more, found on hummocks in peatlands in southern Argentina and Chile, as well as in the Falkland Islands (Malvinas), where it is often locally abundant.[1]

Although collected by Banks and Solander, it was described as a new species from specimens collected by the Forsters, father and son (see Pls 22 and 47), on Cook's second voyage. Some of their specimens found their way to Abraham Bäck (1713–1795), the surgeon to the king of Sweden, and from him to the younger Linnaeus (also Carl; 1741–1783), who described this and other Forster plants in his *Supplementum plantarum* (1782), but attributed them to Bäck and not the Forsters.

Marsippospermum (from the Latin *marsipium*, *marsupium*, a pouch, bag or purse) is a genus of four species of temperate South America, with one in New Zealand.

Marsippospermum grandiflorum (L.f.) Hook., *Icones Plantarum* 6: t. 533 (1843)

Copper plate by Daniel Mackenzie, based on Parkinson's 1769 watercolour; BF 735; Diment et al., 1987: TF74

1. Moore, 1983, p. 319

20.

SPONDIAS DULCIS
ambarella, Anacardiaceae

Banks and Solander collected material of this fruit tree in the Society Islands, in what is now French Polynesia, where *Endeavour* arrived in April 1769. Solander named it 'Spondias dulcis' (*dulcis* meaning sweet), but this name was appropriated by Stanfield Parkinson, without acknowledgment, in his unauthorized 1773 book based on his brother Sydney's manuscripts. It was therefore one of the first botanical discoveries of the voyage to be published.

Parkinson wrote of the 'E avee', as he called it:

> This is a large stately tree, and often grows to the height of forty or fifty feet: the fruit, which, I believe, is peculiar to these isles, is of an oval shape, yellow when ripe, and grows in bunches of three or four, and is about the size of a middling apple, with a large stringy core: it is a very wholsome [sic] and palatable fruit, improving on the taste, which is nearest that of a mangoe [sic]; it is strongly impregnated with turpentine, and makes excellent pies when green. The wood serves for building canoes, and for several other purposes.[1]

Though its origin is unknown, the tree is apparently native in New Guinea rain forests. In the same family as the mango, the genus *Spondias* (from the Greek word Theophrastus used for a wild plum)[2] comprises about ten tree species from tropical Asia to tropical America. They produce resins that are collected by euglossine, or orchid, bees for constructing their nests. The fruits (drupes) of several species are valued, especially those of *Spondias mombin*, yellow mombin, from America, which are eaten fresh and used in ice-cream and liqueurs.

Spondias dulcis Parkinson, *Journal of a Voyage to the South Seas*: 39 (1773)
Copper plate by Daniel Mackenzie, based on Parkinson's 1769
watercolour; BF 595; Diment et al., 1987: SI1/18
1. Parkinson, 1784, p. 39
2. Mabberley, 2014, p. 814

21.

TACCA LEONTOPETALOIDES
Tahiti arrowroot, Taccaceae

Solander's name for this crop plant collected in French Polynesia was 'Chaitea tacca', *taka* being a vernacular name. Banks wrote of it in August 1769:

> a root of the Salop [salep] kind Calld by the inhabitants *Pea* [*pia*]...a certain quantity of a Paste [used in the manufacture of clothing] made of the root... which serves them also for food.[1]

Tahiti arrowroot is a beach-plant found throughout the Pacific region and is culti-vated there for the starch obtained from its rhizomes, which resembles that of the unrelated arrowroot of commerce, once the bitter principle taccalin is removed. It was formerly used like cornflour and as a laundry starch. The leaves are still used in hat-making.

The genus *Tacca* comprises at least 13 species found in the Old World tropics.[2] Their fly-pollinated flowers heat up to 40°C (104°F), volatilizing an attractive scent from slender 'whiskers' (bracts) that are most familiar in the house plant *T. integrifolia*, the bat flower or bat lily, grown in Europe and North America.

Tacca leontopetaloides (L.) Kuntze, *Revisio Generum Plantarum* 2: 704 (1891)

Copper plate by William Tringham, based on Parkinson's 1769 watercolour; BF 669; Diment et al., 1987: SI2/48

1. Beaglehole, 1963, 1, pp. 343, 356
2. Mabberley, 2014, p. 837

22.

CRATEVA RELIGIOSA
barna, Capparaceae

Barna is a deciduous shrub or tree, native in the Indopacific region and growing to 15 m (50 ft) tall. In Tahiti, Parkinson noted: 'The fruit of this shrub they lay upon their corpses, and hang it upon their burial whattas.'[1] The bark is used in the treatment of urinary disorders, as it contains an active principle called lupeol, while the fruit is rich in vitamin C.

Although Solander gave it the manuscript name 'Crateva frondosa', Georg Forster (1754–1794), who was on Cook's second voyage, gave it today's scientific name, no doubt referring to the ritual Parkinson wrote of.

Crateva, commemorating Crateuas (or Cratevas; 111–64 BCE), botanist and physician to Mithridates VI ('the Great') in what is now northern Turkey,[2] is a genus of ten tropical species (five restricted to Madagascar) known as garlic pears, some of them potherbs and cultivated ornamentals.[3]

Crateva religiosa G. Forst., *De Plantis Esculentis*: 45 (1786)

Copper plate by Gerard Sibelius, based on Parkinson's 1769 watercolour; BF 586; Diment et al., 1987: SI1/3

1. Parkinson, 1784, pp. 39–40
2. N. G. L. Hammond and H. H. Scullard, *The Oxford Classical Dictionary* (Oxford, Clarendon, 1970), p. 297
3. Mabberley, 2014, p. 226

23.

THESPESIA POPULNEA
mahoe, Malvaceae

A pantropical tree of the shoreline, mahoe is now planted widely as a street tree, though it is invasive in the southeastern United States.[1] In 1770 it was introduced in England, where it is a greenhouse plant. Its flowers, which turn from yellow to purple in 24 hours, are pollinated by sunbirds and insects.

Parkinson noted in his journal that:

> This beautiful tree is planted in all Morais, being held Sacred to the Tané: they also make use of it as an emblem of peace; and always bring it in their hands when they meet with strange people.[2]

Solander's manuscript name, 'Thespesia populnea', was not published until 1807. The use of the Greek word *thespesios,* divine, no doubt refers to the practice Parkinson described; *populneus,* like a poplar (*Populus,* Salicaceae), alludes to the appearance of the leaves. Parkinson's finished drawing of this plant can be seen on p. 299.

Thespesia is in the same tribe as cotton, and it was therefore eradicated from cotton-growing areas because it acts as a host to the cotton-stainer, an insect that discolours young cotton fibres. Its hard wood, which takes a fine polish, is used to make bowls (notably for serving hoppers, a type of crepe, in Sri Lanka), gunstocks and wheel-frames.

There are some 17 species of *Thespesia* in the tropics.[3] Several are cultivated as ornamentals, notably the African *T. garckeana,* which has edible fruit, while others produce useful fibre resembling sunn hemp (*Crotalaria juncea,* Leguminosae), especially *T. lampas* of the Old World tropics.

Thespesia populnea (L.) Correa in *Annales du Muséum National d'Histoire Naturelle Paris* 9: 290 + t. 8, fig. 1 (1807)

Copper plate by Daniel Mackenzie, based on Parkinson's 1769 watercolour; BF 591; Diment et al., 1987: SI1/12

1. Mabberley, 1998, p. 40
2. Parkinson, 1784, p. 42
3. Mabberley, 2014, p. 854

24.

SESBANIA GRANDIFLORA
bakphul, Leguminosae

Bakphul is a small tree up to some 12 m (40 ft) tall, bearing red, pink or white flowers up to 10 cm (4 in.) long, which are followed by pods to over 50 cm (20 in.) in length. Found throughout tropical Asia to the Pacific, it is naturalized in the Caribbean and was introduced into European horticulture in 1768.

During their stay in French Polynesia, Parkinson noted that:

> This shrub grows wild, in great abundance, on the island of Toopbai [Tupai]; and is planted on the other islands to shade their houses; and the flower of it, which is very beautiful, they often stick in their ears.[1]

The leaves are eaten as a vegetable, as are the pods when young; both the leaves and bark figure in local medicine.[2]

Sesbania, the Latinized form of the Arabic word *sesban*, used for *S. sesban*, is a genus of some 60 species of warm and usually wet countries. Some make good firewood, notably *S. sesban* (formerly used for gunpowder charcoal) and *S. aculeata* of the Old World tropics. The latter is also a possible source of guar gum, while others, including *S. grandiflora*, are widely cultivated as ornamentals.

Sesbania grandiflora (L.) Poir., *Encyclopédie Méthodique. Botanique* 7: 127 (1806)

Copper plate by Daniel Mackenzie, based on Parkinson's 1769 watercolour; BF 598; Diment et al., 1987: SI1/22

1. Parkinson, 1784, p. 43
2. Mabberley, 2014, p. 791

25.

INOCARPUS FAGIFER
Tahitian chestnut, Leguminosae

While travelling around the islands of what is now French Polynesia, Banks noted in June 1769:

> But fertile as this countrey was we did no[t] get or even see a single breadfruit, the trees were intirely bared, the people seemed to live intirely on Ahee which were plentiful here.[1]

Tahitian chestnut, or *ahee* as Banks recorded, is a Pacific tree up to 20 m (66 ft) tall or more, growing in many kinds of lowland forest, including mangrove, and widely naturalized. Its leaves, flowers and fruits do not much resemble most Leguminosae, but it is closely related to rosewood, *Dalbergia* species, and padouk, *Pterocarpus* species.[2] Its trunk has characteristic buttresses and the wood is used in construction and for firewood. The fragrant flowers appear November–December and the fleshy mesocarp of the fruits is eaten by cockatoos and bats, thus dispersing the large seeds, which are edible once cooked.

The tree was introduced into cultivation in England as early as 1793, and is grown under glass in temperate countries.[3]

Either Sydney Parkinson's brother, Stanfield, or his ghostwriter, William Kenrick (1725–1779), seems to have mistranscribed Solander's manuscript name 'Amotum fagiferum', rendering it *Aniotum*, and it became one of the first scientific names coined on the voyage to be published.[4]

Inocarpus, from Greek *inos*, fibre, and *karpon*, fruit, is a genus of three species found from Malesia (the region including Malaysia, Indonesia, the Philippines and New Guinea) to the Pacific; the Latin *fagifer* means bearing beech (*Fagus*)-like fruits.

Inocarpus fagifer (Parkinson) Fosb. in *Journal of the Washington Academy of Sciences* 31: 95 (1941)

Copper plate by Gerard Sibelius, based on Parkinson's 1769 watercolour; BF 601; Diment et al., 1987: SI1/26

1. Beaglehole, 1963, 1, pp. 297–98
2. Mabberley, 2014, p. 431
3. Chittenden, 1951, 2, p. 1051
4. Parkinson, 1784, p. 39

26.

BENINCASA HISPIDA
wax gourd, Cucurbitaceae

The wax or white gourd, or petha, is not known outside cultivation, that is, it is a cultigen, though it is thought to have an Asian origin.[1] A fast-growing annual climber – in three hours the shoots can increase by as much as 2.3 cm (almost 1 in.) in length – its large, fleshy fruits, which are spherical to oblong and hispid (hairy), become waxy on maturation.

The fruit is boiled as a vegetable in curries and soups, and can be pickled or candied; the shoots, tendrils and leaves are used as a potherb. The plant also features in local medicine, while the hollowed-out waxy gourds were used as containers for scented coconut oil in Polynesia before European contact, as Parkinson described:

> The fruit of this tree is about the size of a small orange, very hard, and quite round, serving them, instead of bottles, to put their monoe or oil in.[2]

Solander gave it the manuscript name 'Cucurbita pruriens' because of the irritant hairs on the young fruit, which no doubt act as a deterrent to grazing animals. The name was used by Parkinson, but without enough descriptive matter to make it validly published.

The generic name commemorates the Flemish Joseph Goedenhuitze (1535–1596), later known as Giuseppe (Casabona) Benincasa, a director of the Pisa Botanic Garden.

Benincasa hispida (Thunb.) Cogn. in DC., *Monographie Phanerogamarum* 3: 513 (1881)

Copper plate by Daniel Mackenzie, based on Parkinson's 1769 watercolour; BF 606; Diment et al., 1987: SI1/34

1. Mabberley, 2014, p. 99
2. Parkinson, 1784, p. 44

27.

LUFFA CYLINDRICA
loofah, Cucurbitaceae

The loofah, or vegetable sponge, is a scrambler from the tropics of the Old World. Its young fruits are eaten as a vegetable, as are those of the Asian *Luffa acutangula*, the sing-kwa, or sinqua (melon),[1] while the bleached vascular system of the mature fruit is the loofah of bathrooms. This vascular system is also used in engine filters, linings for steel helmets, insulation and bath mats, besides as a matrix in bioreactors for ethanol production.[2]

Luffa, from the Arabic name for the plant, is a genus of eight species in the tropics, with five in the Old World and three in the Americas; *cylindricus* refers to the shape of the fruits.

Luffa cylindrica (L.) M. Roem., *Familiarum Naturalium Regni Vegetabilis Synopses Monographicae* 2: 63 (1846)

Copper plate by Gabriel Smith, based on Parkinson's 1769 watercolour; BF 608; Diment et al., 1987: SI1/36

1. Mabberley, 2014, p. 504

2. N. Filipowicz et al., 'Revisiting *Luffa* (Cucurbitaceae) 25 years after C. Heiser: species boundaries and applications of names tested with plastid and nuclear DNA sequences', *Systematic Botany* 39, 2014, pp. 205–15

28.

CANAVALIA ROSEA
beach bean, Leguminosae

A trailing vine, beach bean is a common pantropical beach-plant. It is pollinated by carpenter bees and its seeds are spread by sea. Through these 'drift seeds' it was one of first pioneers on Krakatau after the catastrophic 1883 eruption. Seeds even reach Britain, though by the time of their arrival they are no longer viable.

Solander's manuscript name for the Polynesian plant was 'Glycine rosea', the specific epithet referring to the flower colour; this name was also used by Swedish botanist Olof Swartz (1760–1818) in his first published description of the Jamaican type specimen as *Dolichos roseus* (1788).

Canavalia, the Latinized form of the Konkani name *kanavali* of southern India, is a genus of some 60 tropical species, found especially in the Americas, with Hawaii having six endemic species.[1] They provide green manure and stock feed as well as some edible beans and a tobacco substitute.

Canavalia rosea (Sw.) DC., *Prodromus Systematis Naturalis Regni Vegetabilis* 2: 404 (1825)

Copper plate by Daniel Mackenzie, based on Parkinson's 1769 watercolour; BF 597; Diment et al., 1987: SI1/21

1. Mabberley, 2014, p. 146

29.

CYRTANDRA GLABRA
Gesneriaceae

Cyrtandra glabra is an endangered species native in French Polynesia. The material Banks and Solander collected was used by the Gaertners (father and son, Josef and Karl Friedrich; see also Pls 2 and 56) in their work, and was the basis for the new species the younger Gaertner described in 1807.

The name *Cyrtandra*, from the Greek *kurtos*, curbed, and *andros*, male, refers to the two stamens. The genus contains around 600 species, some of which are tree-like, found mainly in Borneo and New Guinea (each with 150), as well as in China, south Japan, and the Nicobars to the Pacific islands. Many hybrids occur in Hawaii. The family Gesneriaceae includes familiar house plants such as African violets and other species of *Streptocarpus*, originally from Africa, as well as gloxinias (*Sinningia speciosa*) from Brazil.

Cyrtandra glabra C. F. Gaertn., *Supplementum Carpologiae*: 234 + t. 224 fig. 4 (1807)
Copper plate by John Roberts, based on Parkinson's 1769 watercolour;
BF 634; Diment et al., 1987: SI2/10

30.

SOLANUM VIRIDE
uporo, Solanaceae

In his journal Parkinson wrote: 'The leaves of this plant, baked, are eaten as greens.'[1] Uporo is native from Fiji to Tonga and Samoa, but has been carried as far east as Hawaii. The large-leaved cultivar in villages in Fiji known as 'Anthropophagorum'[2] (meaning man-eating) has tomato-like edible fruits, which are used in ceremonies and are the basis of so-called 'Cannibal Chutney', a Fijian novelty.[3]

Solanum, the Latin name for a plant, possibly the weedy *S. nigrum*, is an enormous, economically important genus of perhaps 1,400 species, found from coasts to upland forest and semi-desert throughout almost all the world. They range from trees, such as the tree tomato (*S. betaceum* from South America), to shrubs and herbs, sometimes climbing and often prickly, the prickliness being associated with marsupial grazing in Australia, for example. They contain alkaloids and so are often toxic, though the fruits of many cultivated species, such as the tomato (*S. lycopersicum*) and aubergine (*S. melongena*), are edible. *Solanum tuberosum* is the potato, derived from wild species in the Andes.

Solanum viride Sol. ex G. Forst., *De Plantis Esculentis*: 72 (1786)
Copper plate by Gabriel Smith, based on Parkinson's 1769 watercolour;
BF 633; Diment et al., 1987: SI2/9
1. Parkinson, 1784, p. 38
2. A. C. Smith, *Flora Vitiensis nova: A New Flora of Fiji*, vol. 5 (Lawai, Hawaii, National Tropical Botanical Garden, 1991), pp. 18–21
3. Mabberley, 2014, pp. 804–06 and 4th ed., 2017

31.
GARDENIA TAITENSIS
tiare, Rubiaceae

It is surprising that such a conspicuous plant as tiare was not named until 1830. Solander, using the name *Gardenia florida* in his manuscripts, confused it with the well-known gardenia or Cape jasmine, *Gardenia augusta* (*G. florida*, *G. jasminoides*), an Asian species cultivated for over a thousand years in China, but long thought to have come from South Africa.

In his journal, Banks recorded that tiare was planted around houses in Polynesia and that women put the sweetly scented flowers in their hair or through holes in their ears.[1] In Vanuatu, *Gardenia tannaensis* is also grown for its flowers.[2] Tiare is now the national flower of both French Polynesia and the Cook Islands, though it was probably introduced there from further west, despite the specific name *taitensis*, 'from Tahiti'. Today the flowers are used in some commercial scents.

Gardenia, named after Dr Alexander Garden (1730–1791), a correspondent of Linnaeus and the first grower of the gardenia in the United States, is a genus of about 140 species of the warmer parts of the Old World. A number of them are of medicinal significance, and some have apparently insecticidal qualities.

Gardenia taitensis DC., *Prodromus Systematis Naturalis Regni Vegetabilis*
4: 380 (1830)
Copper plate by Daniel Mackenzie, based on Parkinson's 1769
watercolour; BF 615; Diment et al., 1987: SI1/46
1. Beaglehole, 1963, 1, pp. 325, 338
2. Mabberley, 2014, p. 350 and 4th ed., 2017

32.

CERBERA MANGHAS
sea mango, Apocynaceae

Sea mango is an evergreen tree that can grow to 25 m (80 ft) tall, though it is usually much smaller. Native from the Seychelles eastwards to French Polynesia, it is found growing in coastal, especially mangrove, forests. In his journal Parkinson noted that, 'This plant has a pretty large white flower like that of an oleander. Of the wood of this tree they make their pahaoos, or drums.'[1]

Elsewhere, the soft wood is also used for charcoal, as well as for carving some of the brightly coloured masks typical of Sri Lanka.[2] Sea mango has been widely cultivated for its attractive, fragrant flowers, but the leaves and fruits contain the toxic cardiac glycoside cerberin, which has been used in poisoning and suicides. The specific name *manghas* refers to the mango-like fruit.

Cerbera, after Cerberus, the three-headed dog guarding the gateway to the Underworld in classical mythology, perhaps referring either to the scales over the stamens at the red corolla throat in *C. manghas* or to the toxic principles, is a genus of just two species, the second being *C. floribunda* of New Guinea and northeastern Australia. The fruit of the latter is blue and is eaten by cassowaries, which then disperse the seeds in their droppings.

Cerbera manghas L. *Species Plantarum* 1: 208 (1753)

Copper plate by Gerard Sibelius, based on Parkinson's 1769 watercolour; BF 622; Diment et al., 1987: SI1/53

1. Parkinson, 1784, p. 38

2. Mabberley, 2014, p. 169; D. J. Middleton, 'Cerbera', in E. Soepadmo et al. (eds), *Tree Flora of Sabah and Sarawak*, 5 (Kuala Lumpur, Forest Research Institute Malaysia, 2004), pp. 23–27

33.

HELIOTROPIUM ARBOREUM
tahinu, Boraginaceae

A small tree or shrub typical of the littoral from the western Indian Ocean (Seychelles) to Polynesia, tahinu is also found inland on saline or calcareous soils. Long known as *Tournefortia argentea*, it has now been identified as a species of *Heliotropium*.[1]

As with many other Boraginaceae, such as alkanet (*Anchusa tinctoria*) of the Mediterranean, tahinu is a source of a red dye.[2] It also has medicinal qualities, and in the Seychelles the leaves are smoked.[3] Its wood is used in handicrafts.

Heliotropium, from the Greek *helios*, sun, and *trope*, turning, referring to an old (erroneous) idea that the heads of the flowers move with the sun, is a genus of about 350 species of trees, climbers and especially herbs containing alkaloids. The alkaloids are so deterrent to grazing that East African *Heliotropium* species growing in places where locusts swarm survive unharmed. Most familiar in cultivation is *H. arborescens* from Peru; known as heliotrope or cherry pie, this is a common bedding plant in Europe, where in southern parts it is used in scent-making.

Heliotropium arboreum (Blanco) Mabb., *Mabberley's Plant-book* ed. 4: 1101 (2017)

Copper plate by Gabriel Smith, based on Parkinson's 1769 watercolour; BF 624; Diment et al., 1987: SI1/57

1. Mabberley, 2014, p. 397 and 4th ed., 2017

2. Beaglehole, 1963, 1, p. 358

3. Staples and Herbst, 2005, p. 199

34.
IPOMOEA BATATAS
sweet potato, Convolvulaceae

Originally a New World crop ('kumar' in Peru), sweet potato was brought to Polynesia ('kumara') before Europeans arrived there and was then taken to New Zealand by Māori. The swollen tubers are the source of edible starch; the Māori grew no cereals and sweet potato became their staple crop.[1] There are many cultivars, the early Hawaiians, for instance, having 230, all except 24 of which are now lost.

Sweet potato has a hybrid origin, being hexaploid (having six sets of chromosomes); its closest relations are *I. tabascana* (tetraploid, with four sets of chromosomes) and *I. trifida* from tropical America. A major food source, notably in Asia (especially Japan, but also as dang myun noodles in Korea) and the United States, where it is called yam, it is the fifth most important root crop, with an annual world production amounting to more than 100 million tonnes.

With its natural fibres, sweet potato starch is used in biodegradable plastic for Toyota cars, and is also an alcohol source. It was the first 'potato' in Europe: Linnaeus even adopted the Caribbean name 'batatas' when giving it a scientific name. No doubt because of its shape, Henry VIII considered it an aphrodisiac, and Shakespeare has the bawdy Falstaff say 'Let the sky rain potatoes'. The word potato was later transferred to the unrelated *Solanum tuberosum*, the potato of Europe – it was an over-reliance on this that led to the Great Famine in Ireland when the crop was destroyed by blight. Some ornamental cultivars of *Ipomoea batatas* are used in hanging baskets, notably the dark-leaved 'Blackie' and lurid, pale ones.

Ipomoea, apparently derived from the Greek *ips*, worm, used by Linnaeus for *Convolvulus*, and *homois*, similar to or like, is a genus of perhaps 650 species found in all warmer parts of the world. Many are grown as ornamental climbers, particularly *I. tricolor* from Central America, which is also a source of hallucinogenic ergoline alkaloids popularized in the 1960s as 'morning glory', a name referring to the short-lived flowers. This name is also used for many other species, especially *I. nil*, which featured widely in the decorative arts of the Japanese Edo period.

Ipomoea batatas (L.) Lam., *Tableau Encyclopédique et Methodique. Botanique* 1: 465 (1793)

Copper plate by Gabriel Smith, based on Parkinson's 1769 watercolour; BF 627; Diment et al., 1987: SI2/3

1. Mabberley, 2014, pp. 432–33 and 4th ed., 2017

35.
PIPER METHYSTICUM
kava, Piperaceae

Solander's manuscript name for this plant was 'Piper inebrians', and Parkinson noted in his journal, 'The expressed juice of this plant they drink to intoxicate themselves.'[1] Similarly, the current epithet, *methysticum*, is from the Greek word for intoxicating. The cultivated kava, one of the most celebrated plants of the Pacific, is now known to comprise a series of sterile cultivars derived from wild plants in Papua New Guinea, the Solomon Islands and Vanuatu. They are usually male, the rare female plants apparently never setting seed.[2]

The roots of kava are the source of a narcotic sedative drink that is served in special bowls to welcome guests and has been used in ceremonies for over 3,000 years. To prepare it, the roots are first chewed, formerly by women and children, then ground or pounded, before being mixed with water or coconut milk and strained. Missionaries tried to eradicate kava, but now special bars serve it and it is a cash crop in Vanuatu and Fiji.

The effective principle is a lactone, one of a group of compounds binding to receptors associated with euphoria and wellbeing.[3] It is not addictive and is used in the treatment of generalized anxiety disorder,[4] insomnia and in tablets taken on long flights.

Piper, pepper, from an Indian word via Greek, is a genus of perhaps 2,000 species from the tropics, by far the most significant being *P. nigrum*, pepper, originally from southern India and Sri Lanka, the most used of all spices.

Piper methysticum G. Forst., *De Plantis Esculentis*: 76 (1786)

Copper plate by Jean-Baptiste Michell, based on Parkinson's 1769 watercolour; BF 642; Diment et al., 1987: SI2/18

1. Parkinson, 1784, p. 37

2. Staples and Herbst, 2005, p. 456

3. Mabberley, 2014, pp. 670–71

4. J. Sarris et al., 'Kava in the treatment of generalized anxiety disorder: a double-blind, randomized, placebo-controlled study', *Journal of Clinical Psychopharmacology* 33, 2013, pp. 643–48

36.
ALEURITES MOLUCCANUS
candlenut, Euphorbiaceae

Describing the candlenut, Parkinson wrote in his journal:

> Of the bark of this tree, soaked in water, they make that gummy substance which they put upon their dark-coloured cloth to make it glossy, and keep out the rain. The fruit of this tree is a sort of nut, which yields a very fat kernel, of which they make their black dye, used in Tataowing [tattooing], by burning them, and receiving the smoke. Strung upon a reed or stick they serve instead of candles, and give a very good light.[1]

Solander gave the tree the manuscript name 'Telopea perspicua', with *telopos* in Greek meaning seen far away, as the pale foliage is visible from a distance. However, that generic name was eventually to be used for a similarly striking plant from Australia, the red-flowered waratah, *Telopea speciosissima*, the state flower of New South Wales.

Although native to tropical Southeast Asia, the candlenut was introduced across the Pacific by the Polynesians, as it will thrive on otherwise useless land.[2] Somewhat perversely, then, it is the official tree of the State of Hawaii. The seeds are used in *lei* (garlands) there, and oil from the seeds (lumbang oil) was once produced commercially for use on both skin and hair, as well as in polish for wood. In Asia it is still used in curry and commercial shampoos. The tree was introduced into cultivation in England in 1793.[3]

Aleurites comes from the Greek *aleuron*, meaning flour, as the tree appears as if dusted with it. The genus comprises just two species from the Indopacific.

Aleurites moluccanus (L.) Willd., *Species Plantarum* 4: 590 (1805)

Copper plate by Gerard Sibelius, based on Parkinson's 1769 watercolour; BF 654; Diment et al., 1987: SI2/31

1. Parkinson, 1784, p. 44
2. Mabberley, 1998, p. 42
3. Chittenden, 1951, I, p. 72

37.

CASUARINA EQUISETIFOLIA
beefwood, Casuarinaceae

A pioneer seashore tree of the coasts of the Indopacific region, beefwood is a common evergreen growing up to 35 m (115 ft) tall. It is now widely planted and is invasive in the Caribbean and South Africa. Trees bear both male and female flowers, unlike most *Casuarina* species, which produce them on different trees.[1] It is planted as a windbreak or as trimmed hedges, though its woody female cones are painful to foot-traffic on beaches, and is even grown as bonsai.[2]

Banks recorded that the tree was a source of a red dye and that its hard wood was used for tools for beating bark-cloth (tapa),[3] while Parkinson elaborated:

> This is one of the best woods they have; it is very hard and heavy, and coloured like mahogany. They make their clubs, lances, cloth-beaters, and several other knick-knacks and utensils of it.[4]

Today the wood is used for roof shingles and is the 'best firewood in the world', burning with great heat.[5]

Casuarina, like *Casuarinus*, cassowary, allegedly because the tree's drooping branchlets resemble cassowary feathers, is a genus of 17 species from the Indopacific region. They are notable for their bacterial root-symbionts, species of *Frankia*, which fix atmospheric nitrogen, thereby allowing the plants to colonize poor, sandy soils. *Casuarina* species are possibly allelopathic, meaning they produce chemicals that inhibit the growth of other plants. The epithet *equisetifolius* indicates that the shoots resemble horsetails, species of *Equisetum*, that name being derived from *equus*, horse, and *seta*, bristle.

Casuarina equisetifolia L., *Amoenitates Academici seu dissertationes variae physicae, medicae...* 4: 143 (1759)

Copper plate by Gabriel Smith, based on Parkinson's 1769 watercolour; BF 663; Diment et al., 1987: SI2/42

1. Mabberley, 2014, p. 159
2. Staples and Herbst, 2005, p. 229
3. Beaglehole, 1963, 1, pp. 355, 357
4. Parkinson, 1784, p. 44
5. Mabberley, 2014, p. 159

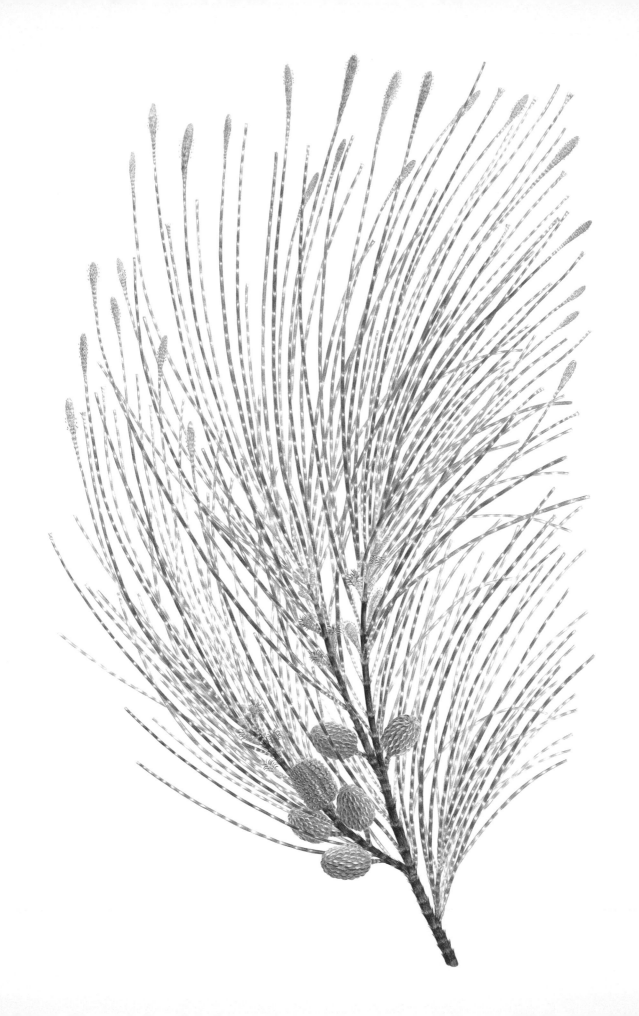

38.
CORDYLINE FRUTICOSA
ti, Asparagaceae

Ti is a sparsely branched pachycaul (thick-stemmed) tree up to 4 m (13 ft) tall, native to the western Pacific but introduced to Hawaii and New Zealand by Polynesians. It has scented flowers and is widely planted for ornament; the coloured leaves are sold as foliage in the international cut-flower market.[1] Many cultivars, including reddish and variegated ones, were introduced into the horticultural trade in Europe in the nineteenth century and grown as 'dracaenas' – with scores of scientific names. In the Pacific they are planted as hedges and windbreaks. Ti is often associated with 'good luck', and in Hawaii is traditionally planted at the four corners of a house or other building.[2]

The swollen root-tubers are sweet-tasting and can be fermented. In his journal, Parkinson noted: 'Of this plant there are five different sorts, yielding a large root, which is eaten, and counted very good food, by the islanders of the South-seas.'[3] The strap-like leaves are used to thatch houses and also for making skirts such as the Hawaiian *hula* and traditional dress in New Guinea.[4]

Cordyline, from Greek *kordyle*, a club, referring to the shape of the fleshy roots, is a genus of about 20 species from Australasia and the Pacific, with one in tropical America, some of which are cultivated as 'cabbage trees'; *fruticosus* means shrubby.

Cordyline fruticosa (L.) A. Chev., *Catalogue des Plantes du Jardin Botanique de Saigon*: 66 (1919)

Copper plate by Gerard Sibelius, based on Parkinson's 1769 watercolour; BF 671; Diment et al., 1987: SI2/49a

1. Staples and Herbst, 2005, p. 581
2. Staples and Herbst, 2005, p. 581
3. Parkinson, 1784, p. 38
4. Mabberley, 2014, p. 216

39.
SOPHORA TETRAPTERA
kōwhai, Leguminosae

By early October 1769 *Endeavour* had reached North Island, New Zealand, and Banks and Solander began collecting as soon as possible. Kōwhai and its close allies are found in Chile and North Island, New Zealand, along streams and in lowland forest edges. In New Zealand, *Sophora tetraptera* is a tree up to 12 m (40 ft) tall, with useful timber. Following the yellow flowers, the unusual four-winged pods are up to 18 cm (7 in.) long, and narrow tightly between each seed.

Parkinson sketched a specimen at Teoneroa (Te Oneroa), which Cook named Poverty Bay, in October 1769, adding the following colour instructions on his drawing:

> The flowers yellow the capsules of a greenish downy Orange the buds greenish
> yellow, the carina [keel] + alae [wings] of a paler yellow than the vexillum [standard]

Solander named it 'Sophora tetraptera' (four-winged, referring to the fruits), but that name was to be published by Johann Sebastian Mueller (1715–1790; two of whose sons, John and James, worked on Parkinson's drawings for Banks). He drew a plant that flowered at the Chelsea Physic Garden in 1779 from material Banks had brought home (see illustration below).

Sophora derives from *sophera*, an Arabic name for a tree with pea-flowers.[1] The genus comprises some 50 species of largely north temperate trees.[2] *Sophora toromiro* was formerly found on Easter Island, where it was the only species suitable for building and carving, but was reduced to one tree by 1917 and exterminated by grazing by 1962. However, plants were raised from seeds from herbarium specimens collected by Thor Heyerdahl, so that it now survives in at least 18 botanic gardens and is being re-introduced to the island.

Sophora tetraptera J. S. Muell., [*Icones Novae*]: t. 1 (1780)
Copper plate by Gerard Sibelius, based on an undated Frederick Nodder watercolour, derived from Parkinson's drawing; BF 430; Diment et al., 1987: NZ1/38
1. Chittenden, 1951, 4, p. 1984
2. Mabberley, 2014, p. 807

40.

SCANDIA ROSIFOLIA
koheriki, Umbelliferae

Restricted to the North Island of New Zealand, koheriki is a perennial herb or subshrub up 1 m (3 ft) tall.[1] It is found growing from the coast up to a height of around 1,400 m (4,600 ft; subalpine), commonly on cliffs, banks or among rocks, for instance, in river gorges.

Because of its strong scent when bruised, Solander gave it the manuscript name 'Ligusticum aromaticum', and *Scandia* today is still considered to be in the same tribe as *Ligusticum* (lovage). It is notable for its stipules (small leaf-like growths at the base of a leaf stalk), which are otherwise unknown in native New Zealand umbellifers.

Scandia, alluding to its scandent or climbing habit, is a genus in need of revision; *rosifolius* refers to having leaves like those of a rose.

Scandia rosifolia (Hook.f.) J. W. Dawson in *New Zealand Journal of Botany* 5: 410 (1967)

N.B. *Scandia* has been included in *Gingidia* but it is the older name

Copper plate by Gabriel Smith, based on John Miller's 1774 watercolour, derived from Parkinson's surviving pencil drawing made at 'Taoneroa'; BF 461; Diment et al., 1987: NZ2/74

1. Allan, 1982, p. 505

41.

CLEMATIS FORSTERI
pōānanga, Ranunculaceae

A common climber in New Zealand, *Clematis forsteri* was collected by Banks and Solander at several landfalls; Parkinson drew it at Teoneroa in October 1769. It is a liane up to about 5 m (16 ft), growing in lowland forest edges and other open areas, and is recognizable by its bright green leaves with slightly lobed leaflets and its 5–8 creamy white sepals (it has no petals).[1] That Solander's manuscript name was 'Clematis odorata' suggests the flowers are scented. The specific name, *forsteri*, commemorates Georg Forster (see Pl. 22, p. 62), who accompanied his father as naturalist on Cook's second voyage.

There are perhaps nine species of *Clematis* in New Zealand, all of which are found nowhere else; they are generally dioecious (having male and female flowers on different plants). Of these, *Clematis afoliata* is remarkable for leaves that are reduced to petioles (leaf-stalks) and petiolules (the stalk of a leaflet), with full leaves developing only in young plants or in the shade.

Clematis, from the Greek word *klema*, used for various climbers, is a genus of over 300 species in the north temperate regions and extending to South America, Madagascar and Oceania, as well as the mountains of tropical Africa.[2] Most familiar in cultivation are climbers derived from the Asian species *C. florida*, which flowers on old wood in summer, *C. patens*, which flowers on old wood in spring, and especially the hybrid *C. ×jackmanii* (*C. lanuginosa*, not known in the wild, × *C. viticella*, from the Mediterranean and southwest Asia), which arose in 1858 at Jackman's nursery in Woking, England, and which flowers on new wood in summer and autumn.

Clematis forsteri J. F. Gmel., *Systema Naturae* 2: 873 (1791)
Copper plate by Gerard Sibelius, based on Frederick Nodder's 1778 watercolour, derived from Parkinson's surviving pencil drawing made at 'Taoneroa'; BF 402; Diment et al., 1987: NZ1/1

1. Allan, 1982, p. 167; P. B. Heenan and J. Cartman, 'Reinstatement of *Clematis petriei* (Ranunculaceae), and typification and variation of *C. forsteri*', *New Zealand Journal of Botany* 38, 2000, pp. 575–85
2. Mabberley, 2014, p. 194

42.
BRACHYGLOTTIS REPANDA
rangiora, Compositae

Banks and Solander collected rangiora at Teoneroa and subsequent landfalls. Parkinson annotated his pencil outline drawing with the description, 'the upper side of the leaves grass green the veins a little ting'd w^t purple the under side white with a glaucus [sic] cast the upper side of the young leaves more yellow & a little downy'.

A common, fast-growing shrub or tree up to 6 m (20 ft) or more tall, rangiora[1] has large leaves that are white on the lower surface, as Parkinson noted; the specific epithet *repandus* refers to their wavy edges. Often a pioneer species in ecological succession, rangiora is found in coastal to lower montane shrubland and open forest.

Because of their soft undersides, its leaves have been used as lavatory paper; one such leaf has even successfully served as a postcard.[2] The plant figures in Māori medicine, and was introduced into cultivation in Britain in 1890.[3]

Brachyglottis, from the Greek *brachy*, short, and *glottis*, tongue, is a genus of controversial limits and geographical distribution. Most familar in cultivation outside New Zealand is the shrubby *Brachyglottis ×jubar* Dunedin Group ('Dunedin Hybrids'), especially 'Sunshine' (*B. compacta × B. laxifolia*, both from New Zealand), a widely planted evergreen in towns grown as '*Senecio greyi*'.

Brachyglottis repanda Forst. & G. Forst., *Characteres Generum Plantarum*: 92 + t. 46 (1776)

Copper plate by Gerard Sibelius, based on Frederick Nodder's undated watercolour, derived from Parkinson's surviving pencil drawing; BF 487; Diment et al., 1987: NZ2/103

1. Allan, 1982, p. 757
2. http://pukeariki.com/Heritage-Collections/Spotlight-on-the-Heritage-Collection/id/210/title/leaf-postcard – accessed 15 May 2017
3. Chittenden, 1951, 1, p. 305

43.

PELARGONIUM INODORUM
kopata, Geraniaceae

This plant is another that Banks and Solander collected at a number of localities, beginning at Teoneroa in October 1769. Parkinson annotated his pencil sketch with the colour instructions: 'The flowers a pale crimson the marks on the petala very deep [?] the leaves grass green rather pale, the capsulae and calyx pale green the stalk and petiole deeply ting'd w^t red'.

Kopata is common in lowland to montane grassland throughout New Zealand and is also found in Australia, where there are five other species.[1] It is a sprawling annual to biennial herb, more or less scented, hence '*inodorus*', with the characteristic musky smell of 'geraniums'. When described as a new species in cultivation in Berlin, it was thought possibly to have come from the Cape, where there are 148 *Pelargonium* species, 79 of which are only found there.

Pelargonium, from *pelargos*, stork, since the fruit resembles a stork's bill, is a genus of perhaps 280 species from tropical and especially southern Africa, with two species in the eastern Mediterranean to Iraq, and one each from Socotra, St Helena and Tristan da Cunha.[2] These include the 'geraniums' of greenhouses, but differ from true *Geranium* in their irregular flowers and the fact that only five to seven of the ten stamens are fertile. Most important worldwide are *P.* × *hortorum* (zonal pelargoniums), *P.* × *domesticum* (regals), of complicated hybrid origin, and *P. peltatum* (ivy-leaved), the familiar hanging basket 'geranium'. Also popular are species with highly aromatic leaves due to their essential oils, reminiscent of lemon, peppermint, pennyroyal, nutmeg, strawberry, mint, camphor, apple, ginger, rue and so on. The oils are thought to be a deterrent to animal-grazers, though some are used as the basis for scent and soap.

Pelargonium inodorum Willd., *Hortus Berolinensis* 1: t. 34 (1804)

Copper plate by Gerard Sibelius, based on Frederick Nodder's undated watercolour, derived from Parkinson's surviving pencil drawing; BF 423; Diment et al., 1987: NZ1/24

1. Allan, 1982, p. 237

2. Mabberley, 2014, p. 641

44.

CORYNOCARPUS LAEVIGATUS
karaka, Corynocarpaceae

Karaka is the Māori word for yellow, referring in this case to the plant's orange-yellow fruit. A canopy tree up to 15 m (50 ft) tall,[1] it is a major component of coastal forest throughout New Zealand, though it is probably native only in the north, having been dispersed from there by Māori.[2] Parkinson annotated his pencil drawing with the description, 'the petalae of the flower white. the fruit a shining grass green the Pedunculi pale tawny brown'.

There are separate male and female trees, though the 'males' sometimes produce fruits.[3] The fruit, which is dispersed by reptiles, is toxic to dogs as it contains karakin, an alkaloid, but when carefully prepared the pulp is edible to humans and was an important Māori food-source.[4] The tree was introduced into cultivation in England in 1823,[5] and is now naturalized and invasive in Hawaii, following the unwise seeding of Kaui by air in 1929.[6]

In a family of its own, *Corynocarpus*, from the Greek *koryne*, a club, and *karpos*, fruit, comprises just five species in the southwest Pacific; *laevigatus* is Latin for smooth.

Corynocarpus laevigatus Forst. & G. Forst., *Characteres Generum Plantarum*: 32 + t. 16 (1776)

Copper plate by Gabriel Smith, based on John Miller's 1774 drawing, derived from Parkinson's surviving pencil drawing; BF 427; Diment et al., 1987: NZ1/35

1. Allan, 1982, p. 407

2. R. A. Atherton et al., 'A molecular investigation into the origin and relationships of karaka/kōpi (*Corynocarpus laevigatus*) in New Zealand', *Journal of the Royal Society of New Zealand* 45, 2015, pp. 212–20

3. P. J. Garnock-Jones et al., 'Gynodioecy, sexual dimorphism and erratic fruiting in *Corynocarpus laevigatus* (Corynocarpaceae)', *Australian Journal of Botany* 55, 2007, pp. 803–08

4. W. Skey, 'Preliminary notes on the isolation of the bitter substance of the nut of the Karaka tree (Corynocarpus laevigata [sic])', *Transactions and Proceedings of the New Zealand Institute* 4, 1871, pp. 316–21

5. Chittenden, 1951, 2, p. 554

6. Mabberley, 2014, p. 221

NEW ZEALAND, TEONEROA (POVERTY BAY), 8–11 OCTOBER 1769

104

45.

CLIANTHUS PUNICEUS
kakabeak, Leguminosae

First encountered by Banks and Solander at Tegadu (Anaura) Bay, North Island, in October 1769, this spectacular evergreen shrub grows to 4 m (13 ft) or more tall. Long cultivated by Māori,[1] who selected superior forms, its natural variation and distribution on North Island are probably now obscured.

Solander named it 'Clianthus', from the Greek *kleos*, glory, and *anthos* flower; *puniceus*, meaning blood red, refers to the flowers. But his name was not to be published until 1836. The red form was introduced into cultivation in Europe by 1831; plants with creamy white flowers are also grown.

Kakabeak belongs in the same tribe as Sturt's desert-pea, *Swainsona formosa* (formerly included in *Clianthus*), a distinctive scarlet-flowered creeping plant of arid Australia. This was found in 1699 by the explorer-pirate William Dampier (1651–1715), one of the first plants indisputably collected by Europeans on that continent. Dampier's specimens are preserved at the University of Oxford.

Clianthus puniceus (G. Don) Lindl., *Edwards's Botanical Register* 21: t. 1775 (1836)

Copper plate by Daniel Mackenzie, based on an unsigned watercolour, derived from Parkinson's pencil drawing; BF 432; Diment et al., 1987: NZ1/40

1. Mabberley, 2014, p. 195

46.

FUCHSIA EXCORTICATA
kōtukutuku, Onagraceae

Largest of all fuchsias, kōtukutuku is a common, often deciduous, tree up to 15 m (50 ft) tall found throughout New Zealand; it grows to altitudes of about 1,000 m (3,300 ft), especially along watercourses. It is easily spotted because its bark develops red papery strips, which peel off to reveal the paler inner bark, as referred to in the specific epithet, *excorticatus*.

Banks and Solander collected it at a number of places, but first at Tegadu (Anaura) Bay, and it was apparently there that Parkinson made his field sketch, noting on it:

> the calyx deep Crimson on the inside as are also the filaments & stile the top of which is yellow The petals dark purple the outside of the calyx paler & ting'd w^t green the anthera yellow ting'd w^t red the upper part of the leaves dark grass green The under part white w^t a cast of green & vein'd w^t green the capsule green the stalk gray green.

Solander gave it the manuscript name *Agapanthus*, but that name was subsequently published for the familiar cultivated species of a genus of South African Amaryllidaceae (see *Aleurites*, Pl. 36, p. 88, for a similar case). When formally describing it, the Forsters named it *Skinnera excorticata* after their and Banks' friend, the botanist Richard Skinner (?1729–1795), but it was soon realized that it was truly a fuchsia.

The flowers are pollinated by endemic honeyeaters (bellbirds and tuis),[1] while the juicy fruit was eaten by both Māori and European settlers. Today the trees are much attacked by brushtail possums, which were introduced from Australia in 1837 to establish a fur-trade. It seems to be one of their preferred food sources, and they will browse it so intensively that the consequent defoliation can cause a tree's death. Possum-control measures may reverse the decline of this important species.

The genus *Fuchsia* is named after Leonhart Fuchs (1501–1566), a German doctor in Tübingen and a 'father of botany'. New Zealand has four of the 106 recognized species, including the smallest of all, the creeping *F. procumbens* of North Island.[2] Most familiar elsewhere are cultivated hybrids grown in hanging baskets and as standards, especially *F. × hybrida*, which probably has several South American species in its ancestry. *Fuchsia magellanica*, from southern South America, especially 'Riccartonii', is grown for hedging in the Azores, Isle of Man and Ireland, where it is naturalized, and it has now become invasive in Australia and Hawaii.

Fuchsia excorticata (Forst. & G. Forst.) L.f., *Supplementum Plantarum*: 217 (1782)

Copper plate by Gabriel Smith, based on James Miller's 1775 watercolour, derived from Parkinson's surviving pencil drawing; BF 452; Diment et al., 1987: NZ1/63

1. A. W. Robertson et al., 'Assessing pollination and fruit dispersal in *Fuchsia excorticata* (Onagraceae)', *New Zealand Journal of Botany* 46, 2008, pp. 299–314

2. Mabberley, 2014, p. 346

NEW ZEALAND, TEGADU (ANAURA) BAY, 20–22 OCTOBER 1769

47.

HEDYCARYA ARBOREA
porokaiwhiri, Monimiaceae

Porokaiwhiri is a common tree in New Zealand, growing in lowland forest up to montane forest in the North Island. Separate male and female trees can both reach up to 12 m (40 ft) tall, with clear boles below the first branch.[1]

Banks and Solander collected specimens of this tree at a number of places, but first at Tegadu (Anaura) Bay. Parkinson noted on his pencil sketch: 'the leaves grass green on the underside pale yellow green the flowers & foot stalks pale green the stamina white w^t a cast of green the stalks black-green'.

On 10 November 1774, Johann Reinhold Forster (1729–1798), scientist on Cook's second voyage, wrote:

> I luckily found the Female flowers & large Berries to the plant we found two days ago, & which smells remarkably sweet, something like Auricula or Lily of the Valley: the Berries, Leaves and the Bark, have all something of the same Smell, but fainter: the whole air is embalmed if you happen to stand under or near such a Tree in Flower.[2]

These sweet-smelling flowers are now known to be pollinated by thrips.[3]

Hedycarya, from the Greek *hedys*, sweet, and *karyon*, nut, is a genus of 11 dioecious species from the southwest Pacific.[4] *Hedycarya angustifolia* of eastern Australia provides a timber for cabinetwork.

Hedycarya arborea Forst. & G. Forst.f., *Characteres Generum Plantarum*: 128 + t. 64 (1776)

Copper plate by Daniel Mackenzie, based on Frederick Nodder's 1780 watercolour, derived from Parkinson's surviving pencil drawing; BF 467; Diment et al., 1987: NZ2/80

1. Allan, 1982, p. 138

2. Hoare, 1982, pp. 682–83

3. S. A. Norton, 'Thrips pollination in the lowland forest of New Zealand', *New Zealand Journal of Ecology* 7, 1984, 157–63

4. Mabberley, 2014, p. 394

48.

ENTELEA ARBORESCENS
whau, Malvaceae

The Māori name for this plant, whau, appears cognate with the Polynesian word for hibiscus, to which *Entelea* is indeed related. Whau is a fast-growing shrub or tree up to some 6 m (20 ft) tall, found in coastal and other lowland habitats.[1] Its seeds, produced in large numbers from its bristly capsules, are long-lived and are stimulated by fire to germinate.[2]

Banks and Solander collected whau at several localities, first at Tegadu (Anaura) Bay. Parkinson described its colouring on his pencil sketch as:

> the leaves a fresh green vein'd w^t paler the under side of the leaves more Glaucus [sic] w^t pale high veins the flower white calyx & peduncles downy white w^t a cast of Green, the stamina yellow The capsulae green.

The only species in its genus, *Entelea*, from Greek *enteles*, perfect, as all stamens are fertile, has very light wood (with a specific gravity lower than that of cork), which is used by Māori for fishing-floats.[3] It was introduced into cultivation in England in 1820.[4]

Entelea arborescens R. Br. in Sims, *Curtis's Botanical Magazine* 51: t. 2480 (1824)

Copper plate by Gerard Sibelius, based on Frederick Nodder's ?1776 watercolour, derived from Parkinson's surviving pencil drawing; BF 418; Diment et al., 1987: NZ1/19

1. Allan, 1982, pp. 335–36
2. L. H. Millener, 'A study of *Entelea arborescens* R. Br. ("Whau"): Part I. Ecology', *Transactions and Proceedings of the Royal Society of New Zealand* 76, 1946–47, pp. 267–88
3. Mabberley, 2014, p. 307
4. Chittenden, 1951, 2, pp. 746–47

49.

SENECIO RUFIGLANDULOSUS
pūhāureroa, Compositae

Pūhāureroa is a herbaceous plant found throughout much of New Zealand. It has reddish, glandular hairs, hence the specific epithet, *rufiglandulosus*. Parkinson noted on his pencil sketch:

> the flowers bright yellow, the stalks a yellow green the upper side of the leaves grass green faintly ting'd w^t bluish purple about the veins the underside a Glaucus [sic] green & the veins faint blue purple which tinges the rest of the leaf, a little.

Senecio, from Latin *senex*, old man, probably referring to the plumed fruits, is a huge genus of perhaps a thousand species of trees, shrubs, climbers and herbs found throughout much of the world,[1] especially as weeds, such as groundsel, *S. vulgaris*.

Senecio rufiglandulosus Colenso in *Transactions and Proceedings of the New Zealand Institute* 28: 599 (1895)

Copper plate by Daniel Mackenzie, based on Frederick Nodder's undated watercolour, derived from Parkinson's surviving pencil drawing; BF 488; Diment et al., 1987: NZ2/104

1. Mabberley, 2014, p. 788

50.

DYSOXYLUM SPECTABILE
kohekohe, Meliaceae

Banks and Solander first encountered this winter-flowering tree at Tolaga Bay, North Island, New Zealand, in October 1769. Solander named it 'Trichilia cauliflora', the specific name referring to the flowers borne on the trunk (deriving from the Latin for stem and flower), but his name was never published and Georg Forster's *T. spectabilis* of 1786 instead provides the basis for the current name.

Kohekohe grows to some 15 m (50 ft) tall in coastal forests throughout the North Island. Female or hermaphrodite trees have waxy, bird-pollinated flowers followed by capsules of seeds coated with orange to scarlet arils (a fleshy covering); other trees are strictly male.[1] Its bitter leaves were formerly used in local medicine and as a substitute for hops.[2]

The genus *Dysoxylum* (referring to the unpleasant smell of the wood) belongs to the mahogany family and comprises some 80 tree species found from tropical Asia to the Pacific.[3] Important timber trees include *D. fraserianum*, Australian rosewood, and *D. loureiroi*, which has sandalwood-scented wood used for coffins and incense sticks, as well as *D. mollissimum*, red bean, which was once the largest of all trees in Java.

Dysoxylum spectabile (G. Forst.) Hook.f., *Handbook of the New Zealand Flora*: 41 (1864)

Copper plate by Gerard Sibelius, based on Frederick Nodder's undated watercolour, derived from Parkinson's surviving pencil drawing; BF 425; Diment et al., 1987: NZ1/29

1. J. E. Braggins et al., 'Sexual arrangements in kohekohe (*Dysoxylum spectabile*, Meliaceae)', *Telopea* 8, 1999, pp. 315–24

2. J. D. Hooker, *Handbook of the New Zealand Flora* (London, Lovell Reeve & Co., 1864), vol. 1, p. 41

3. Mabberley, 2014, p. 294

51.
VITEX LUCENS
pūriri, Labiatae

Although Solander called this ornamental tree 'Ephialis drupacea', it was not formally described until 1838, by the botanist and explorer Allan Cunningham (1791–1839), as *Vitex littoralis*. However, that name had already been coined for a different tree, hence today's name. Parkinson noted of it: 'The flowers crimson rather deep, the red side cover'd w^t down the filaments white Anthera black the stile white'.

When describing it as new, using Banks and Solander material as well as his own, Cunningham wrote,

> A tree of very irregular growth on the rocky shores of the Bay of Islands, growing frequently within the range of salt water. That able [if notorious] missionary, the Rev. W[illiam] Yate observes that, 'this tree from its hardness and durability has been denominated the New Zealand oak, and indeed it seems to answer all the purposes of that prince of trees. The wood is of dark brown colour, close in the grain, and takes a good polish; it splits freely, works well and derives no injury from exposure to the damp, twenty years experience having proved that in that period it will not rot, though in a wet soil and underground. For ship building it is (like the teak which belongs to the same order) a most valuable wood; as the injury which it has received from being perforated in various places, by a large grub peculiar to the tree, does not essentially diminish its value for the timbers of ships or the knees of boats. It grows from fifteen to twenty feet without a branch, and varying from twelve to twenty feet in circumference'.[1]

Pūriri can grow to 20 m (66 ft) tall, with a trunk up to 150 cm (5 ft) in diameter, and is closely allied to the lignum vitae, *V. lignum-vitae*, of Australia.[2] The genus *Vitex* (which is the Latin name for the chaste tree of southern Europe, *V. agnus-castus*, its fruit being used to alleviate PMT and regulate menstrual cycles)[3] comprises some 250 largely tropical tree species. Several have valuable timbers (often known as fiddlewood), such as New Guinea teak (*V. cofassus*), used for carving and drums, and milla (*V. pinnata*). The specific epithet, *lucens*, shining, refers to the glossy leaves.

Vitex lucens Kirk in *Transactions and Proceedings of the New Zealand Institute* 29: 525 (1897)

Copper plate by Daniel Mackenzie, based on an undated Frederick Nodder watercolour, derived from Parkinson's surviving pencil drawing; BF 525; Diment et al. (1987): NZ3/141

1. A. Cunningham, 'Florae Insularum Novae Zelandiae Precursor; or a specimen of the botany of the islands of New Zealand', *Annals of Natural History* 1, 1838, pp. 455–62; quote from pp. 461–62. The grub referred to is no doubt the pūriri moth (*Aenetus virescens*), the country's largest moth, though not in fact restricted to pūriri.

2. D. J. Mabberley, 'On *Neorapinia* (*Vitex* sensu lato, Labiatae-Viticoideae)', *Telopea* 7, 1998, pp. 313–17

3. Mabberley, 2014, pp. 900–01

52.

KNIGHTIA EXCELSA
rewarewa, Proteaceae

Material of rewarewa was first collected by Banks and Solander at Tolaga Bay, North Island. Solander named it 'Brabeium sparsum', that is, related to *Brabejum stellatifolium* (Proteaceae), the 'wild almond' of South Africa. Gabriel Smith's engraving was published by Robert Brown (1773–1858; see Pl. 105, p. 220) in his description of his new genus *Knightia*, which commemorates Banks' friend, Thomas Knight (1758–1838), the noted pomologist and pioneering plant physiologist.

Restricted to the lowland and lower montane forests of North Island, rewarewa is the sole species of *Knightia*. It forms an emergent tree up to 30 m (100 ft) tall, with a trunk up to 1 m (3 ft) or more across and upright (fastigiate) branches. Its beautifully figured timber is used in cabinet-making.[1] The striking red flowers are up to *c.* 3.5 cm (1½ in.) long and are pollinated by birds (tuis), though their smell of sour milk suggests that bats may be involved too.[2] Introduced birds and even rats may also play a role, thus aiding survival of the tree when its original pollinators have been reduced or have disappeared altogether.[3] Commercial rewarewa honey has a rather malt flavour.

Knightia excelsa R. Br. in *Transactions of the Linnean Society of London* 10: 194 + t. 2 (1810)

Copper plate by Gabriel Smith, based on Parkinson's 1770 watercolour; BF 540; Diment et al., 1987: NZ3/155

1. Mabberley, 2014, p. 455

2. R. O. Gardner, 'Notes on rewarewa (*Knightia excelsa*)', 1987 – see bts. nzpcn.org.nz/bts_pdf/Auck_1987_42_2_72-73.pdf – accessed 15 May 2017

3. D. E. Pattemore and D. S. Wilcove, 'Invasive rats and recent colonist birds partially compensate for the loss of endemic New Zealand pollinators', *Proceedings of the Royal Society B* 279, 2012, pp. 1597–1605

53.
SCHEFFLERA DIGITATA
patē, Araliaceae

Restricted to New Zealand and the only *Schefflera* species found there, patē is a common, possibly dioecious (having separate male and female plants), small tree in lowland and other forests up to 1,000 m (3,300 ft) in altitude.[1] It is notable for its compound leaves, which are shaped like an open hand, as referred to in its specific name *digitata*. Banks and Solander collected it in a number of places, but first at Tolaga Bay. Parkinson noted on his pencil drawing, 'the buds stalks + petala very pale green the receptaculum pea green'.

Patē is often the host for *Dactylanthus taylorii*, the only root-parasite flowering plant native in New Zealand,[2] whose smelly, nectar-rich flowers are visited by short-tailed bats, but are also now attacked by introduced Australian possums (see *Fuchsia excorticata*, Pl. 46, p. 108). When cleaned of any such parasite tissue, the disc-like host root is one of the 'wood roses' of curios.

Schefflera, commemorating Johann Peter Ernst Scheffler (1739–1809), doctor, mineralogist and botanist of Gdansk, Poland, is, in the narrow sense, a genus of just eight species of the southwest Pacific. In the current sense, however, it comprises about 550 species throughout the tropics, including house plants such as *S. actinophylla* (the umbrella tree of New Guinea and tropical Australia) and *S. arboricola* from Hainan and Taiwan.[3] *Schefflera morototoni* (jereton) from tropical America yields timber used for pulp, drums and matches, while its seeds are used in maracas and made into women's aprons.

Schefflera digitata Forst. & G. Forst., *Characteres Generum Plantarum*: 46
+ t. 23 (1776)

Copper plate by Gabriel Smith, based on John Miller's 1774 watercolour, derived from Parkinson's surviving pencil drawing; BF 466; Diment et al., 1987: NZ2/79

1. Allan, 1982, p. 432
2. Mabberley, 2014, p. 251
3. Mabberley, 2014, p. 775

54.

LEPIDIUM OLERACEUM
nau or Cook's scurvy-grass, Cruciferae

Banks and Solander collected what they called 'Lepidium frondosum' at a number of landings, and Parkinson drew it at Opoorage (Mercury Bay) in November 1769. Nau was probably fed to the ship's company, as, eaten raw or cooked, it is rich in vitamin C, and during the voyage Cook was anxious to limit scurvy in his crew – 'cress' and 'scurvy grass' were a boon to the men.

Today nau is one of the threatened plants of New Zealand because it thrives only on high-fertility soils that experience regular cycles of disturbance caused by the now much reduced indigenous sea birds in their nesting grounds. It is also eaten by cattle and other livestock, and is still under pressure from over-collecting by humans. It is therefore largely restricted to rock stacks, islets and the windy headlands of rodent-free offshore islands.[1]

Lepidium, the classical name for cress,[2] is a cosmopolitan genus of some 250 species; *oleraceus* means 'of the vegetable garden'. Numerous *Lepidium* species are important in salads and other dishes, notably the Mediterranean species *L. latifolium* (dittander) and especially *L. sativum* (cress), which is usually eaten at the seedling stage, with mustard sown four days later ('mustard and cress'). *Lepidium meyenii* (maca) from the Andes was formerly a cultivated salad plant, but also allegedly an aphrodisiac, with its roots eaten as porridge and fermented to make alcoholic drinks; today it is dried and sold as a fashionable 'superfood'.

Lepidium oleraceum G. Forst. ex Sparrm. in *Nova Acta Regiae Societatis Scientiarum Upsaliensis* 3: 193 (1780)

Copper plate by Daniel Mackenzie, based on Frederick Nodder's undated watercolour, derived from Parkinson's surviving pencil drawing; BF 410; Diment et al., 1987: NZ 1/9

1. J. Sawyer and P. de Lange, '*Lepidium oleraceum* – a threatened herb of coastal Wellington', *Wellington Botanical Society Bulletin* 50, 2007, pp. 30–36

2. Mabberley, 2014, p. 480

55.

GLEICHENIA DICARPA
tangle fern, Gleicheniaceae

Named 'Pteris lobulata' by Banks and Solander when they collected it at Opoorage, where Parkinson made his pencil drawing, this fern is found from the Malay Archipelago to the western Pacific. It grows throughout New Zealand, from the coast to subalpine regions in wet places, sometimes forming almost impenetrable stands, hence the common name.[1]

Gleichenia, which commemorates the German biologist Wilhelm Friedrich von Gleichen-Russwurm (1717–1783), is a genus of some ten species largely in the Old World tropics; *dicarpus*, paired fruits, here refers to the spore-clusters.

Gleichenia dicarpa R. Br., *Prodromus Florae Novae Hollandiae*: 161 (1810)

Copper engraving by Gerard Sibelius, based on John Miller's undated watercolour, derived from Parkinson's surviving pencil drawing; BF 563; Diment et al., 1987: NZ4/192

1. http://www.nzpcn.org.nz/flora_details.aspx?ID=1946 – accessed 15 May 2017

56.
METROSIDEROS EXCELSA
pōhutukawa, Myrtaceae

Also known as the New Zealand Christmas tree (it flowers in mid-December), pōhutukawa grows in exposed habitats in North Island and can reach 20 m (66 ft) or more in height, with a trunk up to 2 m (6½ ft) in diameter.[1] The prominent and numerous stamens give the flowers their bright red, or occasionally orange, pinkish, yellow or white, colour.

An important tree to Māori, it is under attack from possums introduced from Australia. Its timber was formerly used in boat-building. A number of atypical forms are in cultivation, 'Parnell' being a floriferous, multi-branched tree, and there are also some rather less attractive variegated cultivars. It is the floral emblem of La Coruña in Spain because of an old specimen growing there, but is invasive in Cape *fynbos*.

Banks' generic name, *Metrosideros*, is from the Greek *metra*, core, and *sideros*, iron, referring to the hard heartwood; Solander's specific name, '*excelsa*', meaning tall, was published by Josef Gaertner (see also Pl. 2, p. 24), who was made welcome in Banks' house to study the fruits and seeds of the *Endeavour* specimens.

Metrosideros comprises more than 60 species of trees, shrubs and woody climbers (some stranglers) in the Pacific region, with just one found in South Africa.[2] In Hawaii the timber of *M. polymorpha* is used for construction, and formerly for religious figurines, while that of *M. robusta* (rātā) of New Zealand is made into telegraph poles.

Metrosideros excelsa Sol. ex Gaertn., *De Fructibus et Seminibus Plantarum*
1: 172 + t. 34 f. 8 (1788)

Copper plate by Gabriel Smith, based on an unsigned watercolour,
derived from Parkinson's surviving pencil drawing; BF 445; Diment et al.,
1987: NZ1/56

1. Allan, 1982, p. 325

2. Mabberley, 2014, p. 541

57.

RORIPPA DIVARICATA

matangaoa, Cruciferae

Matangaoa is found only in New Zealand, where it is a threatened plant. It survives on disturbed ground in just a few localities, notably where native sea birds stir up the soil, but also in wooded places including pine plantations.[1]

Banks and Solander collected what they called 'Sisymbrium divaricatum' in at least three places, including Tolaga Bay, but Parkinson's pencil sketch was made at Opoorage. Today this plant is being promoted as a salad vegetable in New Zealand.[2]

Rorippa, a Latinized name from the Old Saxon (German) *rorippen*, used for watercress (*Nasturtium* spp.), is a widespread genus of about 85 species; *divaricatus* means straggly, referring to the growth habit of matangaoa.

Rorippa divaricata (Hook.f.) Garnock-Jones & Jonsell in *New Zealand Journal of Botany* 26: 479 (1988)

Copper plate by Robert Blyth, based on Frederick Nodder's 1770s drawing, derived from Parkinson's surviving pencil drawing; BF 406; Diment et al., 1987: NZ1/5

1. http://www.nzpcn.org.nz/flora_details.aspx?ID=91 – accessed 15 May 2017

2. P. J. Garnock-Jones and B. Jonsell, '*Rorippa divaricata* (Brassicaceae): a new combination', *New Zealand Journal of Botany* 26, 1988, pp. 479–80

58.

OLEARIA PANICULATA

akiraho, Compositae

Common in lowland and lower montane shrubland and forest edges throughout much of New Zealand, akiraho is a shrub or tree up to 6 m (20 ft) tall,[1] with wavy-edged leaves that are white underneath, and fragrant flowers. It is often planted as a fast-growing hedge plant there.

Banks and Solander collected their 'Solidago undulata' at Opoorage, which is where Parkinson made his pencil sketch. The Forsters also collected it on Cook's second voyage and published a description naming it *Shawia paniculata* after Thomas Shaw (1694–1751) of Oxford, a traveller and plant collector.

Olearia is from the Latinized name (Olearius) of the seventeenth-century German botanist Johann Gottfried Ölschläger (1635–1711); *paniculatus* refers to the flower-heads borne in panicles. The genus comprises some 180 species of trees and shrubs, known as tree daisies or daisy bushes; 130 of them are found in Australia, the others in New Guinea and New Zealand.[2] Some are timber trees and many are cultivated as ornamentals around the world, including the New Zealand *O. albida*, which is remarkable for having more than 400 chromosomes.

Olearia paniculata (Forst. & G. Forst.) Druce in *(Report), Botanical Society and Exchange Club of the British Isles* 4, suppl. 2: 638 (1917)

Copper plate by Gerard Sibelius, based on Frederick Nodder's 1779 watercolour, derived from Parkinson's surviving pencil drawing; BF 479; Diment et al., 1987: NZ2/93

1. Allan, 1982, p. 661

2. Mabberley, 2014, p. 599

59.
METROSIDEROS ALBIFLORA
akatea or white rātā, Myrtaceae

Banks and Solander collected their 'Metrosideros albiflora' at Opoorage, where Parkinson made his pencil sketch. A robust liane or vine growing up to 20 m (66 ft) long or more, akatea is restricted to northern parts of the North Island of New Zealand, where it is usually found in kauri forests.[1]

Its large, fluffy white flowers, which appear August to November, are held in clusters of six to ten. The plant had some traditional uses in medicine and as cordage.

For information on the genus, see *Metrosideros excelsa* (Pl. 56, p. 128); *albiflorus* means white-flowered.

Metrosideros albiflora Sol. ex Gaertn., *De Fructibus et Seminibus Plantarum* 1: 172 + t. 34, f. 11 (1788)

Copper plate by Gerard Sibelius, based on a watercolour by an unknown hand, derived from Parkinson's surviving pencil drawing; BF 441; Diment et al., 1987: NZ1/49

1. Allan, 1982, p. 327

60.
BRACHYGLOTTIS KIRKII
kohurangi, Compositae

Kohurangi is a usually epiphytic shrub growing to 1.5 m or even 3 m (5 or 10 ft) tall, with brittle branches[1] and fleshy leaves; its white, daisy-like flowers appear in August to October. Banks and Solander collected what they called 'Cineraria glastifolia' at Opoorage, and Parkinson made his pencil drawing there. It is restricted to the North Island of New Zealand and is now in decline because it is a highly attractive food for feral animals such as possums, deer and goats, and is intolerant of browsing.

For information on the genus, see *Brachyglottis repanda* (Pl. 42, p. 100); *kirkii* commemorates Thomas Kirk (1828–1898), an outstanding New Zealand botanist.

Brachyglottis kirkii (Kirk) C. J. Webb in *New Zealand Journal of Botany* 25: 150 (1987)

Copper plate by Daniel Mackenzie, based on Frederick Nodder's 1779 watercolour, derived from Parkinson's surviving pencil drawing; BF 477; Diment et al., 1987: NZ2/91

1. Allan, 1982, p. 748

61.

EUPHORBIA GLAUCA
waiū-atua, Euphorbiaceae

The only native *Euphorbia* species in New Zealand, Solander's 'Euphorbia purpurea' is a perennial herb with erect stems up to 1 m (3 ft) tall.[1] It is restricted to New Zealand and the Chatham Islands, where it grows on coastal sands and rocks, but is now in decline. Its Māori name is the same as, or very similar to, that of *Rhabdothamnus solandri* (see Pl. 62, p. 138) and other plants.

Euphorbia is named after Euphorbus, the Greek doctor to King Juba II of Numidia (northwest Africa) in the first century BCE/CE;[2] *glaucus* refers to the bluish-grey colour of the leaves. The genus comprises some 1,900 species found throughout the world. They range from succulent trees to annual herbs, and all contain a toxic white latex. Many are weedy, but most familiar as a cultivated plant is the poinsettia, *E. pulcherrima*, from Mexico, huge numbers of which are sold at Christmas. *Euphorbia antisyphilitica*, the candelilla of southwest North America, produces a wax that is refined for use in polishes or creams for leather, furniture and babies, in lipstick and lip balm, and for coating certain sweets; when mixed with rubber it is used for electric insulation materials, as well as in waterproofing fabrics and paper; when mixed with paraffin it is made into candles.

Euphorbia glauca G. Forst., *Florulae Insularum Australium Prodromus*: 36 (1786)

Copper engraving by Daniel Mackenzie, based on Frederick Nodder's undated watercolour, derived from Parkinson's surviving pencil drawing; BF 547; Diment et al., 1987: NZ3/163

1. Allan, 1982, p. 346

2. Mabberley, 2014, p. 325

62.

RHABDOTHAMNUS SOLANDRI
kaikaiatua, or waiuatua, Gesneriaceae

Rhabdothamnus solandri is the only species of the Gesneriaceae family native to New Zealand and is restricted to North Island. Its closest relations are other shrubby genera such as *Fieldia* in Australia. Banks and Solander collected it at Opoorage on 15 November 1769, and this formed part of the material used to describe the species as new almost 70 years later.

Kaikaiatua is usually found on rocky sites in forests, where it grows to some 2 m (6½ ft) tall.[1] The red-streaked yellow flowers are pollinated by birds, but because of the local extinction of many of these by introduced animals on the mainland, pollination and therefore seed-set is less successful there than on the offshore islands, where bird populations have been maintained.[2]

The genus *Rhabdothamnus*, from *rhabdos*, a rod, and *thamnos*, a shrub, referring to its twiggy habit, comprises just this one species, commemorating its collector, Daniel Solander.

Rhabdothamnus solandri A. Cunn. in *Annals of Natural History* 1: 460 (1838)

Copper plate by Gerard Sibelius, based on Frederick Nodder's undated watercolour, derived from Parkinson's surviving pencil drawing; BF 523; Diment et al., 1987: NZ3/139

1. Allan, 1982, pp. 953–54

2. S. H. Anderson et al., 'Cascading effects of bird functional extinction reduce pollination and plant density', *Science* 331, 2011, pp. 1068–71

63.

PASSIFLORA TETRANDRA
kōhia, Passifloraceae

Banks and Solander collected kōhia first at Opoorage, and then later at Oohoorage (Hauraki Bay), where the expedition stayed for a few days, from 19 to 22 November 1769. Their name, 'Passiflora tetrandra', was not to be published until almost 60 years later.

Kōhia is a climber growing to 10 m (33 ft)[1] and is found throughout New Zealand. It bears male and female flowers on different plants (dioecious). The fruits are not edible (see *Passiflora aurantia*, Pl. 93, p. 196, for commercial species with edible ones), but the seed oil[2] was used by Māori for medicine and scent.

Passiflora refers to the *flos Passionis* of the Spanish missionaries in South America,[3] who saw the flower's three styles as signifying the nails of the Crucifixion, the five stamens as the wounds of Jesus Christ and the corona as his crown of thorns; the petals and sepals together represented the apostles (not including Peter and Judas), and the lobed leaves and tendrils the hands and scourges of Jesus' persecutors. Kōhia's specific name, *tetrandra*, meaning four males, refers to the fact that this species has only four stamens.

There are perhaps 500 species of passionflower, most of them found in South America, with just a few in the Pacific.

Passiflora tetrandra Banks ex DC., *Prodromus Systematis Naturalis Regni Vegetabilis* 3: 323 (1828)

Copper plate by Gerard Sibelius, based on Frederick Nodder's undated watercolour, derived from Parkinson's surviving pencil drawing; BF 453; Diment et al., 1987: NZ2/64a

1. Allan, 1982, pp. 318–19

2. S. G. Brooker, 'New Zealand plant fats. Parts II and III. Part II: The oil of *Dysoxylum spectabile* Hook. Part III: The oil of *Tetrapathaea tetrandra* Cheesm.', *Transactions of the Royal Society of New Zealand* 88, 1960, pp. 157–59

3. Mabberley, 1998, p. 80

64.

LASTREOPSIS VELUTINA
velvet fern, Dryopteridaceae

This fern is found only in the lowland forest of both North and South Island in New Zealand,[1] though it is rather uncommon in the latter. Banks and Solander collected what they called 'Polypodium speluncae' (*spelunca* meaning a cave in Latin), first at Opoorage in early November 1769, and later at Totara nui in January–February 1770.

Lastreopsis, meaning resembling *Lastrea*, a fern genus named after Charles Delastre (1792–1859), a French botanist, comprises 28 species in the tropics and south temperate zone, especially Australia.[2]

Lastreopsis velutina (A. Rich.) Tindale in *Victorian Naturalist* 73: 184 (1957)

Copper engraving by Gerard Sibelius, based on John Miller's watercolour, derived from a lost Parkinson field drawing; BF 578; Diment et al., 1987: NZ4/209

1. Allan, 1982, p. 91

2. Mabberley, 2014, p. 469 and 4th ed., 2017

65.
GERANIUM SOLANDERI
Geraniaceae

Banks and Solander collected what they called 'Geranium pilosum' at a number of sites in New Zealand, beginning at Teoneroa in early October 1769, with the last gathered at Motu aro Island in November–December of that year. On his pencil sketch, Parkinson noted: 'the flowers reddish purple somewhat pale'.

Geranium solanderi (by the time *G. pilosum* was published another plant had been given that name, so the new name commemorates its collector) is a perennial herb with a woody, turnip-like rootstock up to 2 cm (just under 1 in.) in diameter. It is native throughout the lowland grasslands of New Zealand, where it is now in decline as a result of grazing by rabbits, but it is also widespread in Australia.[1]

Geranium, from Greek *geranion*, derived from *geranos*, crane, an allusion to the beaked fruits (hence the English name cranesbill), is a genus of about 430 species in the temperate regions and also the mountains of the tropics.[2] They are usually rabbit-proof (unlike *G. solanderi*) perennials or annuals, but shrubby species are found in Hawaii and also Madeira and the Canary Islands. Before 1789, *Pelargonium* species (see *P. inodorum*, Pl. 43, p. 102) were included in this genus, which is why they are called 'geraniums' in English, even now.

Geranium solanderi Carolin in *Proceedings of the Linnean Society of New South Wales* 89: 350 (1964)

Copper plate by Gerard Sibelius, based on Frederick Nodder's watercolour, derived from Parkinson's surviving pencil drawing made at 'Motuaru'; BF 422; Diment et al., 1987: NZ1/23

1. Allan, 1982, p. 234; R. O. Gardner, '*Geranium solanderi* and allies in New Zealand', *New Zealand Journal of Botany* 22, 1984, pp. 127–34

2. Mabberley, 2014, p. 356 and 4th ed., 2017

66.

CONVOLVULUS TUGURIORUM
pōwhiwhi, Convolvulaceae

This perennial, herbaceous climber was found by Banks and Solander at Motu aro Island, and they gave it the manuscript name 'Convolvulus versatilis'. Parkinson described it on his field drawing as 'The flowers pale blush colour & the nerves white'.

Pōwhiwhi (a name applied to other climbers as well) is common in lowland areas of New Zealand,[1] where it can be encountered growing on bare lava, and is also found in southern South America. In cultivation its rhizomes, as with many *Convolvulus* species, can become invasive.

Convolvulus is from the Latin *convolvere*, to twine around; *tuguriorum*, of huts, alludes to the plant's habit of growing over such structures. The genus *Convolvulus*, including *Calystegia*, to which pōwhiwhi has been referred, has about 125 species found throughout the world.[2] Although many are weedy, *Convolvulus japonicus*, and especially its double-flowered form, 'Flore Pleno', is favoured in Chinese gardens, while *C. sylvaticus* of the eastern Mediterranean was possibly the origin of the lotus-flower motif of the ancient Greeks. *Convolvulus soldanella*, found on seashores worldwide, including New Zealand, is a scurvy-grass substitute, while *C. scammonia* of southwestern Asia is scammony, the source of a drastic purgative.

Convolvulus tuguriorum G. Forst., *Florulae Insularum Australium Prodromus*: 14 (1786)

Copper plate by William Tringham, based on John Miller's 1773 watercolour, derived from Parkinson's surviving pencil drawing; BF 512; Diment et al., 1987: NZ3/128

1. Allan, 1982, p. 837
2. Mabberley, 2014, p. 214

67.

ACIPHYLLA SQUARROSA
taramea, Umbelliferae

Taramea, also known as speargrass or Spaniard, forms tussocks up to 1 m (3 ft) high and grows from the coast to the mountains of New Zealand. Banks and Solander found it at Totara nui (Queen Charlotte Sound) in January–February 1770. Because of the very sharp tips to the lobes of its leaves they gave it the manuscript name 'Laserpitium spinosissimum'. This ferocious armament may have been a deterrent to the now extinct moas (compare *Pereskia grandifolia*, Pl. 4, p. 28).

Like the other 38 species of *Aciphylla*, taramea[1] is dioecious (having separate male and female plants), with sweet-smelling flowers. Except for two species in Australia, *Aciphylla* – its name is from the Latin *acicula*, needle, and the Greek *phyllum*, leaf – is restricted to New Zealand; *squarrosus*, rough or scaly, refers to the leaves.

Aciphylla squarrosa Forst. & G. Forst., *Characteres Generum Plantarum*: 136 + t. 68 (1776)

Copper plate by Gerard Sibelius, based on John Miller's 1772 watercolour, derived from Parkinson's surviving pencil drawing; BF 457; Diment et al., 1987: NZ2/70

1. Allan, 1982, pp. 480–81

68.

COPROSMA AUTUMNALIS
kanono, Rubiaceae

A common and variable understorey shrub or tree up to 6 m (20 ft) tall, kanono is found growing in lowland to lower montane forests of New Zealand.[1] Banks and Solander gave it the manuscript name 'Pelaphia grandifolia'.

Coprosma, from *kopros*, faeces, and *osme*, smell, alludes to the foetid smell of the bruised tissue of many of its species; *autumnalis* refers to the autumn-flowering habit described by botanist-cleric William Colenso (1811–1899). The genus comprises about 100 species of dioecious herbs, shrubs and trees from southern China to Hawaii, South America and Tristan da Cunha.[2] Some 15 of the New Zealand species are tangled, twiggy 'divaricate' shrubs, of which there are 51 species in 23 different plant families there, the most twiggy ones called 'mickeymick' (Māori mingimingi). It has been argued that this growth habit is associated with defence against grazing by now extinct moas (see also *Aciphylla squarrosa*, Pl. 67, p. 148).

Coprosma autumnalis Colenso in *Transactions and Proceedings of the New Zealand Institute* 19: 263 (1887); this has lately been called *C. grandifolia* Hook.f., but that is a superfluous name for *Ronabea australis* A. Rich. (*C. australis* (A. Rich.) Robinson), now known to be a synonym of *C. lucida* Forst. & G. Forst. (M. F. Large and D. J. Mabberley unpubl.)

Copper plate by Gerard Sibelius, based on Frederick Nodder's undated watercolour, derived from Parkinson's surviving pencil drawing; BF 469; Diment et al., 1987: NZ2/83

1. Allan, 1982, p. 582
2. Mabberley, 2014, p. 215

69.

SOLANUM AVICULARE
poroporo, Solanaceae

Although Banks and Solander gave this plant the manuscript name 'Solanum lanceum', alluding to the spear-shaped leaves, Georg Forster provided the currently accepted name, *avicularis*, referring to small birds.

Poroporo[1] grows into a soft-wooded shrub or small tree up to about 3 m (10 ft) tall, found at forest edges and in shrubland throughout much of New Zealand; it flowers and fruits most of the year. It is also native to New Guinea, New Caledonia and Australia, where it is known as kangaroo apple.[2] The ripe fruits are edible, though green ones are poisonous. It was introduced into England in 1772 and today is grown in eastern Europe as well as New Zealand as a source of solasodine, for producing cortisone and other steroid drugs.

For information on the genus *Solanum*, see *S. viride* (Pl. 30, p. 73).

Solanum aviculare G. Forst., *De Plantis Esculentis*: 42 (1786)

Copper plate by William Tringham, based on John Miller's 1774 watercolour, derived from Parkinson's surviving pencil drawing; BF 517; Diment et al., 1987: NZ3/132

1. Allan, 1982, p. 834
2. R. W. Purdie et al., '*Solanum aviculare*', *Flora of Australia* 29, 1982, pp. 110–11

70.

MELICYTUS RAMIFLORUS
māhoe, Violaceae

Māhoe is a widespread shrub or small tree up to 15 m (50 ft) tall,[1] with greyish-white bark. It is found in coastal to montane forests throughout New Zealand. Though dioecious (with separate male and female individuals),[2] there are more male trees than female. Its flowers, borne on the branches (hence *ramiflorus*, from Latin *rami*, branches), are fragrant and insect-pollinated. The dark blue or purple fruits are taken by New Zealand pigeons and silvereyes. By contrast, *Melicytus alpinus* bears white fruits on the underside of prostrate stems, and it is thought these are dispersed by reptiles.[3] *Melicytus ramiflorus* is still cultivated in Europe; its timber was formerly used for gunpowder.

Melicytus, Greek *meli*, honey, and *kytos*, a hollow vessel, alluding to the hollow nectaries in the flowers, comprises eight or nine species from the Solomon Islands to eastern Australia, New Zealand and Fiji.

Melicytus ramiflorus Forst. & G. Forst., *Characteres Generum Plantarum*: 124 + t. 62 (1776)

Copper plate by Gerard Sibelius, based on Parkinson's 1770 watercolour; BF 411; Diment et al., 1987: NZ1/10

1. Allan, 1982, p. 192

2. M. H. Powlesland, 'Reproductive biology of three species of *Melicytus* (Violaceae) in New Zealand', *New Zealand Journal of Botany* 22, 1984, pp. 81–94

3. Mabberley, 2014, p. 536

71.

ASTELIA HASTATA
kahakaha, Asteliaceae

Once assigned to the genus *Collospermum*, this plant was originally given the manuscript name 'Astelia furfuracea' by Banks and Solander, in Banks' new genus *Astelia*, to which it is now returned.[1]

Kahakaha is a common epiphyte in New Zealand's forests in North Island and the northern part of South Island. It is a large, tufted plant, with leaves to 170 cm (6½ ft) long and a 'tank' at its heart. It often occurs in considerable colonies, which can accumulate plant debris around them to such an extent that the weight may cause the fracture of the limb on which they are growing. The mature red fruits are taken by tuis and pigeons.[2]

The genus *Astelia*, from Greek *a*, without, and *stele*, a pillar, that is, stemless, is now considered to comprise some 30 species from the western Indian Ocean through the Pacific to Chile.

Astelia hastata Colenso in *Transactions and Proceedings of the New Zealand Institute* 19: 265 (1887)

Copper plate by Frederick Nodder based on an unsigned, undated watercolour, derived from Parkinson's surviving pencil drawing; BF 557; Diment et al., 1987: NZ4/180

1. J. L. Birch, 'A revision of infrageneric classification in *Astelia* Banks & Sol. ex R.Br. (Asteliaceae)', *PhytoKeys* 52, 2015, pp. 105–32

2. http://www.pukekura.org.nz/index.php?page=collospermum-hastatum---the-widow-maker – accessed 15 May 2017

72.

SONCHUS NOVAE-ZELANDIAE
Compositae

Parkinson drew this dandelion-like plant at Totara nui in January–February 1770, and Banks and Solander gave the collected specimens the manuscript name 'Hieracium fragile'. These were to become type specimens when the plant was first given a published scientific name in 1864, almost a century after they had been gathered. This species was later placed in its own genus, *Kirkianella*, but this is no longer recognized as distinct.

Today this small plant is apparently threatened by introduced weeds, notably the European *Pilosella officinarum* (mouse-ear hawkweed, Compositae) and is restricted to Three Kings Islands and South Island, where it grows up to 1,200 m (3,950 ft) above sea level, often in sea bird colonies or other open habitats.

The genus *Sonchus*, from a Greek plant called *sonchos*, comprises about 80 species;[1] the herbaceous ones are known as milk thistles because of their copious white latex. Their young leaves are edible and according to legend were eaten by Theseus before he set off from Athens to kill the Minotaur in Crete. Although many species are weedy, in particular *S. oleraceus* (sowthistle) from Europe, *S. grandifolius* is a spectacular native of New Zealand, known only from the Chatham Islands, with leaves up to 1 m (3 ft) long. On Juan Fernández, off Chile, some species are, or were (a number are already extinct), palm-like plants; a surviving one is *S. brassicifolius*, which was reduced to three wild plants in the 1980s but is now planted as a street tree in Chile.

Sonchus novae-zelandiae (Hook.f.) B. D. Jacks., *Index Kewensis* 4: 945 (1895)

Copper plate by Gerard Sibelius, based on Frederick Nodder's 1770s watercolour, derived from Parkinson's surviving pencil drawing made at 'Totarra nue or Queen Charlottes Sound'; BF 495; Diment et al., 1987: NZ2/111

1. Mabberley, 2014, p. 807

73.
VERONICA SALICIFOLIA
koromiko, Plantaginaceae

While in New Zealand, Banks and Solander collected koromiko several times, first at Tolaga Bay in October 1769, and finally at Totara nui in early 1770. They gave it the manuscript name 'Veronica glabella'.

Koromiko is a much-branched shrub to 5 m (16 ft) tall, native to South Island and the Stewart Islands of New Zealand and to southern Chile. The narrow leaves (hence *salicifolius*, from *Salix*, willow – that is, with leaves like those of willows) are used for diarrhoea. It is the hardiest shrubby veronica (hebe), and is widely cultivated in European gardens; it is now naturalized in southwest England.[1]

In Australasia there are 90 woody species formerly referred to the genus *Hebe*. It is believed that the New Zealand ones originated from a single long-distance intro-duction from Australia. Many New Zealand hebes are now cultivated worldwide, notably several derived from *Veronica speciosa,* such as the shrubby *V. ×franciscana,* a hybrid with *V. elliptica,* a species native from New Zealand to South America and now commonly used as hedging in southern Britain.

The generic name *Veronica* commemorates St Veronica, who is said to have handed her veil to Jesus to wipe his face with as he carried the cross to Golgotha. It is alleged that this very 'vernicle', with Jesus' features miraculously impressed on it, is that preserved as a relic in St Peter's Basilica in Rome.[2] And it has been sug-gested that this story could be linked to the common English name, 'speedwell', that is 'goodbye', given to European species because the flower petals fall as soon as a sprig is picked. However, the Latin name ultimately derives from the classical Greek name Pherenike, 'bearer of victory'.

The genus comprises some 450 species, largely herbs, including nine weeds, found across almost all the north temperate zone. Among these are *Veronica filiformis,* with rooting stems, introduced from southwest Asia in 1838 and now a persistent weed in lawns in Britain and the United States, especially common in churchyards. Another weed, *V. persica,* has a complex genetic history. Deriving from *V. polita* from northern Iran, which spread to Europe as a Neolithic weed and crossed with *V. ceratocarpa* from the Caucasus and Iran, it has complete sets of chromosomes from both parents, with four sets in all, i.e. being tetraploid.

Veronica salicifolia G. Forst., *Florulae Insularum Australium Prodromus*: 3 (1786)

Copper plate by Daniel Mackenzie, based on Parkinson's 1770 watercolour; BF 520; Diment et al., 1987: NZ3/136

1. Mabberley, 2014, p. 896; C. Stace, *New Flora of the British Isles* (Cambridge, Cambridge University Press, 1991), p. 727
2. *Oxford English Dictionary*: vernicle

74.
PLANTAGO RAOULII
kopakopa, Plantaginaceae

Parkinson drew this plantain, which Solander called 'Plantago erecta' in his manuscripts, at Totara nui. Growing in shaded, usually moist, habitats throughout New Zealand, it forms a rosette up to 16 cm (over 6 in.) across.[1]

Plantago is the Latin name for plantains; *raoulii* commemorates Étienne Raoul (1815–1852), a French naval surgeon and naturalist, who spent three years in New Zealand from 1840.

The genus comprises some 200 species spread across the world.[2] Many are weedy, especially *Plantago lanceolata*, ribwort plantain, perhaps originally a plant of sea-cliffs, and *P. major*, common plantain, perhaps originally a marsh plant and now used in Chinese herbalism for influenza and colds. Some species have seeds that are mucilaginous when wetted and act as efficient laxatives, especially *P. afra*, psyllium, and *P. indica*, which lowers cholesterol and so is added to cereals and pasta; *P. ovata*, isphagul, is used in the treatment of dysentery and for bowel regulation. No doubt the efficacious compounds aid the dispersal of the seeds by preventing them from being digested by animals, which eat whole plants at a time.[3]

Plantago raoulii Decne in DC., *Prodromus Systematis Naturalis Regni Vegetabilis* 13 (1): 703 (1852)

Copper plate by John Lee, based on Parkinson's 1770 watercolour; BF 527; Diment et al., 1987: NZ3/142b

1. Allan, 1982, p. 784

2. Mabberley, 2014, p. 676 and 4th ed., 2017

3. Mabberley, 1992, p. 149

75.
TETRAGONIA TETRAGONOIDES
kōkihi, Aizoaceae

Kōkihi is a sprawling herb[1] with glistening, succulent foliage. It is frequently found on stony beaches and sand dunes around New Zealand, but also in Japan, Australia and South America. Banks and Solander first encountered it at Teoneroa in early October 1769 and several times later, collecting their last specimens in New Zealand at Totara nui in early 1770.

Later, at Botany Bay in Australia, Banks wrote of it,

> We dind today upon the sting-ray and his tripe…We had with it a dish of leaves of tetragonia cornuta [sic] boild, which eat as well as spinage [spinach] or very near it.[2]

Banks was to introduce it into cultivation in Europe, where it was first described as *Demidovia tetragonoides* in 1781 from plants grown in St Petersburg, before Banks' own name for it was published. Though high in oxalates, it is widely grown as spinach, especially in sites too hot for true spinach; it is therefore known as New Zealand spinach, and also as warrigal greens in Australia.

Tetragonia, from *tetra*, four, and *gonia*, an angle, from the shape of the fruits, is a genus of 57 species from the tropics and warm countries, especially South Africa and North America.[3]

Tetragonia tetragonoides (Pall.) Kuntze, *Revisio Genenerum Plantarum* 1: 264 (1891)

Copper plate of 1782 by Gerard Sibelius, based on Frederick Nodder's undated watercolour, derived from Parkinson's pencil drawing made at 'Totarra nue'; BF 532; Diment et al., 1987: NZ3/147

1. Allan, 1982, p. 204
2. Beaglehole, 1963, 2, p. 61
3. Mabberley, 2014, p. 849

76.
URTICA FEROX
ongaonga, Urticaceae

In his manuscripts Solander called this plant 'Urtica hastata' ('hastata' meaning spear-shaped). Ongaonga is a shrub up to 3 m (10 ft) tall, which can grow in large patches. Ferocious, stiff hairs (*ferox* is fierce in Latin) on the leaves and stems can cause long-lasting stings. The hairs have bulb-like projections that break off, leaving a sharp bevelled edge which pierces the skin and injects the active compounds histamine, serotonin and acetylcholine in such amounts that a human fatality has been recorded. Ongaonga is the main larval food-plant of the New Zealand red admiral, just as European species of nettles are for red admiral, peacock and small tortoiseshell butterflies.

Urtica, from Latin *urere*, to sting, comprises some 80 species of nettles found almost throughout the world.[1] The young shoots of some can be eaten like spinach (nettle pudding) and are used in certain English and Dutch cheeses, and they are also sources of fibre, especially for making fishermen's nets. The widely introduced *U. dioica* was used in prehistoric times for binding arrowheads to shafts, and later, until the eighteenth century, was woven into cloth; fabric made from nettle fibres was revived during the First World War to make German military uniforms (40 kg/88 lb of nettles were needed for one shirt) when there was a shortage of cotton.

Urtica ferox G. Forst., *Florulae Insularum Australium Prodromus*: 66 (1786)

Copper plate by Gerard Sibelius, based on Frederick Nodder's undated watercolour, derived from Parkinson's surviving pencil drawing made at 'Totarra nue'; BF 550; Diment et al., 1987: NZ3/168

1. Mabberley, 2014, p. 888

77.
ACTINOTUS HELIANTHI
flannel flower, Umbelliferae

In April 1770 *Endeavour* reached the coast of Australia. Banks and Solander collected 132 plant species at what was to be named Botany Bay, among them the flannel flower.[1]

On his pencil sketch made in early May 1770, Parkinson wrote the colour instructions:

> the radius [bracts] white the tips a little green the disk pale green somewhat grey anthera brownish yellow the buds greenish the upper sides of the leaves grey green cover'd w^t white down the underside almost white with down the whole stalks and buds are also downy.

A shrublet common on sandstone heath in New South Wales and Queensland, the flannel flower is particularly abundant after bushfires. The generic name comes from the Greek *aktinotus*, meaning provided with rays, referring to the head of flowers surrounded by petal-like bracts; the specific name is from the Latin for 'sunflower'.

Cultivars selected in New South Wales are used in the cut-flower trade, as well as grown in gardens. With the waratah, *Telopea speciosissima*, this plant has been one of the most significant floral features in Australian art since colonial times. It was introduced into cultivation in England in 1821.[2]

Delay in publication meant that Solander's manuscript name, 'Involucrata candida', referring to the whorl of bracts making up an 'involucre' around the head of tiny flowers, was never used, and the French naturalist and explorer Jacques de Labillardière (1755–1834; see also Pl. 88, p. 186) bestowed its current Latin name in 1805. The genus *Actinotus* comprises 17 species, with 16 in Australia and one in New Zealand.[3]

Actinotus helianthi Labill., *Novae Hollandiae Plantarum Specimen* 1: 67 + t. 92 (1805)

Copper plate by Gabriel Smith, based on John Miller's 1774 watercolour, derived from Parkinson's surviving pencil drawing made at 'Botany Bay'; BF 141; Diment et al., 1984: A3/162

1. D. Benson and G. Eldershaw, 'Backdrop to encounter: the 1770 landscape of Botany Bay, the plants collected by Banks and Solander and rehabilitation of natural vegetation at Kurnell', *Cunninghamia* 10, 2007, pp. 113–37

2. Chittenden, 1951, 1, p. 36

3. Mabberley, 2014, p. 12

AUSTRALIA, BOTANY BAY, 28 APRIL–6 MAY 1770

78.

BANKSIA SERRATA
saw banksia, Proteaceae

Saw banksia was first collected by Banks and Solander at Botany Bay in April–May 1770. It is one of four species, three from Botany Bay and one from what is now Queensland, of the new genus *Banksia*, named in Banks' honour, to be described by Linnaeus' son Carl in 1782, after he had worked in Banks' herbarium in London. Solander had named it 'Leucadendrum serratifolium', indicating that he thought it was related to the South African genus *Leucadendron*, but this was later altered to 'Leucadendron serratum' by an unknown hand; both specific names refer to the saw-tooth margins of the leaves.

Reaching up to 16 m (53 ft) in height, saw banksia is a common tree on the eastern seaboard of Australia. After fires, its dormant buds resprout from beneath the thick warty bark (epicormic). The fruiting heads are said to be the bad 'Banksia Men' of May Gibbs' classic Australian children's book series, *Snugglepot and Cuddlepie*. The tree is cultivated in warm countries and also under glass in northern Europe, with a number of selected cultivars available, including 'Pygmy Possum', which is only 60 cm (2 ft) tall.[1]

Banksia (including *Dryandra*) comprises some 170 species in Australia, with just one extending to New Guinea (as well as fossils in New Zealand), 150 being restricted to southwestern Australia alone.[2] Aboriginal people use the nectar as high-energy food ('sugar bag').

Banksia serrata L.f., *Supplementum Plantarum*: 126 (1782)

Copper plate by Gabriel Smith, based on John Miller's 1773 watercolour, derived from Parkinson's pencil drawing made at 'Botany Bay'; BF 285; Diment et al., 1984: A7/326

1. R. Spencer, *Horticultural Flora of South-Eastern Australia* 3 (Sydney, University of New South Wales Press, 2002), p. 268
2. Mabberley, 2014, p. 90

79.

XYLOMELUM PYRIFORME
marridugara, woody pear, Proteaceae

Banks and Solander named marridugara[1] 'Leucadendroides pyrifera', since they thought it resembled the South African genus *Leucadendron*. The specific epithet refers to the fact that the fruit superficially looks like a European pear (*Pyrus*); *pyriformis*, meaning pear-shaped, was coined by Josef Gaertner (see Pl. 2, p. 24).

Marridugara grows into a shrub or small tree, sometimes reaching 15 m (50 ft) tall, in eastern New South Wales.[2] After fires, fresh shoots emerge from beneath the bark (epicormics) or from an underground stock (a lignotuber). At the same time, the persistent fruits open, dispersing the seeds. Its wood was formerly used for gunstocks in Australia and it was introduced in England as an ornamental plant in 1869.[3]

Xylomelum, from the Greek *xylon*, wood, and *melon*, apple or other tree-fruit, is a genus of six species from both southwest and southeast Australia.[4]

Xylomelum pyriforme (Gaertn.) J. Knight, *On the cultivation of plants belonging to the natural order of Proteeae*: 105 (1809)

Copper plate by Gabriel Smith, based on John Miller's 1773 watercolour, derived from Parkinson's surviving pencil drawing made at 'Botany Bay'; BF 275; Diment et al., 1984: A7/315

1. One of the few specific plant-names to have come down to us from the original language of the area: see J. Troy, *The Sydney Language* (Canberra, 1994)

2. Harden, 2002, p. 78

3. Chittenden, 1951, 4, p. 2296

4. Mabberley, 2014, p. 916

80.

BANKSIA INTEGRIFOLIA
Proteaceae

As with *Banksia serrata* (Pl. 78, p. 168), Banks and Solander regarded this tree as belonging in the same genus as certain South African Proteaceae, giving it the manuscript name 'Leucadendrum integrifolium', that is, with entire leaves (in contrast with *B. serrata*). Their specimens were again the basis of a new species described by the younger Linnaeus.

Banksia integrifolia is usually a tree to 25 m (80 ft) tall, growing from coastal eastern Australia to the nearby mountains. Its flowers are visited by a wide range of insects, birds, bats and non-flying mammals,[1] which seek the copious nectar and thus aid in pollination. Unlike some other *Banksia* species, it does not require fire to release its seeds. It is cultivated in Australia and was introduced in England by 1824.[2]

It is instructive to compare the different painters' treatment of Parkinson's drawings of the two banksias.

Banksia integrifolia L.f., *Supplementum Plantarum*: 127 (1782)

Copper plate by Charles White, based on an anonymous watercolour, derived from Parkinson's surviving pencil drawing made at 'Botany Bay'; BF 284; Diment et al., 1984: A7/325

1. S. A. Cunningham, 'Experimental evidence for pollination of *Banksia* spp. by non-flying mammals', *Oecologia* 87, 1991, pp. 86–90

2. Chittenden, 1951, 1, p. 234

81.

CORREA ALBA
Rutaceae

Correa alba is an erect shrub[1] up to about 1.5 m (5 ft) tall, growing in sandy and rocky places along the coasts of southeastern Australia. Its leaves have been used to make an aromatic hot drink, 'Cape Barren tea'.[2] When Parkinson drew the specimens of this plant collected by Banks and Solander at Botany Bay, he added the colour notes 'The flowers white the stamina before blown Fawn colour after yellow'.

In 1793 Banks gave some seeds to James Vere, who had a large garden at Kensington Gore, near the present Royal Albert Hall in London.[3] The resulting plants flowered and were named *Correa alba* after José Francisco Correia da Serra (1751–1823), a Portuguese scientist, diplomat and progressive agitator, whom Banks befriended and allowed to work in his herbarium and library; *albus*, white, refers to the flower colour.

The genus *Correa* comprises some 11 Australian species known in horticulture as Australian fuchsias; they all hybridize.[4]

Correa alba Andrews, *The Botanist's Repository* 1: t. 18 (1798)

Copper plate by Gabriel Smith, based on James Miller's 1775 watercolour, derived from Parkinson's pencil drawing made at 'Botany Bay'; BF 34; Diment et al., 1984: A1/39

1. P. H. Weston and G. J. Harden in Harden, 2002, p. 290

2. Mabberley, 2014, p. 219 and 4th ed., 2017

3. H. C. Andrews, *The Botanist's Repository* 1, 1798, Pl. XVIII

4. Mabberley, 2014, p. 219 and 4th ed., 2017

82.

SYNOUM GLANDULOSUM
bastard rosewood, Meliaceae

This tree was named 'Trichilia octandra' by Solander, but was published in 1817 by J. E. Smith (1759–1828), President of the Linnean Society of London, as *T. glandulosa*, the basis of the modern name.

Bastard rosewood, found in coastal regions of eastern Australia, can grow to 20 m (66 ft) tall or more, but is usually much smaller. Its seeds are remarkable for being partly enveloped in a joint aril, or fleshy covering (hence the name *Synoum* derived from Greek *syn-*, together, and *oon*, egg),[1] which is attractive to birds. It is the only species in its genus.

The dark red, rose-scented timber[2] has many uses, including as sawn timber for general house-framing, and for flooring and mouldings. It is also used for cabinet-work, shop and office fixtures, panelling, turnery and carving, and as structural plywood, scaffold planks, particleboard and fibreboard, as well as for wood wool and paper products.

Synoum glandulosum (Sm.) A. Juss. in *Mémoires du Muséum d'Histoire Naturelle* 19: 227 (1832)

Copper plate by Daniel Mackenzie, based on Frederick Nodder's 1777 watercolour, derived from Parkinson's pencil drawing made at 'Botany Bay'; BF 39; Diment et al., 1984: A1/45

1. Mabberley, 2013, p. 20

2. Mabberley, 2014, p. 835

AUSTRALIA, BOTANY BAY, 28 APRIL–6 MAY 1770

83.

BOSSIAEA HETEROPHYLLA
Leguminosae

On his pencil sketch of what Banks and Solander called 'Genista speciosa', Parkinson described the plant's colouring for working up later:

> The Vexillum [standard or top petal] & Alae [wings or lateral petals] bright yellow the V. stained w[t] red [?] and the bottom w[t] red the Carina [the keel, formed by the bottom pair of petals] a dark red. turning paler towards the base.

Delay in publication meant that the Banks and Solander name was once again superseded, and the formal description was based on French material originating in Sydney in 1792. Independently, the plant was introduced into cultivation in England the same year.[1] The generic name commemorates Joseph Boissieu de la Martinière (1758–1788), a French doctor-naturalist who accompanied La Pérouse (1741–1788) on his voyage to the Pacific, and was presumed drowned with him when the expedition's vessels disappeared off the Solomon Islands.

Bossiaea heterophylla forms an upright shrub up to about 1 m (3 ft) tall and grows south from Queensland to Wilsons Promontory in Victoria, eastern Australia, usually on sandy soils in heath or woodland near the coast.[2] The specific epithet *heterophyllus*, with different leaves, refers to the variable leaf-shape.

The genus *Bossiaea* comprises 78 species found in the temperate parts of Australia, especially in the southwest.[3] The different colours of the species' flowers attract a range of pollinators – the yellow flowers are pollinated by bees and the red ones by birds.

Bossiaea heterophylla Vent., *Description des Plantes Nouvelles*: 7 + t. 7 (1800)

Copper engraving by Robert Blyth, based on Frederick Nodder's 1777 watercolour, derived from Parkinson's surviving pencil drawing made at 'Botany Bay'; BF 54; Diment et al., 1984: A2/61

1. Chittenden, 1951, 1, p. 301

2. T. A. James and G. J. Harden in Harden, 2002, p. 514

3. Mabberley, 2014, p. 115 and 4th ed., 2017

AUSTRALIA, BOTANY BAY, 28 APRIL–6 MAY 1770

84.
LOBELIA DENTATA
Campanulaceae

The specific name given to this plant by Banks and Solander, 'Lobelia azurea', is illuminated by Parkinson's colour note on his pencil sketch: 'The flower a delicate ultramarine the base of the petala white. The upperside of the Calyx ting'd w^t dirty purple the stalk & leaves grass green'.

Lobelia dentata is a slender herb to about 40 cm (16 in.) tall,[1] growing in eucalypt woodland in eastern New South Wales and Victoria. It is particularly abundant after bushfires, when its dazzling blue flowers bring some cheer following the flames' devastations. How its minute seeds survive such catastrophes is unclear.

Yet again, the delay in publication meant that Banks' and Solander's manuscript name was superseded, this time by the Spanish. The first formal description, with *dentatus* referring to the toothed leaves, was based on materials collected in 1792 by Luis Née (1734–1803) in the Sydney area, during the Malaspina Expedition to the Pacific (1789–94).

Lobelia,[2] commemorating Mathias de L'Obel (1538–1616), a Flemish botanist and doctor to James I of England (VI of Scotland), is a large genus likely to be split up. It currently comprises some 415 species, mostly of tropical and warm regions, ranging in size from small herbs to shrubs and pachycaul (thick-stemmed) trees (the Giant Lobelias, found largely in the mountains of the tropics). During development, the flowers twist through 180 degrees, and when they open, the styles push through an anther-tube forcing out the pollen; the stigmas then separate, exposing their receptive surface, free of 'home' pollen. Many lobelias are grown as ornamental garden plants, especially the African *Lobelia erinus*, the common bedding plant with numerous cultivars, of which 'Pendula' is frequently planted in hanging baskets. They contain alkaloids with medicinal applications, particularly the eastern North American *Lobelia inflata* (Indian tobacco), grown for use in chest conditions, and the Chilean *L. tupa*, which contains psychoactive and possibly hallucinogenic compounds and is used in the treatment of toothache, though the overpowering smell can cause nausea.

Lobelia dentata Cav., *Icones et Descriptiones Plantarum* 6: 14 + t. 522 (1800)

Copper plate by Daniel Mackenzie, dated 1783 and based on Frederick Nodder's 1782 watercolour, derived from Parkinson's pencil drawing made at 'Botany Bay'; BF 187; Diment et al., 1984: A5/214

1. B. Wiecek in Harden, 1992, p. 126

2. Mabberley, 2014, p. 497 and 4th ed., 2017

85.

EPACRIS LONGIFLORA
fuchsia heath, Ericaceae

This striking shrub grows up to 2 m (6½ ft) tall in sandy soils, from *Eucalyptus* forest to heath and cliff faces, in New South Wales and Queensland.[1] In drawing Banks' and Solander's 'Ericastrum pulcherrimum', meaning 'the most beautiful heather', Parkinson added the colour notes: 'The leaves grass green something pale below the Calyx pale green ting'd w^r red'.

Although Solander prepared a description, delay in publication meant that his thunder was again stolen, once more by the Spanish. The first published account and name were based on materials collected on the Malaspina Expedition (see Pl. 84, p. 178) when the ships were in Port Jackson. It was introduced into cultivation in England in 1803.

The genus *Epacris* – *epi*, upon, and *akris*, summit, referring to the hilly habitats of some of its species – comprises around 40 species, 38 of them in southeastern Australia and two in New Zealand.[2] Their flowers often have a sweet scent, reminiscent of carnations.

Epacris longiflora Cav., *Icones et Descriptiones Plantarum* 4: 25 + t. 344 (1797)
Copper plate by Charles White, based on James Miller's undated watercolour, derived from Parkinson's surviving pencil drawing made at 'Botany Bay'; BF 197; Diment et al., 1984: A5/225
1. J. M. Powell in Harden, 1992, p. 409
2. Mabberley, 2014, p. 308

86.

BLANDFORDIA NOBILIS
gadigalbudyari, Christmas bells, Blandfordiaceae

One of the most spectacular plants collected at Botany Bay, gadigalbudyari was named 'Alooides polyanthes' by Banks and Solander, in reference to its apparent similarity to the African genus *Aloe*. Parkinson's colour notes to his pencil sketch describe it well:

> The top of the flower yellow which suddenly turns scarlet & this turns darker towards the base of the flower & into a deep red on the stalks the stalks among the flowers & at the top dirty purple the bractea stain'd w^t red. the leaves grass green turning white at the bottom. the stile pale yellow green.

Gadigalbudyari is a tufted perennial herb[1] with strap-like leaves up to 75 cm (30 in.) long; its flowering scapes (stalks), up to 80 cm (32 in.) tall, are produced at Christmas time, hence its common name. The flowers are held in groups of 3 to 20, followed by fruits up to 6 cm (2½ in.) long. It grows on poor sandstone soils and in wet areas in eastern New South Wales, in heathland associated with carnivorous sundews (*Drosera* spp., see Pl. 88, p. 186). In the northern part of its range it appears to hybridize with the even more spectacular *B. grandiflora*. It was introduced into cultivation in England in 1803 and was formally described the following year from coloured drawings and specimens sent to England by John White, Surgeon-General in the colony.

Blandfordia commemorates George Spencer-Churchill (1766–1840), Marquess of Blandford, later 5th Duke of Marlborough, who had an important and extravagant garden at Whiteknights near Reading, Berkshire, England, now the campus of Reading University; *nobilis*, notable or famous, may refer to both him and the plant. There are four species in the genus, all native in eastern Australia.[2] Traditionally they were Aboriginal food plants and are now protected in the wild. Flowers were found in the gut of the first emu shot in Australia (1788).

Blandfordia nobilis Sm., *Exotic Botany*. 1: 5 + t. 4 (1804)

Copper plate by Edward Walker, based on James Miller's 1775 watercolour, derived from Parkinson's pencil drawing made at 'Botany Bay'; BF 325; Diment et al., 1984: A8/375

1. A. L. Quirico in Harden, 1992, p. 68

2. Mabberley, 2014, p. 108

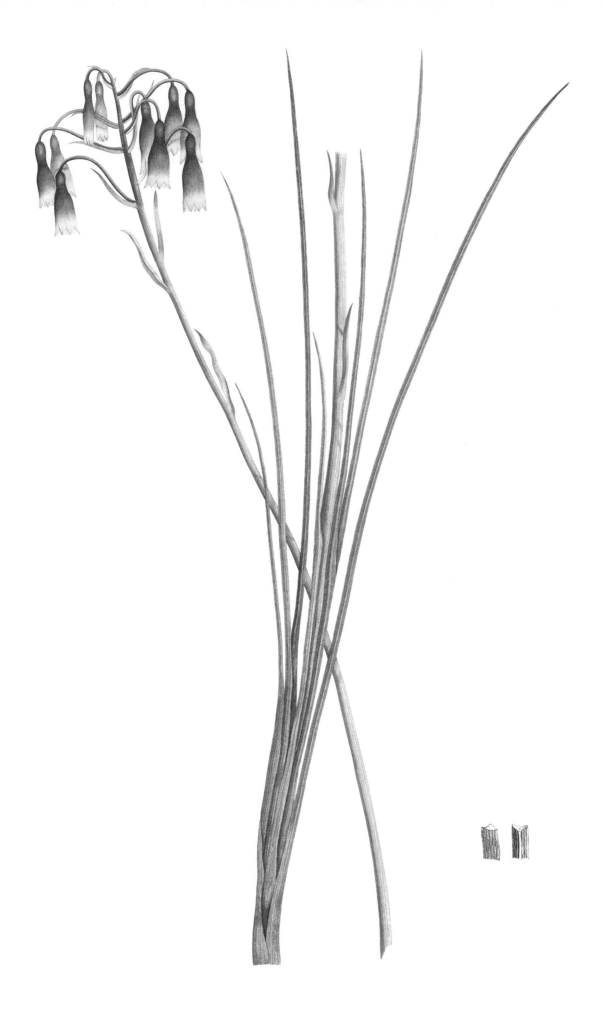

87.
ACACIA TERMINALIS
sunshine wattle, Leguminosae

In the local Sydney language,[1] the word wadanguli is used for wattles generally, and as sunshine wattle is one of the most common, it would have been included under that name. When Banks and Solander collected their 'Mimosa pinnata' at Botany Bay, Parkinson wrote on his pencil sketch: 'The anthera on the blown flower yellow the buds a mixture of straw & orange the leaves on the upperside grass green below much whiter…. stalks a greenish red'. It is the stamens that make up the colour of *Acacia* flowerheads, the petals being very reduced in size.

This wattle is a rather variable shrub or small tree[2] from northern New South Wales to central Victoria and Tasmania, conspicuous in later winter with its golden yellow to cream flowerheads. It cannot set seed after self-pollination, but is visited by bees and small birds, which help exchange pollen between individual plants. Each leaf has a red nectary up to 122 mm (5 in.) long on its petiole (stalk), which, especially in the morning, exudes a nectar containing the sugar hexose and rich in amino acids, attractive to birds.[3]

Acacia, the Greek name for the African *Vachellia* (*Acacia*) *nilotica*, perhaps derives from *akis*, a sharp point,[4] referring to the plant's spiny stipules; the significance of *terminalis* is unclear, but is presumed to refer to the position of the inflorescences. There are some 1,468 described species of *Acacia* from the tropical and warm parts of the Old World, especially Australia, which has about 1,053. *Acacia pycnantha* (golden wattle) is the Australian national emblem. Many provide important products including timber, fuel, forage and tanbark, and they are also cultivated as ornamental trees, though some have become pestilential weeds. Most familiar in Europe is *A. dealbata* (blue or silver wattle), the florists' 'mimosa', imported to London from southern France in winter.

Acacia terminalis (Salisb.) J. F. Macbr. in *Contributions from the Gray Herbarium of Harvard University* 59: 7 (1919)

Copper plate by Frederick Nodder, based on his 1781 watercolour, derived from Parkinson's surviving pencil drawing made at 'Botany Bay'; BF 95; Diment et al., 1984: A2/107

1. See J. Troy, *The Sydney Language* (Canberra, 1994)

2. P. G. Kodela and M. D. Tindale in *Flora of Australia* 11A, 2001, pp. 220–21

3. R. B. Knox et al., 'Extrafloral nectaries as adaptations for bird pollination in *Acacia terminalis*', *American Journal of Botany* 62, 1985, pp. 1185–96; this is recorded in at least two other *Acacia* spp.

4. *Oxford English Dictionary*: acacia

AUSTRALIA, BOTANY BAY, 28 APRIL–6 MAY 1770

88.

DROSERA PEDATA
forked sundew, Droseraceae

On his pencil drawing of this striking carnivorous plant Parkinson wrote, 'The flowers white germen green Anthera yellow the leaves yellow green the stalks the same ting'd w[t] red, especially at ye bottom & top', which was fortunate because dried specimens turn black. In his manuscripts Solander named it 'Drosera dichotoma', the specific name referring to its forked leaves. This sundew has long been known as *Drosera binata* Labill. (with 'binata' referring to the same characteristic), but that name was published by Jacques de Labillardière (see Pl. 77, p. 166) just a few weeks later later than *D. pedata* was. As naturalist on Bruni d'Entrecasteaux's voyage to the Pacific, Labillardière had collected the plant in Tasmania in January 1793,[1] but in Java his collections were seized by the British and presented to Queen Charlotte.[2] Only through the diplomacy of his friend, Joseph Banks, were they returned to him in 1796.

This perennial species is widespread from eastern Australia to New Zealand. It grows to 50 cm (20 in.) tall and is the only species to have leaves that are forked, sometimes, indeed, twice forked, with selected forms having even more divided ones with up to 36 'points'; *pedatus*, referring to the leaves, means with divided with leaflets from the same point, with the lateral ones divided again. It was accidentally introduced into cultivation in Britain in 1823, when, at the Royal Botanic Gardens, Kew, 'it sprung up among some earth imported from New Holland'.[3] It is now perhaps the most commonly seen exotic species grown in Europe and is readily propagated from root cuttings.[4]

Drosera is from the Greek *droseros*, dewy, referring to the glistening, gland-tipped hairs on the leaves. It is a genus of about 100 species (sundews) found in wet places worldwide,[5] but especially the southern hemisphere, with southwest Australia alone having 68. They have round to linear leaf-blades with gland-tipped red or greenish hairs. When irritated by insects the hairs are capable of movement, and can hold and digest the victims. In some species at least this promotes flowering. Some are of local medicinal significance due to quinones, for instance 'Herbae Droserae' (*D. rotundifolia*), which is used for whooping cough and asthma in Europe.

Drosera pedata Pers., *Synopsis Plantarum* 1: 357 (1805)
Copper plate by Gerard Sibelius, based on John Cleveley's watercolour, derived from Parkinson's surviving pencil drawing made at 'Botany Bay'; BF 100; Diment et al., 1984: A3/113

1. E. Duyker, *Citizen Labillardière* (Carlton, Victoria, Miegunyah Press, 2003), pp. 140–41
2. Ibid., pp. 197, 206–11
3. W. J. Hooker in S. Curtis, *Curtis's Botanical Magazine* 58, 1831, t. 3082
4. Chittenden, 1951, 2, p. 715
5. Mabberley, 2014, p. 289

AUSTRALIA, BOTANY BAY, 28 APRIL–6 MAY 1770

89.

HIBBERTIA SCANDENS
snake climber, Dilleniaceae

Banks and Solander first collected this vigorous scrambler,[1] their 'Dilleniastrum reptans', at Botany Bay, and then at their next landfall, Bustard Bay, now partly in Eurimbula National Park in Queensland. The spot where they reached shore is today in the town of Seventeen Seventy.

Snake climber is a native of much of eastern Australia, and was first named *Dillenia scandens* by the German botanist and plant taxonomist Carl Ludwig Willdenow (1765–1812), from herbarium material in Berlin. It had been introduced in England in 1790 and in 1796 was given the name *D. humilis*, without description, by James Donn (1758–1813), Scottish curator of the Cambridge Botanic Garden, in his *Hortus Cantabrigiensis, or a catalogue of plants...cultivated in the Walkerian botanic garden, Cambridge* (1796). Donn had worked at Kew and through Banks' influence was appointed to Cambridge in 1794.[2] The plant is still in cultivation.

Hibbertia commemorates George Hibbert (1757–1837), who owned a private botanic garden at Clapham, now in south London; *scandens* is Latin for climbing. The genus contains about 225 species, 200 of them found in Australia, with some in New Caledonia, one in Madagascar, two in the Malay Archipelago and one in Fiji.[3] The number of stamens per flower ranges from one in some species to over 200. Some are buzz-pollinated, that is, the anthers are induced to release pollen by particular frequencies of the wings of visiting flying insects.

Hibbertia scandens (Willd.) Gilg in Engl. & Prantl, *Natürlichen Pflanzenfamilien* 3(6): 117 (1893)

Copper plate by Daniel Mackenzie, based on Frederick Nodder's 1778 watercolour, derived from Parkinson's surviving pencil drawing made at 'Botany Bay'; BF 3; Diment et al., 1984: A1/3

1. G. J. Harden and J. Everett in Harden, 1990, p. 297
2. Henrey, 1975, 2, p. 238
3. Mabberley, 2014, p. 405 and 4th ed., 2017

90.

ACACIA LEIOCALYX
black wattle, Leguminosae

When they collected this small tree at Bustard Bay, Banks and Solander named it 'Mimosa axillaris'. It is common in eucalypt woods from Queensland south to Sydney, growing up to 7 m (23 ft) tall, with furrowed bark;[1] it is apparently largely pollinated by a beetle restricted to it.[2]

Acacia leiocalyx is a phyllodic species, meaning that after the seedling leaves have fallen, it has only flattened, parallel-veined leaves that are apparently equivalent to the basal parts of pinnate leaves such as those of *A. terminalis*. Other phyllodic acacias include *A. mangium* (mangium) of the eastern Malay Archipelago and tropical Australia, which is the most planted tropical species of *Acacia*, amounting to perhaps 900,000 ha (2,225,000 acres) in Malaysia and Indonesia alone. It is harvested for building timber, fuel and woodchips for pulp and charcoal, including medicinal 'activated charcoal'.

For the origin of the name *Acacia,* see *A. terminalis* (Pl. 87, p. 184); *leiocalyx* is from the Greek *leios*, smooth, referring to the glabrous (hairless) calyx.

Acacia leiocalyx (Domin) Pedley in *Contributions from the Queensland Herbarium* 15: 10 (1974)

Copper plate by Daniel Mackenzie, based on Frederick Nodder's 1781 watercolour, derived from Parkinson's surviving pencil drawing made at 'Bustard Bay'; BF 91; Diment et al., 1984: A2/103

1. M. D. Tindale et al. in *Flora of Australia* 11B, 2001, pp. 164–65

2. T. J. Hawkeswood, 'Observations on *Pyrgoides dryops* (Blackburn) (Coleoptera: Chrysomelidae), a pollen-feeding beetle on *Acacia leiocalyx* (Domin) Pedley, at Brisbane, south-east Queensland', *Victorian Naturalist* 100, 1983, pp. 156–58

91.
DIANELLA CAERULEA
blue flax-lily, Asphodelaceae

In drawing Banks' and Solander's 'Anthericum caeruleum', Parkinson recorded his colour notes on his pencil drawing:

> The flowers & buds pale blue wᵗ a cast of purple the very young buds more purple the anthera pale yellow filaments orange peduncle stain'd wᵗ purple, leaves grass green turnᵍ gradually white at the bottom.

Dianella caerulea is a very variable tuft-forming perennial native to eastern Australia, where it is found in coastal regions and other habitats. It can reach 1 m (3 ft) in height, and its blue flowers (*caeruleus* means dark blue) are followed by edible indigo fruits high in vitamin C, though they are considered toxic by some authorities. In Queensland they are taken by bowerbirds, rosellas, king parrots and honeyeaters.[1]

This species is often cultivated in gardens as it is tough and long-lived; a number of selected cultivars are favoured in civic plantings, in particular the dwarf, clumping Little Jess™. It was one of the earliest Australian plants introduced into cultivation in England, and its describer, John Sims, noted it was

> first raiſed in this country from ſeeds from Port Jackſon, about the year 1783 [apparently the seeds came from Banks in 1771], by our much reſpected friend, the late Mr. CUFF, of Teddington, a gentleman of great zeal and aſſiduity in cultivating plants and promoting the ſcience of Botany, to whoſe liberality the *Brompton Botanic Garden* is indebted for this and many other ſcarce and beautiful plants.[3]

Dianella, a diminutive of Diana, Roman goddess of hunting, is a genus of more than 20 species ranging from East Africa to the Pacific.[4] The dried rhizome of *D. ensifolia* is chewed as a vermifuge, though when fresh it is used as a rat-poison.

Dianella caerulea Sims, *Botanical Magazine* 15: t. 505 (1801)

Copper plate by Jabez Goldar, based on John Cleveley's 1775 watercolour, derived from Parkinson's pencil drawing made at 'Bustard Bay'; BF 322; Diment et al., 1984: A8/372

1. Cooper, 2004, p. 396

2. E. C. Nelson, 'Australian plants cultivated in England before 1788', *Telopea* 2, 1983, pp. 347–53

3. J. Sims, *Botanical Magazine* 15, 1801, t. 505

4. Mabberley, 2014, p. 266 and 4th ed., 2017

AUSTRALIA, BUSTARD BAY, 22–24 MAY 1770

92.

XEROCHRYSUM BRACTEATUM
strawflower, Compositae

Solander's 'Xeranthemum aureum' was collected in what is now southern Queensland; Parkinson made his pencil sketch of it at Bustard Bay.

Also known as golden everlasting, this is a very variable annual or perennial species (or complex of species), widespread in Australia and growing to 1.5 m (5 ft) tall. By 1799 it was being cultivated at Empress Joséphine's garden, Malmaison, near Paris, when it was named *Xeranthemum bracteatum*; it is naturalized on St Helena, allegedly having escaped from Napoleon's garden there.[1]

Strawflowers are still very commonly grown for cutting and drying for long-lasting winter decoration – hence their name 'immortelles' or 'everlastings'. In cultivation, the heads, made up of tiny flowers, are up to 8 cm (3 in.) in diameter. There are many selected forms, often called 'helichrysums', with red, orange, yellow, violet, pink or white persistent papery bracts.[2] Seed races include dwarf Bright Bikinis Series and dwarf Hot Bikini, as well as taller Swiss Giants Mixture and Tall Splendid Mix, forms of which have 'double' flowers in which the central disk florets are replaced by ray florets.

Xeranthemum is now considered to be a strictly Mediterranean genus, and the six Australian species comprise the genus *Xerochrysum*, its name deriving from the Greek *xeros*, dry, and *chrysos*, gold.

Xerochrysum bracteatum (Vent.) Tzvelev in *Novosti Sistematiki Vysshikh Rastenii* 27: 151 (1990)

Copper plate by Gerard Sibelius, based on Frederick Nodder's 1780 watercolour, derived from Parkinson's surviving pencil drawing made at 'Bustard Bay'; BF 167; Diment et al., 1984: A4/193

1. Mabberley, 2014, p. 915

2. Huxley, 1992, 2, p. 527

93.
PASSIFLORA AURANTIA
Passifloraceae

Endeavour reached Thirsty Sound, south of the present-day town of Mackay, Queensland, on 29 May 1770, where Banks and Solander collected what they called 'Passiflora coccinea'. Parkinson noted on his pencil drawing of it:

> The Petala cherry colour small nectaria dark red the large buff colour stained w[t] red near the edge. stile & stigma pale green anther yellow green leaves vivid grass green w[t] small veins the underside pale glaucus [sic] fruit pea green...

Originally described from material from New Caledonia, *Passiflora aurantia* is a widespread species in the western Pacific. Its flowers, creamy white at first and later turning pink and orange-red, last just one day and are followed by fruits 3–4 cm (1–1½ in.) long.[1] Material from Norfolk Island, perhaps ultimately from William Paterson (1755–1810), who was in charge of the penal settlement there, was in cultivation in England before 1800, when Mary Lawrance issued the first printed illustration of it. This was a plate in her very rare passionflower series: 'Pafsiflora adiantifolia/ Norfolk Island Pafsion Flower/ Published by Mifs Lawrance Teacher of Botanical Drawing &c. No 86 Queen Ann Street East. London. Octr 1 1800.... Drawn & Etched by Mifs Lawrance'.[2]

Many hybrids are also cultivated for their edible pulp around the seeds, which is often used in drinks and ices, including 'Panama passion fruit', as well as numerous South American species such as *P. edulis* (purple granadilla), *P. laurifolia* (water lemon or yellow granadilla) and *P. mollissima* (banana passion fruit), while *P. quadrangularis* (granadilla), with a yellow fruit to 30 cm (1 ft) long, is eaten as a vegetable when immature. *Passiflora tarminiana* (banana poka) is now a serious weed in Hawaii, Australia and New Zealand.[3]

For the meaning of *Passiflora* see *P. tetrandra* (Pl. 63, p. 140); *aurantius* is orange-coloured, referring to the flowers.

Passiflora aurantia G. Forst., *Florulae Insularum Australium Prodromus*: 62 (1786)

Copper plate by Daniel Mackenzie, based on Frederick Nodder's 1780 watercolour, derived from Parkinson's surviving pencil drawing made at 'Thirsty Sound'; BF 134; Diment et al., 1984: A3/153

1. P. S. Green, *Oceanic Islands I, Flora of Australia* 49, 1994, p. 126
2. Copy in Lindley Library, Royal Horticultural Society, London
3. Mabberley, 2014, pp. 636–37

94.

PANDOREA PANDORANA
wonga-wonga vine, Bignoniaceae

Among the plants Parkinson sketched at Thirsty Sound was 'Bignonia floribunda', describing it on his pencil drawing as, 'The flower white the inside stript w^t purple. the leaves grass green somewhat glaucus [sic] below the young stalks pale green. Capsula fresh green speck'd w^t white'.

The wonga-wonga vine is a rampant liane growing on larger trees in the forests of the Malay Archipelago and western Pacific, and is now naturalized in New Zealand. It has very finely divided leaves when young, and fruits with winged seeds when mature; its wood was formerly used for spears.

It is a popular garden plant with several cultivars, such as the scented, white-flowered 'Snowbells'. In England it was originally raised in 1793 by the nursery firm Lee and Kennedy of Hammersmith, from seed sent by William Paterson from Norfolk Island, where it had probably been introduced from Sydney.[1] It first flowered in 1798, in James Vere's garden in Kensington Gore, London. On Norfolk Island,

> upon the return of the season, in which the young tendrils begin to shoot, and the leaves begin to appear; within fifteen, or twenty days, the whole plant is entirely covered with a white downy insect, of the genus Aphis, something similar to our blight; which, in a very short time from their first appearance on this plant, become so completely dispersed over every vegetable production, that scarce a green leaf is to be seen through the whole extent of the island. So great a plague was this insect thought to be, from its effects on the vegetation, by those who were sent to colonize the island, that it was considered as one of the principal reasons for abandoning the settlement.[2]

This is alleged to be the reason for the plant's Latin name, *Pandorea pandorana*, from the Greek myth of Pandora. Created by the gods, Pandora was the first mortal woman. She was sent to earth by Zeus with a jar or box, and married Epimetheus, the brother of Prometheus. When she opened her box, she released all the evils that humans suffer from, as punishment by Zeus for Prometheus' theft of fire from the gods to give to mankind.

Pandorea pandorana (Andrews) Steenis in *Bulletin du Jardin Botanique de Buitenzorg* ser. 3, 10: 198 (1928)
Copper plate by Daniel Mackenzie, based on Frederick Nodder's 1778 watercolour, derived from Parkinson's surviving pencil drawing made at 'Thirsty Sound'; BF 243; Diment et al., 1984: A6/274

1. P. S. Green, *Oceanic Islands I, Flora of Australia* 49, 1994, p. 344

2. H. C. Andrews, 'Bignonia pandorana', *Botanist's Repository* 2, 1800, t. 86

95.
EUCALYPTUS CREBRA
red ironbark, Myrtaceae

This eucalypt was given the manuscript name 'Metrosideros salicifolia' by Banks and Solander. When Parkinson drew it, he described its colouring as 'The stamina white receptacle pale green the stalks the same. The leaves a pale blue green w^t a yellowish nerve in the middle'.

Red ironbark is a tree growing to 35 m (115 ft) tall, distributed from the Cairns area of north Queensland to just south of Sydney, where it was known as mugagaru.[1] One of the major trees in the dwindling and threatened Cumberland Plain Woodland west of Sydney, its leaves are a koala food and the flowers an important nectar source in the honey industry.

Ironbarks are so-called because their rough, accumulated bark makes them difficult to fell. The timber of *Eucalyptus crebra* was formerly used for railway sleepers, and part of a plank made from it from the stables of the oldest surviving European house in Australia – Elizabeth Farm, Parramatta, New South Wales, which dates from 1793 – is now in the Museum of Applied Arts and Sciences, Sydney.[2]

Eucalyptus is from the Greek *eu*, well, and *kalypto*, cover (as with a lid), alluding to the united calyx lobes and petals, which form a cap that is shed as the flowers open to reveal the coloured stamens; the specific name derives from *creber*, meaning thickly clustered, referring to the flowers. The genus *Eucalyptus* comprises over 800 species from the Philippines to Australia, with 'eucalypt' fossils known from New Zealand.[3] The great majority of species occur in Australia (gums), where they are the most characteristic genus of the landscape and range from dwarf shrubs with lignotubers and coppice shoots (mallees) to some of the tallest trees known; *E. regnans* in the Styx Valley, Tasmania, is the world's tallest angiosperm ('flowering plant'), at over 100 m (330 ft) tall. More than 200 species have been introduced elsewhere, and they now dominate the scenery of parts of California, East Africa, Sri Lanka, Portugal and Israel. Addis Ababa ('new flower' in Amharic) became the first permanent capital of Ethiopia because gums provided a reliable supply of firewood.

Eucalyptus crebra F. Muell. in *Journal of the Proceedings of the Linnean Society. Botany* 3: 87 (1859)

Copper plate by Robert Blyth, based on Frederick Nodder's 1778 watercolour, derived from Parkinson's pencil drawing made at 'Thirsty Sound'; BF 121; Diment et al., 1984: A3/139

1. See J. Troy, *The Sydney Language* (Canberra, 1994)

2. Object D6911, presented 1905

3. Mabberley, 2014, pp. 321–22 and 4th ed., 2017

96.
PITTOSPORUM FERRUGINEUM SUBSP. LINIFOLIUM
kamut, Pittosporaceae

Banks and Solander found kamut on Palm Island, north of present-day Townsville in Queensland, where they went ashore for just one day, on 7 June 1770. Banks reported 'we made a shift however to gather 14 or 15 new plants'. *Pittosporum ferrugineum* is a small tree growing up to 20 m (66 ft), with golden-brown shoots, though they are not as rusty as the epithet *ferrugineus*, rust-coloured, would suggest; its bark is citrus-smelling when cut.

Kamut is found from India and Southeast Asia to Melanesia, and south to central coastal Queensland, particularly in beach forest. The southern populations south from Cooktown in Australia, referred to the subspecies *linifolium*, are distinguished by their short petioles (leaf stalks) and long peduncles (flower or fruit stalks).[1] The subspecies *ferrugineum* is in cultivation and was introduced in England before 1787 as 'native of Guinea',[2] apparently an error for this Indopacific plant.

Pittosporum, from the Greek *pitta*, pitch, and *spora*, seed, the seeds having a resinous coating, is a genus of about 140 species of evergreen trees and shrubs in tropical and southern Africa to New Zealand and the Pacific,[3] often with sweet-smelling flowers. They include *P. coriaceum*, an element of the Madeiran *laurisilva* (see *Heberdenia bahamensis*, Pl. 2, p. 24), and *P. undulatum* of eastern Australia, an aggressive weed-tree in disturbed forests of many parts of the world.

Pittosporum ferrugineum W.T. Aiton subsp. *linifolium* (A. Cunn.)
Cayzer et al. in *Australian Systematic Botany* 13: 892 (2000)

Copper plate by Charles White, based on John Cleveley's 1774 watercolour, derived from Parkinson's surviving pencil drawing made at 'Palm Island'; BF 13; Diment et al., 1984: A1/14

1. L. W. Cayzer et al., 'Revision of *Pittosporum* (Pittosporaceae) in Australia', *Australian Systematic Botany* 13, 2000, pp. 845–902
2. J. Sims, *Curtis's Botanical Magazine* 46, 1819, t. 2075
3. Mabberley, 2014, p. 674 and 4th ed., 2017

97.

JACQUEMONTIA PANICULATA
Convolvulaceae

Another plant collected by Banks and Solander during their short visit to Palm Island was their 'Convolvulus micranthus'. When Parkinson sketched it, he annotated his drawing with the colour description 'The flowers pale lilac ting'd w^t whitish green at the bottom stamina &c white'.

Jacquemontia paniculata is a sparsely to densely hairy climber found throughout the Old World tropics south to central Queensland in Australia. It grows from sea level up to 550 m (1,800 ft) in different kinds of forest.

The name *Jacquemontia* commemorates Victor Jacquemont (1801–1832), a young French explorer and naturalist who travelled first in the West Indies and then in India, where he died; *paniculatus* means with panicles of flowers. The genus *Jacquemontia* comprises some 80–100 species of liane of tropical and warm countries, especially the Americas.[1]

Jacquemontia paniculata (Burm.f.) H. Hallier in *Botanische Jahrbücher für Systematik, Pflanzengeschichte und Pflanzengeographie* 18: 95 (1893)

Copper engraving by Daniel Mackenzie, based on James Miller's undated watercolour, derived from Parkinson's surviving pencil drawing made at 'Palm Island'; BF 226; Diment et al., 1984: A6/258

1. Mabberley, 2014, p. 440

98.

HOYA AUSTRALIS
Apocynaceae

At their next landfall, Cape Grafton, north of present-day Cairns in Queensland, Banks and Solander collected what they called 'Asclepias crassifolia'. Parkinson sketched it and annotated his pencil drawing with the description 'The flower white with a speck of purple at the base of each petal. the calyx & peduncle white'.

An evergreen climber with succulent stems up to 10 m (33 ft) long, *Hoya australis* grows in exposed places, including forest edges, south to Grafton in northern New South Wales.[1] The strongly honeysuckle-scented flowers produce abundant nectar and are pollinated by the southern dart, a skipper butterfly.[2] In England the plant was introduced into cultivation in 1863.[3]

Hoya commemorates Thomas Hoy (*c.* 1750–1822), head gardener to the Duke of Northumberland at Syon House, Isleworth, near Kew Gardens; *australis* is southern. The genus *Hoya* comprises about 250 species of root-climbers, twiners or sprawling shrubs (known as wax flowers or wax plants) in the Indopacific region.[4] Many are associated with ants – some have specialized leaves that house them, some grow on ants' nests and some root in ant-inhabited cavities in trees. Many are cultivated ornamentals, and as house plants have been shown to remove airborne pollutants. Commonly seen are *H. carnosa* from southern China to Australia, used in Hawaiian *leis* (garlands), and *H. lanceolata* subsp. *bella* from India to Myanmar.

Hoya australis R. Br. ex Traill in *Transactions of the Horticultural Society of London* 7: 28 (1827)

Copper plate by Gerard Sibelius, based on James Miller's undated watercolour, derived from Parkinson's surviving pencil drawing made at 'Cape Grafton'; BF 212; Diment et al., 1984: A5/244

1. J. R. Wheeler in Wheeler et al., 1992, p. 714

2. P. I. Forster, 'Pollination of *Hoya australis* (Asclepiadaceae) by *Ocybadistes walkeri sothis* (Lepidopetra: Hesperidae)', *The Australian Entomologist* 19, 1992, pp. 39–43

3. G. Bentham in *Curtis's Botanical Magazine* ser. 3, 26, 1870, sub t. 5820

4. Mabberley, 2014, p. 415 and 4th ed., 2017

99.
HIBISCUS MERAUKENSIS
Malvaceae

A shrubby plant to 2 m (6½ ft) tall, this mallow is found in the Moluccas and New Guinea south to southeastern Queensland. *Hibiscus* is the Greek name for mallow; *meraukensis* means from Merauk, in New Guinea. On his partially coloured pencil drawing (below) of Banks' and Solander's 'Hibiscus scabrosus' Parkinson noted:

> The flower white w^t a cast of citross [sic] colour at the bottom of each petala deep crimson on the outside pale the stamina and stile dark red purple the parts mark[ed] x are stained w^t carmine.

Hibiscus includes about 675 species, ranging from shrubs to small trees and perennials to herbs in warm temperate to tropical parts of the world. The flowers are white to red, yellow or even bluish, usually with basal maroon spots on the petals. Extrafloral nectaries on the leaves are attractive to defending ants, and are found even in the originally ant-less Hawaii. The fruits are in the form of dry capsules or fleshy fruits.

Many species of *Hibiscus* produce good fibre, such as *H. cannabinus* (kenaf, Ambari or Deccan hemp, Bimlipatum jute), originally from tropical Africa. Its fibre is like jute and is used to make paper, and also now for door-panel insulation in Toyota Prius cars. *Hibiscus tiliaceus* (hau in Hawaii) provides an important fibre for cordage, mats, sails and nets, while its wood is used for bows and canoe outriggers, for firewood and erosion control, as well as in local medicine. Other species are important ornamentals, particularly *H. rosa-sinensis* of unknown origin. *Hibiscus esculentus* (gumbo, okra, lady's fingers) has edible (if slimy) young fruits, while *H. heterophyllus* of eastern Australia is the 'soft' wood used by Aboriginal people in combination with a harder one to make fire.

Hibiscus meraukensis Hochr. in *Rapport Annuel Conservatoire et Jardin Botaniques de la Ville de Genève* 11–12: 8 (1907)
Copper engraving by Gerard Sibelius, based on Frederick Nodder's 1778 watercolour, derived from Parkinson's surviving pencil drawing made at 'Cape Grafton'; BF 23; Diment et al., 1984: A1/24

AUSTRALIA, CAPE GRAFTON, 9–10 JUNE 1770

100.

PLANCHONIA CAREYA
cocky apple, Lecythidaceae

Banks and Solander called this plant 'Eugenia crenata', apparently thinking it belonged in the family Myrtaceae. Parkinson noted on his field drawing: 'The petala & stalk pale whitish green stamina white turning into a fine blush colour about the middle to the bottom anthera cream colour'.

Cocky apple is a deciduous tree growing to 15 m (50 ft) tall, found from New Guinea south to coastal central Queensland.[1] Its flowers open at night and are probably bat-pollinated. The edible fruits are up to 9 cm (3½ in.) long and taste something like quince (*Cydonia oblonga*); they are taken by red-tailed black cockatoos and palm cockatoos.[2] Seedlings grow rapidly and cocky apple can soon colonize neglected grazing land. Because the tree contains saponins, it is the source of an effective fish poison.

The scientific name encapsulates a rather contrasting juxtaposition of human endeavour. *Planchonia* commemorates the oenologist's hero, Jules Émile Planchon (1823–1888), the French botanist who helped save the wine industry in France when it was faced with an apparently catastrophic phylloxera attack; while *careya* commemorates William Carey (1761–1834), a Baptist missionary in India.

Planchonia careya (F. Muell.) R. Knuth in Engl., *Das Pflanzenreich* IV, 219: 56 (1939)

Copper plate by Robert Blyth, based on Frederick Nodder's 1777 watercolour, derived from Parkinson's surviving pencil drawing made at 'Cape Grafton'; BF 128; Diment et al., 1984: A3/146

1. J. R. Wheeler in Wheeler et al., 1992, p. 236

2. Cooper, 2004, p. 268

101.

COCHLOSPERMUM GILLIVRAEI
Australian kapok, Bixaceae

Parkinson's partly coloured drawing of this plant (below) was made at Endeavour River, Queensland. *Endeavour* was beached for repairs here for almost two months in June–August 1770 after running aground on a reef, allowing Banks and Solander time to collect numerous new specimens. The sketch is annotated with Parkinson's instructions on colour:

> The petala & stile pale yellow stamina scarlet anthera gold colour calyx green yellow ting'd and freckl'd w^t red, the buds & stalks the same more or less green for their age the old stalk green red.

Solander called this plant 'Argemonoides ricinifolia', referring to the superficial similarity to the poppy *Argemone* (Papaveraceae), and with leaves like *Ricinus communis*, the castor-oil plant.

Australian kapok is a deciduous tree growing up to 12 m (40 ft) tall, found in rather open forests in northern Australia and New Guinea. It produces its bright yellow, edible flowers in spring, when they often open before the leaves unfold. As with cotton, the seeds are woolly with hairs, though in the true kapok, *Ceiba pentandra* (Malvaceae), the hairs grow from the fruit-wall, rather than from the seeds themselves.

Cochlospermum is from the Greek *cochlos*, spiral shell, and *spermum*, seed, because some species have twisted seeds. The specific name commemorates John MacGillivray (1821–1867), who collected the type specimen on Lizard Island in the Great Barrier Reef when he was the naturalist, along with T. H. Huxley, on HMS *Rattlesnake*, captained by Owen Stanley, in 1846–50.

Cochlospermum comprises 12 species of tropical xeromorphic (with structures adapted to living in dry habitats) trees or shrubs.[1] Some have tuberous underground stems, and often flower when leafless in the dry season. *Cochlospermum religiosum*, the silk-cotton tree of Myanmar and India, flowers as an unbranched pole and is the source of an insoluble gum (karaya or kutira), a tragacanth substitute. It is frequently cultivated near temples in India, and its fig-like form engulfs ruins, as at Angkor (Cambodia).

Cochlospermum gillivraei Benth., *Flora Australiensis* 1: 106 (1863)

Copper plate by Gerard Sibelius based on Frederick Nodder's 1778 watercolour, derived from Parkinson's surviving pencil drawing made at 'Endeavours River'; BF 12; Diment et al., 1984: A1/13

1. Mabberley, 2014, p. 198

102.

ERYTHRINA VESPERTILIO
yulbah, Leguminosae

Named 'Erythrina corallodendron concolor' by Solander, yulbah was not given a scientific name until nearly 80 years later, when explorer Thomas Mitchell (1792–1855) wrote, 'the leaflets are often above four inches broad and not two inches long, not unlike the form of a bat [*Vespertilio*] with its wings extended'. He further noted that 'This, sometimes grew to a tree as much as a foot in diameter; and the natives, who, like Nature herself, may be said to do nothing in vain, had cut one down and carried off the whole of the trunk.'[1] The wood was used for making *woomeras* (spear-throwers), *coolamons* (carrying vessels) and shields.[2]

Restricted to northern and northeastern Australia, yulbah is a straggly deciduous tree with thorny, corky bark, flowering when leafless. Cultivated outdoors in warm countries, it is also grown as a greenhouse shrub, having been introduced to Europe before 1885.[3]

Erythrina (from the Greek *erythros*, red) comprises some 120 bird-pollinated species in warm countries.[4] Many are grown as shade trees and for ornament (coral trees), their seeds used as beads and their timber for outriggers and formerly surfboards and fishing-floats. Most familiar is *E. variegata* from East Africa to the Pacific, especially the Lombardy-poplar-shaped 'Tropical Coral'.

Erythrina vespertilio Benth. in Mitchell, *Journal of an Expedition into the Interior of Tropical Australia*: 218 (1848)

Copper plate by Gerard Sibelius, based on Frederick Nodder's 1777 watercolour, derived from Parkinson's surviving pencil drawing made at 'Endeavours River'; BF 75; Diment et al., 1984: A2/86

1. T. L. Mitchell, *Journal of an Expedition into the Interior of Tropical Australia* (London, Longman, Brown, Green, and Longmans, 1848), pp. 218–19

2. J. H. Maiden, *The Useful Native Plants of Australia* (London, Trübner & Co., and Sydney, Technological Museum of New South Wales, 1889), p. 426

3. Chittenden, 1951, 2, p. 779

4. Mabberley, 2014, pp. 317–18

103.

CASTANOSPERMUM AUSTRALE
black bean, Leguminosae

Parkinson annotated the reverse of his drawing of this plant with his detailed colour notes:

> The vexillum [standard petal] first laid over w^t yellow then stain'd & sprinkl'd w^t scarlet. the res^t of the flower scarlet calyx deep buff colour ting'd at the base w^t green the buds the same colour but somewhat more green.

Solander's manuscript name was 'Sophora caudiciflora', the tree indeed being in the same tribe as *Sophora*, but it was not to be formally named for another 50 years. The Scottish hack-writer Robert Mudie (1777–1842), working with botanist Allan Cunningham's manuscripts, wrote:

> The fruit is not a nut, but a very large and rather handsome pod, not very unlike the pod of a windsor bean…. Within it is lined with silky down; of a white colour, and contains a variable number of seeds or beans, which are, when full grown, much larger than chestnuts…. The odour, especially when they are undergoing the process of roasting, is agreeable, intermediate between that of good oaten cake and a potato newly dug and roasted…. It seems to bear being carried to a distance; for a specimen, which probably had not altogether been ripe, though kept for twelve months, and carried sixteen thousand miles, tasted as fresh, and indeed the same fresh appearance, as if it had been newly gathered.[1]

Growing in coastal forest and on beaches of northeastern Australia, western New Britain and Vanuatu,[2] black bean or Moreton Bay chestnut (the generic name derives from *Castanea*, Latin for chestnut, and Greek, *spermum*, seed) is a tree to 40 m (130 ft) tall, with flowers and pods borne on the trunk. It is grown as a street tree, for example in Sydney, and has decorative timber. The seeds, edible if roasted, have been tested for treatment of prostate cancer and screened as a possible AIDS vaccine, the active principle being the alkaloid castanospermine. In Europe, pots of seedlings are sold as 'lucky beans'.

Castanospermum australe A. Cunn. ex Mudie, *The Picture of Australia*: 149 (1829) and *A Description and History of Vegetable Substances*: 421 (1829)

Copper plate by Gerard Sibelius, based on Frederick Nodder's 1779 watercolour, derived from Parkinson's surviving pencil drawing made at 'Endeavours River'; BF 84; Diment et al., 1984: A2/95

1. D. J. Mabberley, 'Robert Mudie (1777–1842) and Australian botany, or, the saga of the Black Bean', *Australian Systematic Botany Society Newsletter* 70, 1992, 13–15

2. Mabberley, 2014, p. 158

IPOMOEA INDICA
blue morning glory, Convolvulaceae

Parkinson's note on his drawing of this perennial climber captures the colours in detail:

> the flower pale blue wᵗ a cast of pink appearing like a lilac colour turning very pale at the tube which is white outside & in capsula fresh green at the edges & very pale green in the middle.

Ipomoea indica is said to be native in tropical America and to be introduced elsewhere, but it is difficult then to explain its occurrence in Australia before European settlement, suggesting that there is work to be done on the taxonomy of this group of morning glories.

The genus *Ipomoea* (for an explanation of the name, see *Ipomoea batatas*, Pl. 34, p. 84) comprises perhaps 650 species of mostly climbers, with a few trees and succulents, in tropical and warm temperate countries; 327 of them are found in the New World.[1] Some have edible tubers, the most important being *I. batatas*, sweet potato or 'yam', which reached Polynesia from Central America in pre-Columbian times. Others have edible flowers or shoots, especially *I. aquatica* (kangkong, Pl. 145, p. 290), while many are important drug plants or ornamentals such as *I. alba*, moonflower, with large, white, scented night flowers, *I. purpurea* (morning glory) and *I. quamoclit*, with scarlet flowers.

Ipomoea indica (Burm.) Merr., *An Interpretation of Rumphius's Herbarium Amboinense*: 445 (1917)

Copper plate by John Lee, based on John Miller's 1773 watercolour, derived from Parkinson's surviving pencil drawing; BF 223; Diment et al., 1984: A6/254. This was one of the plates Banks sent to Linnaeus.

1. Mabberley, 2014, pp. 432–33

105.
DEPLANCHEA TETRAPHYLLA
Bignoniaceae

Called 'Diplanthera tetraphylla' by Solander, this species was first formally described with that name in 1810, based entirely on Banks' and Solander's collections, by Robert Brown (1773–1858), a Scot who was the naturalist on Matthew Flinders' circumnavigation of Australia in HMS *Investigator* (1801–03) and perhaps the greatest botanist of the nineteenth century.[1]

Restricted to northern Queensland and New Guinea, this is a large rain forest tree with leaves to 60 cm (2 ft) long, held in whorls of four, and with heads of spectacular flowers up to 3.5 cm (almost 1½ in.) across. Birds, probably lorikeets, perch on the inflorescence 'platform' and bend down to take up the copious dark brown nectar exposed in the spoon-shaped lowermost corolla lobes, which apparently act as a visual lure. In so doing, the birds brush against the protruding anthers and stigmas with their throat or breast, picking up pollen.[2] In tropical Australia and elsewhere the tree is cultivated outdoors, while in Europe it is grown in pots or tubs under glass.

The genus *Deplanchea* commemorates Dr Émile Deplanche (1824–1875), surgeon and naturalist in French Guiana and New Caledonia, and comprises five species of trees ranging from the Malay Archipelago to Australia and New Caledonia,[3] where Deplanche collected material of the type species, *D. speciosa*.

Deplanchea tetraphylla (R. Br.) F. Muell., *Second Systematic Census of Australian Plants*: 167 (1889)

Copper plate by Daniel Mackenzie, based on Frederick Nodder's 1778 watercolour, derived from Parkinson's surviving pencil drawing made at 'Endeavours River'; BF 244; Diment et al., 1984: A6/275

1. Mabberley, 1985

2. A. Weber and S. Vogel, 'The pollination syndrome of *Deplanchea tetraphylla* (Bignoniaceae)', *Plant Systematics & Evolution* 154, 1987, pp. 237–50

3. Mabberley, 2014, p. 263

106.

DILLENIA ALATA
red beech, Dilleniaceae

Red beech is a rain forest tree to 15 m (50 ft) tall, native in New Guinea and northern Australia. Its fruits are taken by eclectus parrots.[1]

The genus *Dillenia* comprises some 65 species of trees in the Indopacific region, with just *D. alata* reaching Australia.[2] Their impressive flowers exhibit heteranthery, that is, they have two types of stamens: since the flowers are nectarless, the only reward for pollinators is pollen, and so some stamens have pollen for 'feeding', while others are effective in pollination.[3] In addition, the flowers in at least some species are buzz-pollinated, that is, the stamens release their pollen only when subjected to the wing-beat frequencies of particular insects, in these cases *Xylocopa* (carpenter) bees (see also Pl. 144, p. 285). The most familiar species in tropical landscapes is the widely cultivated *D. suffruticosa* from the Malay Archipelago, which is rarely out of flower.

The genus was named *Dillenia* by Linnaeus after Johann Jacob Dillen, or Dillenius (1684–1747), a German botanist who was professor of botany at Oxford when Linnaeus visited the university in 1736. Linnaeus wrote, somewhat ingratiatingly, '*Dillenia* of all plants has the showiest flowers and fruit, even as Dillenius made a brilliant show among botanists.'[4] The species name *alatus*, meaning winged, refers to the petioles (leaf stalks). For the herbarium sheet of a specimen collected by Banks and Solander, see p. 296.

Dillenia alata (DC.) Martelli in Becc., *Malesia* 3: 157 (1886)

Copper engraving by Gerard Sibelius, based on Frederick Nodder's watercolour, derived from Parkinson's surviving pencil drawing with the note 'The old stalks sordid brown'; BF 1; Diment et al., 1984: A1/1

1. Cooper and Cooper, 2004, p. 150

2. Mabberley, 2014, p. 273 and 4th ed., 2017

3. P. K. Endress, 'Angiosperm floral evolution: morphological developmental framework', *Advances in Botanical Research* 44, 2006, pp. 2–61

4. H. N. Clokie, *An Account of the Herbaria of the Department of Botany in the University of Oxford* (Oxford, Oxford University Press, 1964), p. 34

107.
POLYGALA RHINANTHOIDES
Polygalaceae

Banks and Solander found this annual herb at Endeavour River, the southernmost point of its range south from New Guinea.[1] Solander's manuscript name 'Polygala rhinanthoides' was published some 70 years after the voyage. On his pencil sketch made on the spot Parkinson noted, 'The edge of the petala bright violet colour turning into white towards the bottom'.

The genus *Polygala* has some 200 species found throughout much of the world.[2] Some are grown as ornamentals; the most commonly seen in Mediterranean climates is the shrubby hybrid between two South African species, *P. × dalmaisiana*, which almost continuously produces purplish or rose flowers. Some are useful as oilseeds or are of medicinal interest, especially *Polygala sibirica*, which, combined with liquorice, is used to treat depression, irritability and insomnia in modern Chinese herbalism.

This little tropical plant (around 10–20 cm/4–8 in. tall) is burdened with European allusions: *Polygala* is from the Greek name *polygalon* from *polys*, much (or many), and *gala*, milk, as Mediterranean species were alleged to promote milk secretion in animals, hence the English vernacular name milkwort; *rhinanthoides* means resembling *Rhinanthus* (Orobanchaceae), a genus of hemiparasitic annuals (known as rattles) from the northern hemisphere.

Polygala rhinanthoides Sol. ex Benth., *Flora Australiensis* 1: 140 (1863)

Copper plate by Gerard Sibelius, based on Frederick Nodder's 1778 watercolour, derived from Parkinson's surviving pencil drawing made at 'Endeavours River'; BF 16; Diment et al., 1984: A1/17

1. R. A. Kerrigan, 'A treatment for *Polygala* of northern Australia', *Australian Systematic Botany* 25, 2012, pp. 83–137

2. Mabberley, 2014, p. 688 and 4th ed., 2017

108.

XANTHORRHOEA JOHNSONII
Asphodelaceae

Solander confused this grass-tree collected at Endeavour River with other species, as the name he gave it, 'Acoroides resinifera', was initially used for *Xanthorrhoea resinosa* at Botany Bay. This northern species is now known as *X. johnsonii.*

Banks, in reviewing the plant resources of Australia, no doubt considered the two the same when he wrote:

> a small plant with long narrow grassy leaves and a spike of flowers resembling much that kind of Bulrush which is calld in England Cats tail [*Typha*]; this yeilded [sic] a resin of a bright yellow colour perfectly resembling Gambouge [sic] only that it did not stain; it had a sweet smell but what its properties are the chymists may be able to determine.[1]

The two species are quite different. *Xanthorrhoea resinosa* has a trunk at most 60 cm (2 ft) tall and is found in the Blue Mountains and from Sydney south to eastern Victoria on sand or sandstone. *Xanthorrhoea johnsonii* is often almost stemless, but can reach up to 5 m (16 ft) tall,[2] and grows in eucalypt woodland and heath in Queensland south to the Hunter Valley of New South Wales. It is held to be poisonous to stock, but its foliage ('steel grass') is used commercially in floristry. The species name *johnsonii* commemorates Lawrence (Lawrie) A. S. Johnson (1925–1997), a versatile Australian botanist.

The genus *Xanthorrhoea*, from *xanthos*, yellow, and *rheo*, flow, referring to the yellow resinous gum, comprises 28 species and is restricted to Australia.[3] They are slow-growing, long-lived and fire-tolerant plants, with thick stems that produce resins at the bases of old leaves. This resin, known as acaroid, was formerly used to fix spear-heads to shafts and is still utilized as varnish or lacquer for metals and leather. *Xanthorrhoea semiplana* subsp. *tateana* (yakka) is the basis of the yacca gum industry, on Kangaroo Island, South Australia, which once produced 1,000 tons per annum.

Xanthorrhoea johnsonii A. Lee in *Contributions from the New South Wales National Herbarium* 4: 49 (1966)

Copper plate by Gabriel Smith, based on James Miller's 1775 watercolour, derived from Parkinson's surviving pencil drawing with 'The Stamina pale green upon a ground the colour of Terra. ....' made at 'Endeavours River'; BF 334; Diment et al., 1984: A8/389

1. Beaglehole, 1963, 2, p. 116

2. D. J. Bedford in *Flora of Australia* 46, 1986, pp. 156, 162

3. Mabberley, 2014, p. 914

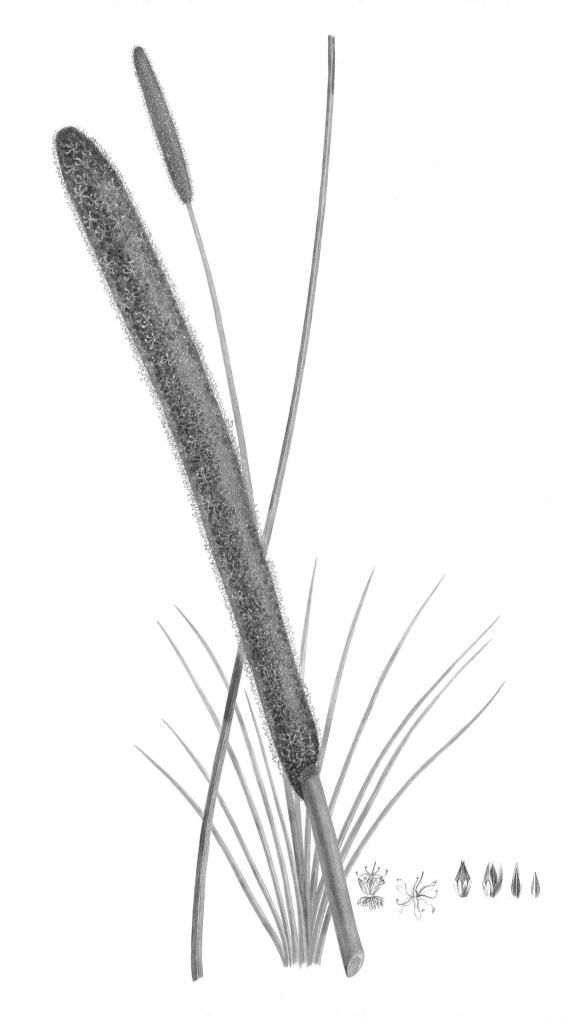

109.

COMESPERMA SECUNDUM
Polygalaceae

On drawing Solander's 'Octanthera secunda', Parkinson added the colour notes to his sketch: 'Capsula Redish Purple, 'Petala & buds white anther yellow'.

Comesperma secundum, found in much of northern Australia, is a twiggy shrub grwoing up to about 1 m (3 ft) tall.[1] The name comes from the Greek *kome*, hair, and *sperma*, seed, referring to the seeds with tufts of hairs; *secundus* alludes to the fact that the flowers grow on one side only of the inflorescences. There are some 40 *Comesperma* species, all found only in Australia. *Comesperma volubile*, a climbing species, is occasionally cultivated as 'love creeper'.

Comesperma secundum Banks ex DC., *Prodromus Systematis Naturalis Regni Vegetabilis* 1: 334 (1824)

Copper plate of 1782 by Gerard Sibelius, based on Frederick Nodder's 1778 watercolour, derived from Parkinson's surviving pencil drawing made at 'Endeavours River'; BF 18; Diment et al., 1984: A1/19

1. J. R. Wheeler in Wheeler et al., 1992, p. 638

110.

LEEA INDICA
bandicoot berry, Vitaceae

The widespread bandicoot berry, a shrubby treelet up to 4 m (13 ft) or so tall with pithy stems, is found from India through to the Pacific, reaching as far south as coastal central Queensland. It is sometimes cultivated as an ornamental elsewhere. In Singapore, the flowers are visited by wasps and other insects, and the fruits are taken by birds – in Queensland wompoo fruit doves eat them.[1]

Leea commemorates James Lee (1715–1795), nurseryman of Hammersmith, near London, who raised many of the earliest Australian plant introductions and popularized them in England and beyond (see also *Pandorea pandorana*, Pl. 94, p. 198). *Leea* is a genus of at least 34 species found in the Old World tropics, though with only two species in Africa.[2] Some are of local medicinal importance, as well as being useful ornamental foliage plants.

Leea indica (Burm.f.) Merr. in *Philippine Journal of Science* 14: 245 (1919)

Copper plate by Gerard Sibelius, based on John Miller's 1774 watercolour, derived from Parkinson's surviving pencil drawing with 'The flower white buds ting'd w' green'; BF 44; Diment et al., 1984: A1/50

1. A. F. S. L. Lok et al., '*Leea* L. (Vitaceae) of Singapore', *Nature in Singapore* 4, 2011, pp. 55–71; Cooper and Cooper, 2004, p. 268

2. Mabberley, 2014, p. 474

III.

DODONAEA VESTITA

Sapindaceae

Solander's 'Dodonaeoides pinnata', a hairy shrub with pinnate leaves, reaches about 1 m (3 ft) in height and is apparently restricted to eastern Queensland on sandstone slopes in open eucalypt forest.[1] The *Endeavour* material was part of that used when the shrub was described as a new species almost 60 years later.[2]

Dodonaea commemorates Rembert Dodoens (1517–1585), a famous Flemish doctor who became professor of medicine at Leiden University, The Netherlands; *vestitus*, means clothed, in this case with hairs. The genus comprises some 68 species from the warmer parts of the world; 61 of them are in Australia, with 59 of those found nowhere else. They are wind-pollinated shrubs and trees, some of them very sticky or viscid.[3] The wood of the very widespread *Dodonaea viscosa*, known as akeake (in New Zealand) or hop-bush, is used for tool handles and makes excellent firewood. It is also grown for ornament, and its fruits and leaves are used in *lei* garlands in Hawaii. A red dye is made there from the winged fruits, which were also allegedly used as hops by early settlers in Australia.

Dodonaea vestita Hook. in Mitchell, *Journal of an Expedition into the Interior of Tropical Australia*: 265 (1848)

Copper plate by Daniel Mackenzie, based on James Miller's 1775 watercolour, derived from Parkinson's surviving pencil drawing made at 'Endeavours River'; BF 46; Diment et al., 1984: A1/52

1. J. G. West, 'A revision of *Dodonaea* Miller (Sapindaceae) in Australia', *Brunonia* 7, 1984, pp. 1–194, especially p. 79
2. G. Bentham, *Flora Australiensis* 1, 1863, p. 484
3. Mabberley, 2014, p. 284

II2.

DODONAEA HISPIDULA

Sapindaceae

A shrub found across tropical Australia, Solander's 'Dodonaeoides villosa' grows up to 3 m (10 ft) high. Its young parts are all densely hairy,[1] hence the specific name *hispidulus*, meaning 'with short bristles'.

Formerly it was referred to *Distichostemon*, from Latin *distichus*, two-ranked, and Greek *stemon*, stamen, referring to the stamens usually being in two groups, but recent analysis shows that the genus is not distinct and the shrub rightly belongs in *Dodonaea*, where it was first put by the Austrian botanist Stephan Endlicher (1804–1809) in 1835.

Dodonaea hispidula Endl., *Atakta Botanica*, t. 30 (1835)

Copper plate by Gabriel Smith, based on John Miller's 1775 watercolour, derived from Parkinson's surviving pencil drawing made at 'Endeavours River'; BF 47; Diment et al., 1984: A1/53

1. B. L. Koch in Wheeler et al., 1992, p. 650

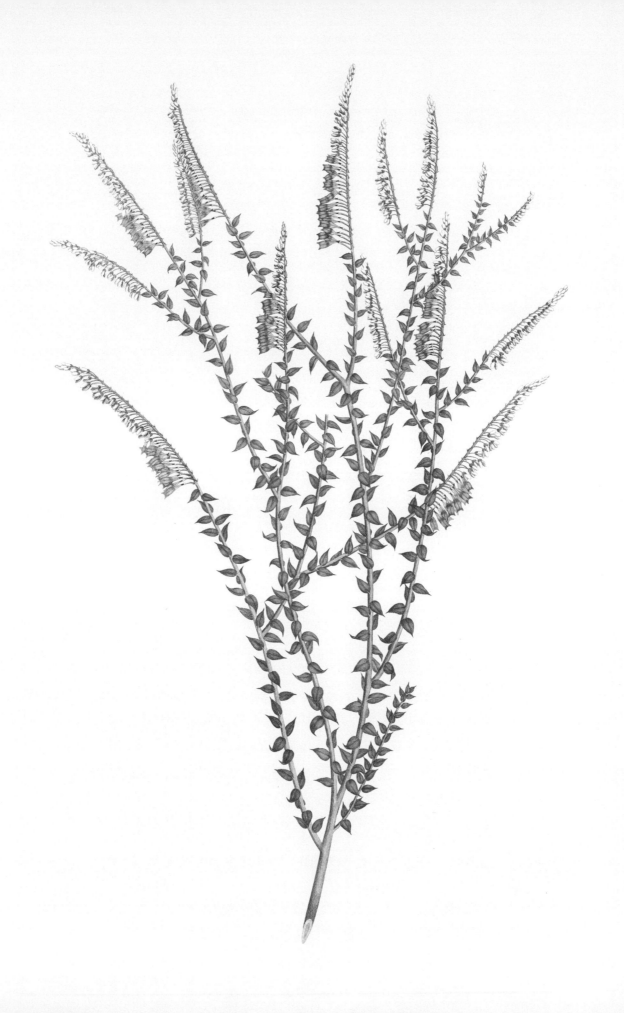

113

BLEPHAROCARYA INVOLUCRIGERA
northern bollygum, Anacardiaceae

The original manuscript name given to this tree was 'Amyroides juglandifolia', the proposed species name referring to its walnut-like leaves. It was not formally described for over another century.

The northern bollygum is a rain forest tree growing up to 40 m (130 ft) tall in northeastern Queensland, between Cape York and the Atherton Tableland. It is dioecious (with separate male and female trees). The small flowers are followed by fruits enclosed in capsule-like woody bracts, alluded to in the specific epithet, *involucrigerus*, which means bearing an involucre or whorl of bracts; these separate to release the seed-like fruitlets, which are eaten by double-eyed fig parrots and king parrots.[1]

There are just two species of *Blepharocarya*, both from Queensland.[2] The genus takes its name from the Greek *blepharon*, eyelid, and *karyon*, nut, another allusion to the fringed involucre around the fruits.

Blepharocarya involucrigera F. Muell., *Fragmenta Phytographiae Australiae* 11: 16 (1878)

Copper plate by Gerard Sibelius, based on John Cleveley's 1775 watercolour, derived from Parkinson's surviving pencil drawing made at 'Endeavours River'; BF 49; Diment et al., 1984: A1/55

1. Cooper and Cooper, 2004, p. 16

2. Mabberley, 2014, p. 109

114.
GOMPHOLOBIUM NITIDUM
Leguminosae

When Parkinson drew Solander's 'Sophoroides microphylla' he noted on his pencil sketch:

> The inside of the vexillum [standard, the large back petal] & alae [wings, the lateral petals] yellow the outside of the vexillum and top of the carina [keel, the united lower pair of petals] olive the bottom of the carina and edge at the top white.

The Banks and Solander material, though given its current name by Solander, was unpublished by him; the specimens were, however, used in the first printed description made over 90 years later by George Bentham (1800–1884), working at Kew Gardens.

One of 44 species of 'wedge peas', *Gompholobium nitidum* is usually found in heathland or grassland and is restricted to northeastern Queensland and Papua New Guinea, while the majority of the others are found in southwestern Australia.[1] The name *Gompholobium* is from Greek *gomphos*, bolt, and *lobos*, pod, alluding to the appearance of the fruits; Latin *nitidus*, shining, refers to the glossy leaflets.

Gompholobium nitidum Sol. ex Benth., *Flora Australiensis* 2: 48 (1864)

Copper plate by Daniel Mackenzie, based on Frederick Nodder's 1779 watercolour, derived from Parkinson's surviving pencil drawing made at 'Endeavours River'; BF 51; Diment et al., 1984: A2/58

1. J. A. Chappill et al., 'Taxonomic revision of *Gompholobium* (Leguminosae: Mirbelieae)', *Australian Systematic Botany* 21, 2008, pp. 67–151

115.

CROTALARIA VERRUCOSA
blue rattlepod, Leguminosae

Blue rattlepod is an attractive blue-flowered shrub growing to about 1.5 m (5 ft) tall, with three- or four-winged stems. It is widespread in tropical Asia, extending south to southeastern Queensland, where it can be found in both forest and farmland.[1]

Banks and Solander named it 'Dolichos stipularis', and Parkinson described its colouring in his notes to his pencil sketch:

> The vexillum [standard, the large top petal] pale blue vein'd w^t deep blue the alae [wings, the two lateral petals] the same but deeper w^t a cast of purple at the edge the carina [keel, the united lower pair of petals] white ting'd w^t green veins blue green the calyx pale green ting'd at the base w^t purple....

It was in cultivation in England by 1730, and was apparently introduced in the Americas, where it escaped. Because it contains pyrrolizidine alkaloids it is poisonous, as are most *Crotalaria* species; the sickness in animals caused by ingesting it is known as crotalism.

Crotalaria is from the Greek *krotalon*, a rattle or clapper, alluding to the seeds rattling in the inflated pods; Latin *verrucosus*, warty, refers to an early description of the leaves. The genus *Crotalaria* comprises perhaps 700 species in the warm parts of the world; of these 511 are found in Africa and Madagascar.[2] Many are sources of fodder and fibres, in particular sunn hemp, *C. juncea*, which is used for cordage, canvas and fishing-nets, being more durable than jute, and also in cigarette-papers.

Crotalaria verrucosa L., *Species Plantarum* 2: 715 (1753)

Copper plate by Daniel Mackenzie, based on Frederick Nodder's 1777 watercolour, derived from Parkinson's pencil drawing made at 'Endeavours River'; BF 55; Diment et al., 1984: A2/62

1. Cooper and Cooper, 2004, p. 206

2. Mabberley, 2014, p. 230

116.

CROTALARIA CALYCINA
hairy rattlepod, Leguminosae

Named 'Crotalaria calyculata' by Banks and Solander, *Crotalaria calycina* is an annual plant growing to 1 m (3 ft) tall found throughout the Old World tropics. In Australia it is often present in seasonally wet areas.[1]

For more on the genus, see *Crotalaria verrucosa* (Pl. 115). Other Australian species include *C. cunninghamii* of inland northern Australia; its fibres are used by Aboriginal people to make 'sandals' for walking on the hot sand of desert Western Australia.

Crotalaria calycina Schrank, *Plantae Rariores Horti Academici Monacensis* 1: t. 12 (1817)

Copper plate by Daniel Mackenzie, based on Frederick Nodder's 1777 watercolour, derived from Parkinson's surviving pencil drawing made at 'Endeavours River'; BF 56; Diment et al., 1984: A2/63

1. J. R. Wheeler in Wheeler, 1992, pp. 380–81

117.

INDIGOFERA PRATENSIS
forest indigo, Leguminosae

A small herbaceous plant, *Indigofera pratensis* is found all across tropical Australia in eucalypt woodlands and grasslands. It produces fresh shoots from a swollen rootstock that withstands fires.

In drawing a specimen, Parkinson noted colour instructions for the final watercolour:

> The vexillum [standard, the large top petal] pale crimson purple w^t some strips of white on the inside the alae [wings, the two lateral petals] same colour but deeper carina [keel, the united lower pair of petals] same but very pale buds pale blue purple calyx very pale green. leaves grass green above w^t lightish veins below glaucus [sic] w^t small dark green veins. stalks yellow green.

Indigofera is from indigo (the Greek word for Indian), the blue dye originally obtained from certain *Indigofera* species, and Latin *ferre*, to bear; *pratensis* means from the meadows. The genus *Indigofera* comprises about 730 species in the warmer parts of the world, with some 500 in Africa alone.[1] These once economically very important dye-plants, especially *I. tinctoria*, produced a dye, 'bleu de Nîmes', the origin of 'denim', which is still used in some hair dyes, Hmong batik and as a food-colouring.

Indigofera pratensis F. Muell., *Essay on the Plants Collected … during Lieut. Smith's Expedition to the Estuary of the Burdekin*: 10 (1860)

Copper plate by Gerard Sibelius, based on Frederick Nodder's 1778 watercolour, derived from Parkinson's surviving pencil drawing made at 'Endeavours River'; BF 61; Diment et al., 1984: A2/69

1. Mabberley, 2014, p. 430 and 4th ed., 2017

118.

VANDASINA RETUSA
ru, Leguminosae

Solander's manuscript name for this plant was 'Glycine retusa', and Parkinson's added colour annotations to his field sketch were: 'The legumen yellow green ting'd w^t red & covered w^t small down'.

Ru is a climber, sometimes rather shrub-like, found in Papua New Guinea and tropical Australia in open forest, including beach forest, usually on sand. Its roots are roasted and eaten by Aboriginal people.

This is the sole species of *Vandasina*, the name commemorating Karel Vandas (1861–1923), a Czech botanist; *retusus* describes the rounded tip of a leaf, here with a small apical point.

Vandasina retusa (Benth.) Rauschert in *Taxon* 31: 559 (1982)
Copper plate by Daniel Mackenzie, based on Frederick Nodder's 1777 watercolour, derived from Parkinson's surviving pencil drawing made at 'Endeavours River'; BF 73; Diment et al., 1984: A2/84

119.

MUCUNA GIGANTEA
Leguminosae

Mucuna gigantea is a deciduous climber found growing in coastal and other rain forests of the Indopacific region south to northern New South Wales.[1] Its stem can reach a diameter of 10 cm (4 in.); the pods following the greenish flowers are covered with golden-brown irritant hairs that are a deterrent to seed-predators.

When drawing Banks' and Solander's 'Dolichos giganteus' Parkinson added the descriptive colour notes to his pencil drawing:

> the calyx & vexillum [standard, the large upper petal] herbaceous green calyx cover'd w^t long & sleek orange hair alae [wings, the lateral petals] & carina [keel, the two united lower petals] greenish white…the capsula fresh green.

Mucuna, from the Brazilian name for these climbers, is a genus of 105 species in the tropics. L-dopa in the seeds has been used in the treatment of Parkinson's disease. *Mucuna pruriens* (cow itch) from tropical Asia, also with irritant hairs, was formerly used as a vermifuge; var. *utilis* (velvet bean) has hairless pods and is grown as fodder and as a cover-crop.

Mucuna gigantea (Willd.) DC., *Prodromus Systematis Naturalis Regni Vegetabilis* 2: 405 (1825)
Copper plate by Gerard Sibelius, based on Frederick Nodder's 1777 watercolour, derived from Parkinson's pencil drawing made at 'Endeavours River'; BF 76; Diment et al., 1984: A2/87
1. Cooper and Cooper, 2004, pp. 213–14

120.

VIGNA VEXILLATA
wild cowpea, Leguminosae

Banks and Solander collected this climber, which Solander was to call 'Phaseolus grandiflorus', at Bustard Bay and Cape Grafton, as well as at Endeavour River. Widespread in tropical regions and extending south to New South Wales,[1] this species is related to the cultivated cowpea (*Vigna unguiculata*), and is grown as a root-crop in Timor and Bali.[2]

The flowers are pollinated by carpenter bees, which make visits of seven to eight seconds. A visiting bee exerts pressure on the left-hand wing petal and the keel, its weight causing the style to emerge and 'hug' it over the top of its head and thorax.[3] Pollen is then deposited on the bee before it is released and visits another flower.

Vigna commemorates Dominico Vigna (d. 1647), professor of botany at the University of Pisa; *vexillatus* is from the Latin for a flag. *Vigna* has 90 tropical species, especially in the Old World.[4] These include several important pulses and green manures: *Vigna angularis* (adzuki or azuki bean), long cultivated for its beans that are boiled or made into curd, and today a constituent of commercial 'washing grains'; *V. mungo* (urd or black gram); *V. radiata* (mung bean, green or golden gram), the seedlings of which are the 'bean sprouts' of markets, and *V. unguiculata* (cowpea), including snake beans, which have an edible pod up to 90 cm (35 in.) long.

Vigna vexillata (L.) A. Rich. in Sagra, *Historia Fiscia Politica y Natural de la Isla de Cuba* 10: 191 (1845)

Copper plate by Robert Blyth, based on Frederick Nodder's 1777 watercolour, derived from Parkinson's surviving pencil drawing made at 'Endeavours River'; BF 80; Diment et al., 1984: A2/91

1. J. R. Wheeler in Wheeler et al., 1992, p. 457

2. A. Karuniawan et al., '*Vigna vexillata* (L.) A. Rich. cultivated as a root crop in Bali and Timor', *Genetic Resources and Crop Evolution* 53, 2006, pp. 213–17

3. I. Hedström and M. Thulin, 'Pollination by a hugging mechanism in *Vigna vexillata* (*Leguminosae-Papilionoideae*)', *Plant Systematics and Evolution* 154, 1986, pp. 275–83

4. Mabberley, 2014, pp. 897–98

121.

DECAISNINA BRITTENII
Loranthaceae

This pendulous mistletoe has a wide range of hosts, including *Parinari nonda* (see Pl. 126, p. 255), across tropical Australia. The Banks and Solander collection was the basis for the original description.

Decaisnina commemorates Joseph Decaisne (1807–1882), director of the Jardin des Plantes, Paris; *brittenii* is after James Britten (1846–1924), a British botanist. There are some 25 species of *Decaisnina* from Java and the Philippines, with one species extending from New Guinea to Tahiti and the Marquesas, an unusual distribution in the family, as few are found on oceanic islands.[1]

Decaisnina brittenii (Blakely) Barlow in *Australian Journal of Botany* 14: 433 (1966)

Copper plate by Daniel Mackenzie, based on John Cleveley's 1774 watercolour, derived from Parkinson's surviving pencil drawing made at 'Endeavours River'; BF 291; Diment et al., 1984: A7/333

1. Mabberley, 2014, p. 259

2. D. J. Mabberley, *Ferdinand Bauer: The Nature of Discovery* (London, Merrell, 1999). The original is Bauer Australian Botanical Drawings 146, Natural History Museum, London.

Finished watercolour of Decaisnina brittenii *by Ferdinand Bauer, London, before 1812, based on his colour-coded pencil sketch (now in Vienna), probably made using material collected at Point Blane, Northern Territory, in January 1803 during Matthew Flinders' Investigator voyage. Banks recruited Bauer as artist on the expedition, which also included the botanist Robert Brown, who was later to inherit Banks' library and herbarium. As an artist, Bauer had the advantage of seeing the living plant in the field and carefully coding its colour according to a scheme of 1,000 shades, which he could 'decode' using a 'painting by numbers' technique back in the studio later.*[2]

AUSTRALIA, ENDEAVOUR RIVER, 17 JUNE–4 AUGUST 1770

122.

DENDROBIUM DISCOLOR
golden orchid, Orchidaceae

Banks and Solander collected this epiphytic orchid at Endeavour River, though it was described as new from plants introduced by Loddiges, London nurserymen, from material introduced by them from Buitenzorg (today's Bogor) in Java. It is native from eastern Indonesia to tropical Australia. Parkinson's unfinished sketch of this plant can be seen on p. 301.

Dendrobium is from *dendron*, tree, and *bios*, life, describing the growing habit of epiphytic orchids; *discolor* means two distinctly different colours, referring to the flowers. The genus *Dendrobium* contains about 1,500 epiphytic species (which grow on other plants), native from tropical Asia to New Guinea (with 560 species) and Australia (with 71), and the Pacific.[1] *Dendrobium sinense* from Hainan is pollinated by hornets (*Vespa bicolor*), which are attracted by its odour resembling that of distressed bees, their prey.

Besides ornamentals, some species are valuable in local medicine or are used in basketwork or for bangles. *Dendrobium moniliforme* from eastern Asia was used by early seventeenth-century Japanese royalty to scent their clothes.

Dendrobium discolor Lindl. in Edwards, *Botanical Register* 27, Misc.: 21 + t. 52 (1841)
Copper plate by Gerard Sibelius, dated 1783 and based on Frederick Nodder's 1780 watercolour, derived from Parkinson's surviving pencil drawing made at 'Endeavours River'; BF 314; Diment et al., 1984: A8/366

1. Mabberley, 2014, pp. 261–62

123.

HAEMODORUM COCCINEUM
scarlet bloodroot, Haemodoraceae

Banks and Solander gave this striking plant the manuscript name 'Wachendastrum corymbosum', reflecting their belief that it was allied to the South African genus *Wachendorfia*, in the same family.

Native to New Guinea and east tropical Australia, scarlet bloodroot produces inflorescences up to 1 m (3 ft) high. It is a promising cut-flower crop in tropical regions and the plant has long been a source of red dyes for bags and baskets.

Haemodorum is from Greek *haema*, blood, and *doron*, gift; *coccineus* is scarlet in Latin. The genus *Haemodorum* has 20 species in Australia, with just *H. coccineum* extending to New Guinea.[1] The rhizomes of *H. corymbosum* and other species of eastern Australia were roasted and eaten by Aboriginal people.

Haemodorum coccineum R. Br., *Prodromus Florae Novae Hollandiae*: 300 (1810)

Copper plate by Thomas Scratchley, based on John Miller's 1773 watercolour, derived from Parkinson's pencil drawing made at 'Endeavours River'; BF 320; Diment et al., 1984: A8/371

1. Mabberley, 2014, p. 385

124.

RHYNCHOSIA ACUMINATISSIMA
Leguminosae

When Parkinson drew 'Glycine racemosa' at 'Endeavour's River', he added the colour instructions to his drawing: 'The flower pale greenish yellow the alae [wings, the lateral petals] more yellow than the rest…the capsula fresh green cover'd wt small hair'.

This small twining herb grows from China and tropical Asia to Australia in rain forest and monsoon forest, extending south to northern New South Wales, where it is very rare. The seeds are metallic blue and its bruised tissues smell of cat's urine.[1]

Rhynchosia is from the Greek *rhynchos*, beak, alluding to the beaked keel of the flowers; Latin *acuminatissimus* is very acuminate, that is, tapering to a narrow point. It is a genus of some 230 species of the tropics, 140 of them in Africa and Madagascar.[2] The seeds of *R. pyramidalis* from Central America are consumed with hallucinogenic mushrooms.

Rhynchosia acuminatissima Miq., *Flora van Nederlandsch Indie* 1(1): 171 (1855)

Copper plate by Daniel Mackenzie, based on Frederick Nodder's 1777 watercolour, derived from Parkinson's surviving pencil drawing made at 'Endeavours River'; BF 83; Diment et al., 1984: A2/94

1. Cooper and Cooper, 2004, p. 215
2. Mabberley, 2014, p. 740 and 4th ed., 2017

125.

ARCHIDENDRON GRANDIFLORUM
Leguminosae

Archidendron grandiflorum, named 'Mimosa grandiflora' when found by Banks and Solander, is a tree up to 20 m (66 ft) tall, native to New Guinea and northern Australia.[1] The fruits are spectacular coiled pods, which split open to reveal black seeds on dangling funicles (stalks) against the orange-red background of the inner fruit-wall.

Archidendron, from the Greek *archi*, chief, and *dendron*, tree, signifies the prominence in the forest of trees in this genus; Latin *grandiflorus* means with large flowers. The genus comprises 94 Indomalesian species, with very many in Borneo; several provide valuable timbers. The strong-smelling seeds of *Archidendron jiringa* (jengkol or ngapi) of Myanmar to Borneo are edible if cooked.

Archidendron grandiflorum (Benth.) I. C. Neilsen in *Nordic Journal of Botany* 2: 481 (1982)

Copper plate by Gerard Sibelius, based on Frederick Nodder's 1781 watercolour, derived from Parkinson's surviving pencil drawing made at 'Endeavours River'; BF 96; Diment et al., 1984: A2/108

1. Cooper and Cooper, 2004, p. 308

126.

PARINARI NONDA
nonda plum, Chrysobalanaceae

Originally named 'Aesculoides parviflora' when collected by Banks and Solander, nonda is a shrub or tree up to 12 m (40 ft) tall, but often is much smaller. It grows in open woodland or forest in tropical Australia, New Guinea and the Solomon Islands. The edible fruits (drupes) are collected by people, but are also taken by palm cockatoos, fruit-doves, red-cheeked parrots, cassowaries and spectacled flying foxes.[1]

Parinari is the local name for a South American species, while *nonda* is the common name in Australia for this plant. The genus *Parinari* comprises 39 tropical species, and in different places the fruits are dispersed by elephants, baboons, agoutis and fish, as well as by bats and many birds including pigeons, rheas and emus. *Parinari curatellifolia* trees of tropical Africa have edible fruit (mobola) and useful timber; David Livingstone's heart is buried beneath such a tree.

Parinari nonda F. Muell. ex Benth., *Flora Australiensis* 2: 426 (1864)

Copper plate by Gerard Sibelius, based on John Cleveley's 1775 watercolour, derived from Parkinson's surviving pencil drawing made at Endeavours River; BF 97; Diment et al., 1984: A3/109

1. Cooper and Cooper, 2004, p. 121

127.

ACMELLA GRANDIFLORA VAR. BRACHYGLOSSA
Compositae

This perennial herb, growing to about 60 cm (2 ft) high, is native to eastern New Guinea and tropical Australia, reaching as far south as the very north of New South Wales. When Parkinson drew Solander's 'Verbesina multiradiata' he noted 'The radius bright yellow disk gold colour' as instructions for the finished watercolour.

Acmella is from a Sinhalese name for another plant in the same family, now known as *Blainvillea acmella*, also formerly referred to the genus *Verbesina*. It is a tropical genus of about 30 species, some now pantropical weeds. *Acmella oleracea* (Brazilian or Pará cress) from South America is a salad vegetable, though it contains a substance called spilanthol, which causes a tingling of the tongue.

Acmella grandiflora (Turcz.) R. K. Jansen var. *brachyglossa* (Benth.)
R. K. Jansen in *Systematic Botany Monographs* 8: 77 (1985)

Copper plate by Daniel Mackenzie, based on Frederick Nodder's 1779 watercolour, derived from Parkinson's surviving pencil drawing; BF 165; Diment et al., 1984: A4/190

128.

PLANCHONELLA OBOVATA
yellow teak, Sapotaceae

Yellow teak, called 'Rhamnoides obtusifolia' when collected by Banks and Solander, is a tree up to 15 m (50 ft) tall, found in the Malay Archipelago and tropical Australia in coastal rain forest and at the edges of mangroves, as well as in other habitats near the sea. In Queensland, the red to black fruits are taken by pied imperial-pigeons, barred cuckoo-shrikes, figbirds and metallic starlings.[1] The wood is useful.

Planchonella commemorates Jules Émile Planchon (see *Planchonia careya*, Pl. 100, p. 210); *obovatus*, egg-shaped, with the widest part towards the apex, refers to the shape of the leaves.

Planchonella obovata (R. Br.) Pierre, *Notes Botaniques Sapotacées*: 35 (1890)

Copper plate by Gabriel Smith, based on James Miller's 1774 watercolour, derived from Parkinson's surviving pencil drawing made at 'Endeavours River'; BF 201; Diment et al., 1984: A5/232

1. Cooper and Cooper, 2004, p. 510

129.

CYNANCHUM VIMINALE SUBSP. AUSTRALE
milkbush, Apocynaceae

Because it is leafless, Solander gave this succulent plant the manuscript name 'Cynanchum aphyllum', the specific name meaning without leaves.

Cynanchum viminale is a common climber in the Old World tropics, with the subspecies *australe* being restricted to Australia.[1] Generally found in arid areas, usually with *Acacia* species, these plants are silver to silvery green upright succulents which mature as woody lianes. The milky latex is caustic, though in places other than Australia the outer stem layers of *C. viminale* are cooked and eaten.[2]

Cynanchum is derived from the Greek *kyon*, dog, and *ancho*, strangle, as some are poisonous, the latex being effective as a fly-killer at least; *viminalis* is Latin for long slender shoots like a willow; *australis* is southern. The genus, including *Sarcostemma*, to which milkbush was long referred, comprises perhaps 250 species of tropical and other warm regions. Just one species is found in Europe, *C. acutum*, the 'convolvulus' of Egyptologists, the latex of which is associated with motherhood and breast-feeding. *Cynanchum sarcomedium* was perhaps a major ingredient of the 'soma', a ritual drink of ancient India.

Cynanchum viminale (L.) Bassi subsp. *australe* (R. Br.) Meve & Liede in *Kew Bulletin* 67: 754 (2012)

Copper plate by Francis Chesham, based on an anonymous watercolour, derived from Parkinson's pencil drawing made at 'Endeavours River'; BF 209; Diment et al., 1984: A5/241

1. P. I. Forster in *Australian Systematic Botany* 5, 1992, p. 67

2. Mabberley, 2014, p. 246

130.

PERSOONIA FALCATA
milky plum, Proteaceae

Material of this plant collected by Banks and Solander at Endeavour River was used in drawing up the original description of it published in 1810 by Robert Brown (see also Pl. 105, p. 220).

Milky plum is a shrub or small tree reaching to 9 m (30 ft) tall and found in northern Australia, most commonly in eucalypt woodland. Its yellow-green fruits (drupes) are edible and have been collected by Aboriginal people for at least 3,500 years.[1]

Persoonia commemorates Christiaan Hendrik Persoon (1761/2–1836), a South African botanist who particularly studied fungi; *falcatus* means sickle-shaped, referring to the leaves. The genus comprises about 100 species restricted to Australia,[2] where it is also known as geebung, snodgollion, snot-goblin or snottygobble, these last three names apparently referring to the appearance of the contents of the fruit when squeezed out. Although the floral parts are usually arranged in four parts, some flowers with five (pentamerous) are occasionally found in *P. falcata*.[3]

A number of other species also have edible fruits, while *Persoonia longifolia* (Barkerbush) of southwestern Australia provides commercially significant foliage for the North American cut-flower market.

Persoonia falcata R. Br. in *Transactions of the Linnean Society* 10: 162 (1810)

Copper plate by Gabriel Smith based on John Miller's 1773 watercolour, derived from Parkinson's pencil drawing made at 'Endeavours River'; BF 272; Diment et al., 1984: A7/312

1. J. Atchison et al., 'Archaeobotany of fruit seed processing in a monsoon savanna environment: evidence from the Keep River region, Northern Territory, Australia, *Journal of Archaeological Science* 32, 2005, pp. 167–81

2. Mabberley, 2014, p. 649 and 4th ed., 2017

3. A. W. Douglas and S. C. Tucker, 'Comparative floral ontogenies among *Persoonioideae* including *Bellendena* (Proteaceae)', *American Journal of Botany* 83, 1996, pp. 1528–55

131.
GREVILLEA PTERIDIFOLIA
golden grevillea, Proteaceae

Reflecting Banks' and Solander's view that this tree was related to the South African genus *Leucadendron*, Solander's manuscript name was 'Leucadendroides crocea'. When Robert Brown (see Pl. 105, p. 220) recognized it as a new species, his description was based on the Banks and Solander collection.

A small tree or large shrub, occasionally prostrate, golden grevillea is restricted to tropical Australia, and has many beneficial properties. Its leaves were used by European settlers to stuff pillows and the nectar is important in Aboriginal culture.[1] The pollen and nectar are favoured food of blossom bats, and the seed-wing is rich in lipid and protein, which are the rewards for ants that disperse the seeds, though the rest of the seed has cyanogenic compounds that potentially can cause cyanide poisoning. Antibiotics extracted from bacteria in the plants are known as kakadumycins and are effective against malarial parasites.[2] The tree is widely cultivated as an ornamental and is the parent of numerous important hybrids with other species.

Grevillea commemorates Charles Francis Greville (1749–1809), politician, collector and a founder of the Horticultural Society of London (whose mistress, Emma Hart, became Lady Hamilton and later Nelson's lover); *pteridifolius* derives from *pteris*, Greek for fern, so with fern-like leaves. The genus comprises 357 species from Sulawesi, New Guinea, New Caledonia, Vanuatu and Australia, where all 357 are found, 350 of them endemic.[3] Pollination in different species is effected by birds and mammals, as well as by nocturnal scarab beetles and many other insects. Some *Grevillea* species provide good timber, especially *G. robusta* (silky oak), a tree up to 40 m (130 ft) tall from eastern Australia, which is also grown for coffee- and tea-shade in many warm countries, and, when a seedling, is much used as a house plant in cold ones.

Grevillea pteridifolia J. Knight, *On the cultivation of the plants belonging to the natural order of Proteeae*: 121 (1809)

Copper plate by Gerard Sibelius, based on John Miller's 1773 watercolour, derived from Parkinson's pencil drawing made at 'Endeavours River'; BF 277; Diment et al., 1984: A7/317

1. R. O. Makinson, 'Proteaceae 2, *Grevillea*', *Flora of Australia* 17A, 2000, pp. 95–96

2. Cooper and Cooper, 2004, p. 126; U. Castillo et al., 'Kakadumycins, novel antibiotics from *Streptomyces* sp NRRL 30566, an endophyte of *Grevillea pteridifolia*', *FEMS Microbiology Letters* 224, 2003, pp. 183–90

3. Mabberley, 2014, p. 375 and 4th ed., 2017

AUSTRALIA, ENDEAVOUR RIVER, 17 JUNE–4 AUGUST 1770

132.

LUMNITZERA LITTOREA
black mangrove, Combretaceae

Solander in his manuscripts called this small tree, which grows up to 8 m (26 ft) tall in drier parts of mangroves, 'Kada Kandel coccinea'. It has knee-shaped pneumatophores or aerial roots, and its seeds are corky, suggesting water-dispersal.[1] Black mangrove is native from East Africa to the Indopacific and has red flowers. The only other species of the genus, *L. racemosa*, has white flowers; pink ones occur at zones of overlap between the species.

Lumnitzera commemorates Stephan Lumnitzer (1750–1806), a German botanist; *littoreus* means 'of the seashore'.

Lumnitzera littorea (Jack) Voigt, *Hortus Suburbanus Calcuttensis*: 39 (1845)
Copper plate by Daniel Mackenzie, based on an unsigned watercolour, derived from Parkinson's surviving pencil drawing made at 'Endeavours River'; BF 105; Diment et al., 1984: A3/121

1. Cooper and Cooper, 2004, p. 126

133.

MELALEUCA VIMINALIS
weeping bottlebrush, Myrtaceae

This spectacular bottlebrush is a shrub or tree up to 15 m (50 ft) tall, with mostly weeping branches. In his manuscripts Solander called it 'Metrosideros viminalis', and Parkinson noted on his field-sketch: 'the Petala & stamina carmine anthera cream colour…Capsula sordid brown. buds ting'd w^t red'.

It is found from northern Australia south to New South Wales in open forest and also rain forest along watercourses, as it is a rheophyte in habit, that is, it grows in or near flowing water. In other parts of the world it is the most commonly grown species of 'callistemon'. Laboratory tests have shown that an oil derived from it has antiparasitic (anthelminthic) properties.

The name *Melaleuca* is from the Greek *melas*, black, and *leukos*, white, perhaps referring to its black trunk and white branches, as exhibited in some species; *viminalis* alludes to its long slender shoots like willow (osier).

Melaleuca (bottlebrushes and paperbarks) is a genus comprising some 300 species in the Indopacific, with around 280 of them in Australia. It is now considered to embrace a number of formerly segregated genera, including *Callistemon*. The fruits often persist and enlarge over many years, and the trees are useful as timber and for medicinal oil. In particular, *M. alternifolia* (tea tree from eastern Australia) has commercial oils traditionally used by Aboriginal people as an antiseptic, and now involved in the treament of acne, athlete's foot and arthritis.

Melaleuca viminalis (Gaertn.) Byrnes in *Austrobaileya* 2: 75 (1984)
Copper plate by Gerard Sibelius, based on Frederick Nodder's 1777 watercolour, derived from Parkinson's surviving pencil drawing made at 'Endeavours River'; BF 114; Diment et al., 1984: A3/130

134.

ASTEROMYRTUS ANGUSTIFOLIA
Myrtaceae

On drawing Solander's 'Melaleuca angustifolia', a name published by Josef Gaertner in 1788, Parkinson added the colour instructions: 'The stamina petala & nectarium white w[t] a cast of green…'.

Banks and Solander collected their specimens at what is now Cooktown, the southernmost part of its distribution.[1] It is a shrub or small tree reaching 10 m (33 ft) tall and growing in forest and heathland, usually on old sand dunes, north to Cape York.

Asteromyrtus is derived from Latin *aster*, star, and *myrtus*, the Greek name for myrtle; *angustifolius* means narrow-leaved (names derived from classical tree-names such as this one are treated as feminine). The genus *Asteromyrtus* comprises 13 species restricted to northern Australia.[2]

Asteromyrtus angustifolia (Gaertn.) Craven in *Australian Systematic Botany* 1: 377 (1989)

Copper plate by Gerard Sibelius, based on Frederick Nodder's 1777 watercolour, derived from Parkinson's surviving pencil drawing made at 'Endeavours River'; BF 116; Diment et al., 1984: A3/132

1. Cooper and Cooper, 2004, p. 341

2. Mabberley, 2014, p. 76 and 4th ed., 2017

135.

TIMONIUS TIMON
timon, Rubiaceae

Timon is a shrub or tree up to 20 m (66 ft) tall, growing in coastal and other forest settings in Indonesia and northern Australia. It produces its small, fragrant, white flowers and fruits much of the year and is monoecious, meaning that separate male and female flowers are borne on the same individual plant.[1] The berries are said to be edible.[2]

Timonius is a Latinization of *timon*, the name for the plant on Ambon Island. The genus has about 170 species ranging from the Seychelles and Mauritius, Sri Lanka and the Andamans, to the Pacific, being particularly rich in New Guinea. Some are 'stranglers', rather like certain kinds of fig trees that start as epiphytes on other trees and eventually engulf their hosts.[3]

Timonius timon (Spreng.) Merr. in *Journal of the Arnold Arboretum* 18: 131 (1937)

Copper plate by Gerard Sibelius, based on James Miller's undated watercolour, derived from Parkinson's surviving pencil drawing made at 'Endeavours River'; BF 147; Diment et al., 1984: A4/168

1. J. R. Wheeler in Wheeler et al., 1992, p. 930

2. Mabberley, 2014, p. 860

3. Mabberley, 1992, p. 105

136.
CLERODENDRUM FLORIBUNDUM
Labiatae

It is not clear why Banks and Solander gave this tree the manuscript name 'Volkameria insectorum', unless its fragrant white flowers were being visited by exceptional numbers of insects. Parkinson sketched it with the colour instructions 'The flowers white anthera brown stile ting'd w^t green'.

Found only in New Guinea and northern Australia, this is generally a small tree, though individuals up to 30 m (100 ft) tall have been recorded. Its spectacular flowers are followed by a black drupe borne on a succulent red star-shaped calyx about 25 mm (1 in.) across.

Clerodendrum is from *kleros*, chance, and *dendron*, tree, apparently due to their variable medicinal attributes; *floribundus* means with abundant flowers. The genus comprises some 150 species of trees and shrubs, as well as perennial and even annual herbs of the tropical and warm Old World.[1] Many are cultivated for ornament or considered important in local medicine. The former include *C. bungei* (from China), a widely grown hardy shrub, as well as *C. chinense* (glory bower, Honolulu or Lady Nugent's rose), from China to the Malay Archipelago – its flowers are offered to Buddha in Cambodia, but it is a serious suckering weed in the Caribbean and Samoa.

Clerodendrum floribundum R. Br., *Prodromus Florae Novae Hollandiae*: 511 (1810)

Copper plate by Gerard Sibelius, based on Frederick Nodder's 1778 watercolour, derived from Parkinson's pencil drawing; BF 254; Diment et al., 1984: A6/287

1. Mabberley, 2014, p. 195

137.
JOSEPHINIA IMPERATRICIS
Pedaliaceae

On 12 August 1770, having 'slept under the shade of a Bush that grew on the Beach very comfortably',[1] Banks explored Lizard Island, in the Great Barrier Reef, near present-day Cooktown. He wrote: 'On it I found some few plants which I had not before seen', one of them being this woody herb, which has white, cream, purple or red flowers and here is at the southeasternmost limit of its essentially Malesian (see Pl. 25, p. 68) distribution.[2]

Recognizing its relationship to *Pedalium* (Pedaliaceae), Solander gave it the manuscript name 'Pedalioides tribulus'. Parkinson sketched it with the colour description, 'The petala on the inside delicate pale crimson the lower labia deep crimson at the edge...'.

During the 1800–04 French Pacific expedition commissioned by Napoleon and led by Nicolas Baudin (who died in 1803), seeds of this unpleasantly aromatic plant were collected and taken back to France by Emmanuel Hamelin (1768–1839), captain of *Le Naturaliste*. The plants soon flowered and were named *Josephinia imperatricis* for Joséphine de Beauharnais (1763–1814), Napoleon's Empress Joséphine (in Latin Josephinia Imperatrix).[3] Her portrait in the Louvre by Pierre-Paul Prud'hon shows her next to a specimen of this plant. Étienne Pierre Ventenat (1757–1808), in his book on Joséphine's garden at Malmaison, wrote,

> L'honneur de dédier un genre à l'auguste Impératrice des Français, devoit être ambitionné par l'auteur du Jardin de la Malmaison – Puisse ce foible hommage rappeler à la postérité la protection éclairée que Sa Majesté accorde à la science et l'éclat dont elle s'embellit![4]

The genus *Josephinia* comprises some three or four species growing in arid areas, extending from East Africa to Australia.[5]

Josephinia imperatricis Vent., *Jardin de la Malmaison* 2: t. 67 (1804)

Copper plate by Gerard Sibelius based on Frederick Nodder's 1778 watercolour, derived from Parkinson's surviving pencil drawing made at 'Lizard Island'; BF 245; Diment et al., 1984: A6/276

1. Beaglehole, 1963, 2, p. 103

2. Beaglehole, 1963, 2, p. 103, n. 2 has one of the new plants being *Blepharocarya involucrigera*, but there are surviving specimens from Endeavour River (Diment et al., 1984: A1/55; see Pl. 113, p. 234)

3. H. Heine, '"Ave Caesar, botanici te salutant"; L'épopée napoléonienne dans la botanique', *Adansonia*, ser. 2, 7, 1967, pp. 115–40

4. 'The honour of naming a genus after the august Empress of the French was a fitting ambition for the author of the Garden of Malmaison. May this small homage remind posterity of the patronage that Her Majesty grants to science and the brilliance with which she shines!'

5. Mabberley, 2014, p. 444

138.
BARRINGTONIA CALYPTRATA
mango pine, Lecythidaceae

Banks wrote that Lizard Island was 'small and Barren; on it was however one small tract of woodland',[1] which is presumably where this plant was collected.

Solander gave it the manuscript name 'Eugenia ramiflora', indicating that he thought (incorrectly) that it belonged in what would now be called Myrtaceae, but also pointing to the fact that the flowers are borne on the branches (*rami*). Parkinson sketched the flowers, noting,

> The petala & stamina white the anthera yellow the buds ting'd w^t green calyx gray green turning pale toward the edge the main stalk of the flower deep green the woody stalk sordid brown.

Mango pine is a deciduous tree up to 30 m (100 ft) tall, with flowers borne on both the branches and the trunk itself, which mature as bluish-green drupes up to 9.5 cm (3¾ in.) long; these are eaten by cassowaries.[2] The tree is found mainly in savanna in New Guinea and on Aru Island, as well as in tropical Australia.

Barringtonia commemorates Daines Barrington (1727–1800), an English antiquary and botanist, and a great friend of Joseph Banks; *calyptratus* means with a cap-like covering, referring to the calyx, which often falls before splitting into lobes.[3] The genus comprises 69 species from East Africa (with just one species) and Madagascar (two) to tropical Asia and the Pacific.[4] Their seeds contain saponins and so are used as fish poison, although when roasted, seeds of several species are eaten by local people.

Barringtonia calyptrata (Miers) F. M. Bailey in *Queensland Agricultural Journal* 18: 125 (1907)

Copper plate by Daniel Mackenzie, based on Frederick Nodder's 1777 watercolour, derived from Parkinson's surviving pencil drawing made at 'Lizzard Isle', Queensland; BF 127; Diment et al., 1984: A3/145

1. Beaglehole, 1963, 2, p. 103

2. Cooper and Cooper, 2004, p. 266

3. G. T. Prance, 'A revision of *Barringtonia* (Lecythidaceae)', *Allertonia* 12, 2013, pp. 1–164

4. Mabberley, 2014, p. 92 and 4th ed., 2017

139.

SYZYGIUM SUBORBICULARE
lady apple, Myrtaceae

While on Lizard Island Banks also collected what Solander was to call 'Eugenia cymosa'. Lady apple is a tree growing up to 12 m (40 ft) or so high, native in New Guinea as well as tropical Australia. Its red or pink berries, often striped white and up to 9 cm (3½ in.) across, are eaten by both palm cockatoos[1] and people.

Syzygium is from Greek *suzugos*, joined, referring to the paired leaves (originally of the allied tropical American *Calyptranthes zuzygium*); *suborbicularis* means almost round, again referring to the leaves.

The genus *Syzygium* contains about 1,120 species distributed from southeastern Africa to the Pacific.[2] They are generally evergreen canopy and emergent trees found growing from shores and swamps to lowland and montane forests. The most important economically is *S. aromaticum*, originally from the Moluccas. Its sun-dried flower buds are the cloves of commerce used widely in flavouring, while the oil (eugenol) derived from them has antibacterial, antiviral (herpes) and analgesic properties much used in the relief of toothache, but is also added to kretek cigarettes in Indonesia (some 30,000 tons per annum). Many other species are grown for their fruits, including the Malaysian *S. aqueum* (water rose-apple), *S. cumini* (jamun, now invasive in Hawaii, South Africa and southeastern United States) and *S. malaccense* (rose or Malay apple). The Australian *S. luehmannii* (riberry) is often included in commercial skin moisturizers, and extracts of the edible fruit of *S. smithii* (lilli-pilli) are used as commercial facial cleansers.

Syzygium suborbiculare (Benth.) T. G. Hartley & L. M. Perry in *Journal of the Arnold Arboretum* 54: 189 (1973)

Copper plate by Gerard Sibelius, based on Frederick Nodder's 1777 watercolour, derived from Parkinson's surviving pencil drawing made at 'Lizzard Island', Queensland; BF 125; Diment et al., 1984: A3/143

1. Cooper and Cooper, 2004, pp. 368–69
2. Mabberley, 2014, pp. 836–37

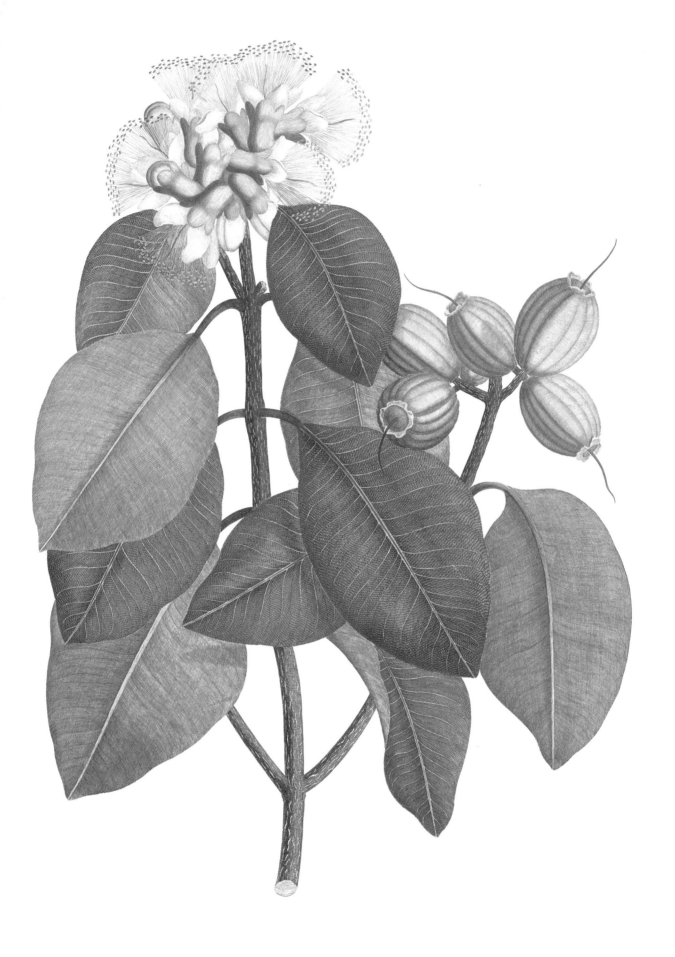

140.

CAPPARIS LUCIDA
coast caper, Capparaceae

On 23 August 1770 *Endeavour* reached Booby Island at the tip of Cape York Peninsula in the Torres Strait. Here Parkinson sketched what Banks named 'Capparis lucida' (*lucidus*, shining, referring to the glossy leaves), adding details of the flower colour – 'stile ting'd w^t red stigma green' – to his drawing. The plant was not formally described from Banks' and Solander's collection until over 50 years later, as *Thylachium lucidum*. It was then 'returned' to *Capparis* by George Bentham, working at Kew in 1863.

A tree growing to 12 m (40 ft) tall, sometimes scrambling, and flowering as a shrub, *Capparis lucida* is found from Java to Australia, as far south as southeastern Queensland, in beach forest, monsoon forest and vine forest. It flowers only at night, with each evanescent, sweet-smelling flower having 50–85 stamens. The red, purple or black fruits are up to 5 cm (2 in.) in diameter and contain many seeds, which are possibly dispersed by bats.[1]

The genus *Capparis* (from the classical Greek name for caper) comprises 150–250 species of trees, shrubs and stranglers found in tropical and warm countries, from rain forests to deserts, with flowers often lasting just one day.[2] The most familiar is *C. spinosa*, cultivated for its flower buds, known as capers, which are pickled as relish, especially in France, being a component of tartare sauce, and also for its fruits, caper berries.

Capparis lucida (DC.) Benth., *Flora Australiensis* 1: 96 (1863)

Copper plate by Daniel Mackenzie, based on Frederick Nodder's 1779 watercolour (with some inaccuracies, corrected in the plate), derived from Parkinson's surviving drawing; BF 6; Diment et al., 1984: A1/8

1. M. Jacobs in *Flora Malesiana* I, 6, 1960, p. 92; Cooper and Cooper, 2004, p. 110

2. Mabberley, 2014, p. 149

141.

CLERODENDRUM PANICULATUM
pagoda flower, Labiatae

On 10 October 1770, *Endeavour* arrived in Batavia, now Jakarta, Java, where Parkinson drew *Clerodendrum paniculatum*. A widely cultivated shrub, it grows to around 3 m (10 ft) tall, with large, lobed leaves up to 40 cm (16 in.) long and 38 cm (15 in.) wide. The striking terminal inflorescence, up to 45 cm (18 in.) long and wide, is made up of red or orange to pale lemon/cream flowers; the blue to black fruits are rarely produced.

Now found throughout tropical and subtropical Asia from Bangladesh to the Moluccas, its original distribution is obscured by widespread cultivation. By 1809 it had been introduced into England from Penang by Thomas Evans of Stepney, London. Often, as in Java and New Guinea (and Central America), the flowers are sterile, with malformed pollen, so these plants must be propagated vegetatively.[1] For a discussion of the genus *Clerodendrum*, see Pl. 136, p. 274.

Clerodendrum paniculatum L., *Mantissa Plantarum* 1: 90 (1767)

Copper plate by Daniel Mackenzie ('1783'), based on Frederick Nodder's 1782 watercolour, derived from Parkinson's surviving pencil drawing; BF 380; Diment et al., 1987: J47

1. D. J. Mabberley, 'Clerodendrum', *Flora of Peninsular Malaysia* (submitted)

142.

LEEA RUBRA
Vitaceae

Specimens of this shrub were collected by Banks and Solander in Batavia. It reaches a height of 1–2 m or even 3 m (3–10 ft) and grows in rain forest, as well as other kinds of habitat from tropical Asia to Australia. Its red, purple or black berries are up to 12 mm (½ in.) across.[1]

Leea commemorates James Lee – see *Leea indica* (Pl. 110, p. 228); *rubra* is from *ruber*, red, the colour of the flowers.

Leea rubra Blume, *Bijdragen tot de Flora van Nederlandsch Indie* 4: 197 (1825)

Copper plate by Daniel Mackenzie, based on James Miller's 1774 watercolour, derived from Parkinson's surviving pencil drawing; BF 364; Diment et al., 1987: J15

1. Cooper and Cooper, 2004, p. 268

143.

MERREMIA GEMELLA
Convolvulaceae

This twining herb, native from Southeast Asia to Australia, has bright yellow flowers, hence Solander's manuscript name, 'Convolvulus flavus', *flavus* being yellow. The stems are used for string in Australia, especially by Aboriginal people for tying up kangaroos for roasting.[1]

Merremia commemorates Blasius Merrem (1761–1824), professor of natural sciences at Marburg, Germany; *gemellus*, twin-born, refers to the paired flowers. The genus *Merremia* comprises about 100 tropical species, some serious weeds in plantations, others cultivated as ornamentals. *Merremia discoidesperma* (Mary's bean), originating in Central America, is the most widespread of all drift-seeds on seashores, while *M. tuberosa* (Brazilian jalap), also originating in Central America but now naturalized around the tropics, was formerly grown for its laxative resins, and its dried fruits with enlarged calyces are still used as the 'wood roses' of dried floral decorations.

Merremia gemella (Burm.f.) H. Hallier in *Botanische Jahrbücher für Systematik, Planzengeschichte und Pflanzengeographie* 16: 552 (1893)

Copper plate by William Smith, based on an anonymous watercolour, derived from Parkinson's surviving pencil drawing; BF 374; Diment et al., 1987: J37

1. Mabberley, 2014, p. 539 and 4th ed., 2017

144.

PELTOPHORUM PTEROCARPUM
yellow poinciana, Leguminosae

Yellow poinciana is a commonly seen deciduous ornamental tree in warm countries. Banks' and Solander's material was collected from south of 'Anger Point', Tanjung Leneng, near Anyer, west of Jakarta.[1]

The tree grows to 25 m (80 ft) or more tall,[2] with rust-covered shoots. The flowers have a grapey scent, especially at night, suggesting bat-pollination, but *Xylocopa* (carpenter) bees carry out buzz-pollination by vibrating their wings at particular frequencies, even though the anthers have slits and not pores as is usual in this method of pollination.[3] In Java the bark is used medicinally and also as the yellow-brown dye *soga* for colouring batik.

Peltophorum is from the Greek *pelte*, a shield, and *phoreo*, to bear, referring to the shape of the stigma; *pteron* is wing and *karpos*, fruit. There are five species in the genus, all tropical, providing timber (brasiletto) and shade trees. Seeds of *P. dubium* from Brazil contain 43.8 per cent protein, and this species has been proposed as a potential future crop.

Peltophorum pterocarpum (DC.) K. Heyne, *De Nuttige Planten van Nederlandsch-Indië* ed. 2, 2: 755 (1927)

Copper plate by Daniel Mackenzie, based on Frederick Nodder's undated watercolour, derived from Parkinson's surviving pencil drawing; BF 366; Diment et al., 1987: J21

1. Beaglehole, 1963, 2, p. 179 n. 5

2. Staples and Herbst, 2005, p. 319

3. R. J. S. Aluri and C. S. Reddi, 'Vibrational pollination in *Peltophorum pterocarpum* (Caesalpiniaceae)', *Journal of Nature Conservation* 8, 1996, pp. 99–100

145.

IPOMOEA AQUATICA
kangkong, Convolvulaceae

Banks and Solander may have encountered this plant on the dining table and in markets as well as in the field during their stay in Java. Kangkong, also known as ong choy, en choi or ong tsoi, is a creeper¹ with hollow stems up to 4 m (13 ft) long, rooting at the nodes, hence, presumably, Solander's manuscript name, 'Convolvulus itinerarius'. Native in the Old World tropics, it has escaped in the Americas, becoming invasive in the southeastern United States.

The plant has been introduced to many countries by Chinese people, who eat the leaves and young shoots either cooked as greens or fresh. Especially favoured, for instance in Hong Kong, is a form with very white stems. Kangkong is rich in vitamin A, but poor in vitamins B and C, iron and calcium.

For an explanation of the name *Ipomoea* see Pl. 34, p. 84; *aquaticus* refers to its watery habitat.

Ipomoea aquatica Forssk., *Flora Aegyptiaco-Arabica* 44 (1775)

Copper plate by William Smith, based on an anonymous watercolour, derived from Parkinson's surviving pencil drawing made in Jakarta (Batavia); BF 375; Diment et al., 1987: J38

1. Staples and Herbst, 2005, p. 247

146.
SARCOLOBUS GLOBOSUS
Apocynaceae

Among the last plants drawn by Parkinson shortly before his tragic death was 'Cynanchoides drupacea'. Parkinson made his sketch from material collected on Princes Island, off the westernmost tip of Java, where *Endeavour* made landfall in January 1771.[1]

This twining shrub of the Asian tropics east to Indonesia is found in a number of habitats including mangrove. Its poisonous seeds have been used as bait to kill pest animals, though in local medicine they are considered to be an effective antimalarial.

Sarcolobus is from *sarx, sarkos*, flesh; *globosus* refers to the fruits. The genus comprises 14 species of the Indopacific region.[2] In West Malaysia the fruit-walls of some species are eaten (once the toxic seeds have been removed) and even candied. The poisons have been used for killing feral dogs, and are said to have exterminated the Javanese tigers.

Sarcolobus globosus Wall. in *Asiatic Researches* 12: 568 (1816). For a discussion of the *Endeavour* material, see R. E. Rintz in *Blumea* 26, 1980, pp. 75–76.

Copper plate by Gabriel Smith, based on John Miller's 1774 watercolour, derived from Parkinson's surviving pencil drawing; BF 372; Diment et al., 1987: J35

1. Beaglehole, 1963, 2, p. 179, n. 1

2. Mabberley, 2014, p. 769

147.
BOESENBERGIA ROTUNDA
Chinese key(s), Zingiberaceae

Parkinson annotated his pencil sketch of Solander's 'Kaempferia erubescens' collected on Princes Island, Java, with the colour instructions, 'The flower very pale crimson [hence Solander's specific epithet] the top of the largest petala deep violet colour'.

Growing up to 50 cm (20 in.) or more tall,[1] Chinese keys has root-tubers and succulent, cylindrical rhizomes, bright yellow within, and is cultivated throughout tropical Asia for spicing food, as well as for medicinal applications to treat rheumatism, ringworm and coughs. Linnaeus considered it a kind of *Curcuma*, and his other species is still called *C. longa*, turmeric.

Boesenbergia commemorates Clara and Walter Boesenberg, the sister and brother-in-law of Otto Kuntze (1843–1907), a German botanist and traveller, who coined the name for them; *rotundus* means round, but in this case the allusion is unclear.

Boesenbergia rotunda (L.) Mansf. in *Kulturpflanze* 6: 239 (1958)

Copper plate by Gabriel Smith, based on John Miller's 1773 watercolour, derived from Parkinson's surviving pencil drawing; BF 389; Diment et al., 1987: J67

1. Staples and Herbst, 2005, p. 769

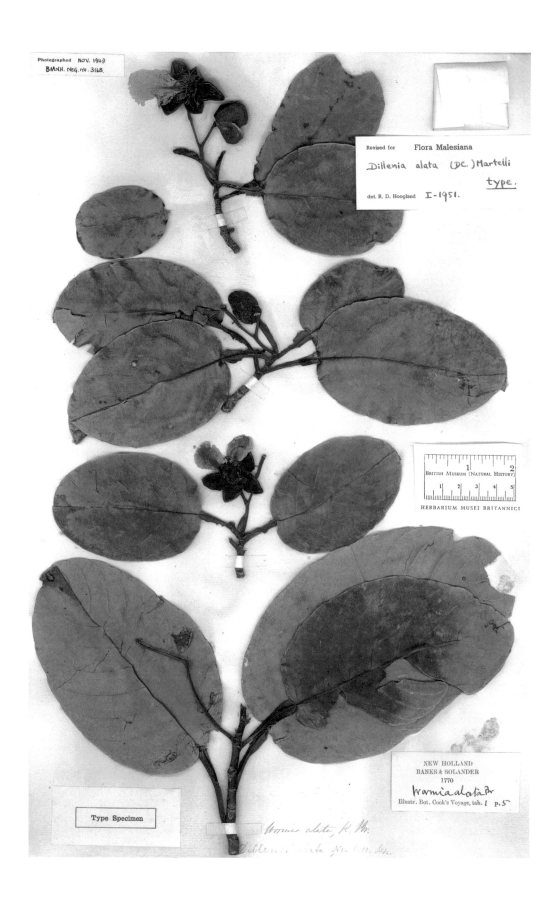

Photographed NOV. 1949
BMNH. NEG. No. 3168.

Revised for   Flora Malesiana

Dillenia alata (DC.) Martelli
                  type.

det. R. D. Hoogland   I-1951.

BRITISH MUSEUM (NATURAL HISTORY)

HERBARIUM MUSEI BRITANNICI

NEW HOLLAND
BANKS & SOLANDER
1770
Wormia alata Br.
Illustr. Bot. Cook's Voyage, tab. *I* p.5

Wormia alata, R. Br.

Type Specimen

The Florilegium 1772–1990

MEL GOODING

May we hope that this strong impulse, which urges forward
this distinguished naturalist to brave the intemperance of
every climate, may also lead him to the discovery of something
highly beneficial to mankind? If he survives, with what delight
shall we peruse his Journals, his Fauna, his Flora?

Gilbert White, letter to Thomas Pennant, 8 October 1768

The unceasing and untiring labours of the naturalists and artists in the great cabin of *Endeavour* had been directed to an end, consciously and conscientiously considered by Banks as necessary from the outset: the preservation of the specimens collected, and the publication of the botanical findings in a manner appropriate to their significance. Banks was happy for others to use in whatever scientific manner seemed appropriate the more than one thousand other natural specimens – ornithological, ichthyological etc. – that were part of the collections made on the voyage (not to mention the great abundance of ethnographic materials and drawings, evidence of material cultures hitherto unknown to European students of human diversity), and these were very soon made available to all who were interested for inspection and study at his house in New Burlington Street, London.

As for the vast collection of botanical specimens – an astounding herbarium of over 30,000 items, representing over 3,600 species, of which over 1,300 were unknown to science – many had been documented in detail, in accordance with strict Linnaean principles, by Banks and his assistant Daniel Solander, with his secretary Herman Spöring, while on board *Endeavour*. As Banks recalled some years later: 'We were well supplied with books on the natural history of the Indies. Storms were seldom strong enough to interrupt our study time, which lasted each day from about 8 a.m. to 2 p.m. and after the smell of food had disappeared, from 4 or 5 p.m. until dark.'[1] Back in London, the indefatigable Solander continued to work on the definitive catalogue, thus initiated, until his death in 1782. He had his own and Banks' shipboard notes for reference, in addition to the meticulous writing up of these by Spöring.

As Solander was well aware, the botanist-collector dealing with a specimen apparently previously unknown, would be faced with uncertainties of identification and definition, and problems of nomenclature. With the benefit of later study and hindsight, his notes were often altered or cancelled in part. He developed a novel system of recording data on paper 'slips', a proto-card-index system, which he adapted and improved directly from Linnaeus' own practice.[2] His work, systematic and scholarly, undertaken intermittently over two decades following the return of *Endeavour*, and copied in fair for publication, would have been the essential text to the definitive realization of Banks' ambitiously projected publication. This was envisaged as comprising 14 magnificent bound folio volumes of the engravings made from Parkinson's botanical drawings, accompanied by descriptions of the plants new to science collected on the voyage.

Sydney Parkinson had, with great skill and no inconsiderable grace and beauty, depicted many of these plant specimens in finished watercolour paintings (269 in all). But when the scale of the flow of collected material made this degree of completion impossible, as occurred frequently on the voyage, he made fine and precise outline drawings (no fewer than 674), with detailed colour notes, which were intended to be finished in colour on his return, in

A herbarium sheet of a specimen of Dillenia alata, *collected by Banks and Solander at Endeavour River, Australia. The plant was dried and pressed, and is now preserved in the Natural History Museum, London. Parkinson made a pencil sketch with colour references, which was then worked up by Frederick Nodder. From this Gerard Sibelius made the engraving reproduced as Plate 106 (see p. 223).*

preparation for engraving and publication. Banks and Solander supervised this work solicitously: 'We worked at the great table in the cabin with our draftsman opposite. We directed his drawing, and made rapid descriptions of our natural history specimens while they were still fresh.'[3] Parkinson was already an experienced botanical artist, and he became a decent field botanist himself, often being responsible in many locations – from Brazil to Java - for the gathering of specimens. This gave his artistic treatment of plants a scientific authority that was to be crucial to the success of the Florilegium.

Parkinson was the son of an Edinburgh Quaker brewer, whose principled generosity finally led to penury. Sydney was apprenticed to a woollen draper, but soon discovered a talent for nature drawing, especially of plants. He exhibited a few works in Edinburgh, but in 1766, to further his career, he moved to London to work as a draughtsman for James Lee, the Edinburgh-born botanist-plantsman who ran 'The Vineyard' nursery at Hammersmith and was much admired for his expertise by Banks. Within a year, Parkinson was working for Banks, painting specimens of various kinds from Banks' expedition to Newfoundland, and he was a natural choice as a natural history artist for the 1768 voyage to the South Seas. As well as his skill, adaptability and energetic application, Parkinson was a young man of extreme integrity and high intelligence, as was evidenced by the range and percipience of his fascinating *Journal of a Voyage to the South Seas*, first published, in vexatious circumstances, in 1773.[4]

Parkinson's added colour references on his linear sketches, indicating the living appearance of leaf, flower and fruit of the plant, and detailed colour notes on the verso for his own future reference, many of which demonstrate a competent knowledge of botanical structure, would prove invaluable to the artists who completed the drawings after his death. One example is the black bean or Moreton Bay chestnut (*Castanospermum australe*; Pl. 103, p. 216) collected during the enforced sojourn in June and July 1770 at Endeavour River, and misnamed by Solander as 'Sophora caudiciflora'. Solander perhaps discerned a similarity in the pinnate foliage and the pendulous flowers and fruit to the so-called Japanese pagoda tree (*Styphnolobium japonicum* (L.); syn. *Sophora japonica*), which had been introduced at Kew as early as 1760; two *Sophora* species had been collected and so-named in New Zealand. Parkinson drew the specimen branch in outline, with colour references, and added on the reverse the meticulous note: 'The vexillum first laid over w^t yellow then stain'd and sprinkled w^t scarlet. the res^t of the flower scarlet calyx deep buff colour ting'd at at the base w^t green the buds the same colour but somewhat more green. The leaves above grass green w^t light veins the underside

ABOVE The frontispiece portrait of Sydney Parkinson in his Journal of a Voyage to the South Seas, *first published in 1773 by his brother, Stanfield.*

OPPOSITE In the early stages of the voyage, Parkinson was able to complete accomplished watercolour paintings of the plants collected by Banks and Solander. This is Thespesia populnea, *which Parkinson also described in his journal; see Pl. 23, p. 64.*

more Glaucus w^t dark veins stalks sordid brown. capsula grass green.' 'Sophora caudiciflora' is written beside this in an unknown hand; and Banks has added 'Endeavours River'.

It was to his great project of publication of the botany of the voyage that Banks applied himself after his return from an expedition to Iceland, undertaken after his disappointment at being excluded from Cook's second voyage in 1772. He had also made a productive short study visit in early 1773 to The Netherlands, where he had met Pierre Lyonnet (1706–1789), the great naturalist-engraver, and his brilliant pupil, Gerard Sibelius (1734–1785), who was later to engrave many of the plates for the Florilegium. This meeting almost certainly crystallized Banks' determination to proceed to publication in appropriate style. He set about at once commissioning the watercolour completion of Parkinson's outline drawings. He turned first to John Frederick Miller (1759–1796) and his brother James (*fl.* 1770s), sons of the gifted botanical artist John Miller (born Johann Sebastian Müller in Nuremberg; 1715–*c*. 1790), who was making his name as the illustrator of Linnaeus' *An Illustration of the Sexual System*

Thespesia populnea.
Otaheite

Sydney Parkinson pinx 1769.

Daniel Solander was Banks' tireless companion, collecting and recording specimens of all kinds during the voyage. A student of Linnaeus, he used his method of ordering the material, both plant and animal, and devised a system of cataloguing the information on loose slips of paper. These 'Solander slips' were later bound into volumes: the entry above, written in Latin, the scientific language of the day, describes the kangaroo. Banks' greyhound chased a pair, but failed to catch them as they bounded over the long grass (Journal, July 1770).

of Linnaeus, issued in part-publication through the 1770s. John Frederick had accompanied Banks to Iceland as an artist, as had John Cleveley (1747–1768), who was also now employed, with Thomas Burgis (*fl.* 1760s–1790s), to create the finished watercolour paintings. The engraving of the plates for eventual publication also began at this time.

Banks was deeply knowledgeable about the current state of botanical art, and personally connected with its leading practitioners, and he considered with great care how best to present the work with the most exact objectivity. He was, moreover, convinced of the importance of fine art work to the presentation of scientific and topographic findings in general, regarding it as integral to the process: a way of knowing and a means of showing. Banks had certainly been engaged in consideration and discussion of these things over many years. On his return from his first voyage, to Newfoundland in 1766, he had commissioned the greatest botanical artist of the time, Georg Dionysius Ehret (1708–1770), to make studies of plants he had collected there.[5] In 1767 he had discerned in the young Parkinson a botanical artist of great promise, and immediately took him into his employ. Banks collected drawings by his friend Paul Sandby (1731–1809), an artist who had begun his professional life as a military surveyor, and whose work thereafter was characterized by an objective clarity and lucid precision that appealed directly to the great naturalist's taste. Johan Zoffany (1733–1810), whom Banks had wanted to accompany him on Cook's second voyage in 1772, was similarly an artist of clear light and sharp definition, although best known for his society portraits. Years later, the topographical artist Joseph Farington (1747–1821) succinctly remarked in his diary: 'Accuracy of drawing seems to be a principal recommendation to Sir Joseph.'[6]

Even so, when it came to landscape and topographical painting, Banks was certainly not above the fashionable taste for the composed 'effects' of the picturesque. He regretted the death of Alexander Buchan, soon after their arrival in Tahiti, partly because it robbed him of the opportunity to bring back to England pictures of the strange and the exotic, as he recorded in his journal for 17 April, 1769:

> I sincerely regret him as an ingenious and good young man, but his Loss to me is irretrevable, my airy dreams of entertaining my freinds in England with the scenes that I am to see here are vanishd. No account of the figures and dresses of men can be satisfactory unless illustrated with figures: had providence spard him a month longer what an advantage would it have been to my undertaking but I must submit.

For Banks, such pictorial records would have been his version of the paintings and engravings brought back from France and Italy by young dilettanti on the conventional Grand Tour. 'Every blockhead does that' he wrote, 'my Grand Tour shall be one round the whole globe.' Following Buchan's death, both Parkinson and Spöring found themselves subsequently pressed into the picturesque delineation of spectacular landscape features, primitive scenes, savages, noble or otherwise, their dwellings, boats and weapons. These might fairly exhibit a degree of the fanciful, though such indulgence was inimical to both of them. For the graphic publication of scientific findings, however, Banks required absolute accuracy and truth to nature.

In this respect he could have found no better an artist than Sydney Parkinson. Parkinson's own books enhanced the more specialized library of Banks and Solander on board *Endeavour*, and remind us that Parkinson was a child of the Edinburgh Enlightenment. He brought not only the Quaker principles of plainness, truth and self-effacing modesty to his work, but also a mind formed by a rounded and broad education, which placed the highest philosophical value on the evidence of the senses, and on close analytic attention to the world of objects. This broadness of culture was reflected in the classical texts – Ovid and Pope's Homer – he took with him, along with Shakespeare and Cervantes.

Most notably, Parkinson's books included *The Analysis of Beauty* (1753) by William Hogarth (1697–1764), whose empirical emphasis on the necessity 'to see with our own eyes' clearly informed Parkinson's observational intensity of approach. The great painter's serpentine 'line of grace' and waving S 'line of beauty' are constantly recurring elements in the rhythmic linearity, lyrically descriptive arabesques and waving leaf surfaces that are essential characteristics of Parkinson's watercolours and outline drawings. In Hogarth's conception, these graphic figures were aspects of the life of forms recurring in art as in nature, recognizable and accessible to what the thinkers of the Scottish Enlightenment in the mid-eighteenth century would call the common sense, the shared empiricism of everyday experience, and the basis of a democratic aesthetic.

It was understood clearly by Parkinson from the outset that he was engaged in a collaborative enterprise, at once of art and of natural philosophy, which began with the meticulous directions from Banks and Solander 'at the great table in the cabin', and would continue with the accurate completion of his drawings – always life-size, and therefore true to immediate experience – and the exactness of their engraving. The realization of his creative efforts, he knew, would be the beautiful and precise engravings that would facilitate the wide dissemination of the astounding botanical discoveries of the epic voyage. After Parkinson's death, Banks himself was determined that the best artists and craftsmen would undertake these tasks, at whatever cost. The final publication of the Florilegium was to be a brilliant revelation of Parkinson's artistic genius, establishing for him a place among the great botanical artists.

Parkinson's down-to-earth 'common-sense' aesthetic gave his artistic inclinations an ethical and epistemological congruity with the natural philosophy of Banks, which was similarly grounded in a combination of wonder at nature's beauty and diversity, and a lucid objectivity, Linnaean in its insistence on the centrality of taxonomy. Both avowedly approached the work of natural philosophy as the revelation of God's beneficence. Linnaeus had famously declared: 'God created; Linnaeus organized.' Banks was not, however, a deep thinker, and his (and Solander's) emphasis on the 'organization' of natural objects, and their devoted and assiduous application of Linnaean binomial nomenclature signified a closer interest in *natura naturata* – nature as manifest, requiring systematic analysis and classification – rather than *natura naturans* – nature as in constant development and change, requiring dynamic theoretical synthesis and an over-arching principle. Joseph Banks, for all the passion and thoroughness of his collection and classification, was no theorist.[7]

From the effective beginning of the grand project in 1773, Banks' house in New Burlington Street was a hive of multifarious activities, scientific and artistic, with the museum-like arrangement and display of natural and ethnographic specimens constantly visited by scholars and the merely curious. Solander and his assistants were engaged on his catalogues, with draughtsman-painters at work on both the completion of drawings and new studies of objects,

Parkinson's unfinished sketch of Dendrobium discolor, *the golden orchid, from Australia. Often the quantity of material to be recorded was so great that Parkinson had no time to complete the watercolours; he would annotate the drawings with detailed colour notes, capturing the essentials of each plant. Plate 122 (p. 251) shows the finished coloured engraving.*

Banks and Solander were voracious collectors of specimens of every kind, not just plants. This tray displays shells they picked up from the beaches of Brazil, Tahiti, New Zealand and Australia.

room] contains an almost numberless collection of animals; quadrupeds, birds, fish, amphibia, reptiles, insects and vermes, most of them new and nondescript [undescribed]....Add to these the choicest collection of drawings in Natural History that perhaps enriched any cabinet, public or private... and all the new genera and species in this vast collection are accurately described, the descriptions fairly transcribed and fit to be put to the press.[8]

In 1776 Banks moved, with his vast collection, to a large corner house at 32 Soho Square, where the work on the Florilegium continued apace, with the gifted Frederick Polydore Nodder (*fl.* 1770–1800) now taking on the task of completing the remainder of the drawings. Nodder's exceptional skills were recognized in his appointment as botanical illustrator to Queen Charlotte, a keen amateur botanist with a close interest in developments at Kew. In addition to Parkinson's own 280 finished studies, 493 were now completed, and many had already been engraved. Over the next few years Nodder made no fewer than 271 finished paintings, including most of the Australian specimens.

Banks was as particular in his choice of engravers as of artists. Certain of the best engravers, in what was a golden period of botanical engraving, were engaged throughout the 1770s with other major projects (Johann Sebastian Müller, or Mueller, for example, as we have seen, was at work on Linnaeus), but Banks was able to employ as many as eighteen engravers in all. Among them he was fortunate in securing for his great work the services of three highly accomplished practitioners, Daniel Mackenzie (*fl.* 1770–1800), Gabriel Smith (1724–1783) and Gerard Sibelius, who between them engraved 564 of the plates. The astonishingly consistent craftsmanship of the engravings in the Florilegium, in its precision of execution, its subtlety and delicacy, is testament to the perfectionism of Banks. Although Banks may have considered the possibilities of hand colouring, at that time he concluded that the fine detail allowed by the engraved monochrome line and tone would better serve the exact reproduction of botanic detail. Scientific utility and artistic beauty must both be served.

Two hundred years later, the printmaker-technicians employed by Alecto lived up to the fine and dedicated work of their eighteenth-century predecessors. Under the meticulous eye of the master printer Edward Egerton-Williams, appointed at only 23 years of age, they proofed the newly cleaned and burnished plates through the ten years it took to edition them for publication. This magnificent final realization of Banks' dream of publication was completed under the closest supervision by Chris Humphries of the Natural

and engravers occupied with their meticulous labours. In December 1772, before the preparations for publication had properly begun, the amazed Keeper of the Ashmolean, Revd William Sheffield (Keeper 1772–95), wrote to the naturalist Gilbert White (1720–1793) of the scene there, despairing of any adequate description:

> it would be attempting to describe within the compass of a letter what can only be done in several folio volumes … His house is a perfect museum, every room contains an inestimable treasure.... First, the Armoury... [which] contains all the warlike instruments, mechanical instruments and utensils of every kind, made use of by the Indians in the South Seas from Terra del Fuego to the Indian Ocean.... The second room contains the different habits and ornaments of several Indian nations they discovered, together with the raw materials of which they are manufactured.... Here is likewise a large collection of insects, several fine specimens of bread and other fruits preserved in spirits; together with a compleat *hortus siccus* [herbarium] of all the plants collected in the course of the voyage. The number of plants is about 3000, 110 of which are new genera, and 1300 that were never seen or heard of before in Europe. What raptures they must have felt to land upon countries where every thing was new to them!...[The third

Joseph Banks' herbarium and library at 32 Soho Square, his London home until his death in 1820. Scholars and researchers came to study his botanical collections here, and Banks' chosen artists and engravers worked on creating the intended great Florilegium. This was never published in Banks' lifetime, and after his death the 743 copper plates, together with his desk and herbarium cabinets, were bequeathed to the British Museum, London. Today they are kept at the Natural History Museum, London.

History Museum, London, who initiated the project, and Joe Studholme, the director of Alecto Historical Editions. Humphries, a botanical taxonomist, biogeographer and theorist of world standing, and an avid lover of botanical art, checked every proof against the original watercolours.

The work of Banks' engravers was enhanced by Egerton-Williams' timely discovery, at the outset, that they could be printed in accurate colour *à la poupée*, a method which entails only one colour inking of the entire plate. Involving the application of all the colours required with small twists of cloth (the *poupée* or 'dolly'), it was a procedure that was invented in the late seventeenth century by the Dutch printmaker Johannes Teyler (1648–*c.* 1709), although Banks appears not to have been aware of the technique.

Why, by the end of the 1780s, did Banks seem to have abandoned the idea of publication? There seems to be no single answer to the question. For throughout that decade, Banks had been intent on proceeding with this scientific

task, if also growing increasingly weary of the responsibility. At enormous cost, 743 plates had been engraved; Solander's edited notes on the collections were nearly ready for publication – only those for New Holland (Australia) were incomplete. However, a number of extraneous circumstances may have contributed to the failure to publish. In 1782 Daniel Solander suffered a stroke while working at the house in Soho Square and died soon after. Banks was deeply upset: his friend had been at the heart of the *Endeavour* publication project. Two years later, still grieving, he wrote to his friend, the Swedish agriculturalist Johan Alströmer: 'This too early loss of a friend I loved during my more mature years, and who I shall always miss, forces me to draw a veil over his passing immediately I cease to speak of it. I can never think of it without feeling such acute pain.'

Even so, Banks at this stage still intended to publish: his letter to Alströmer also states, optimistically: 'As all the descriptions were made when the plants were fresh, little

The herbarium sheet of Banksia serrata, or saw banksia (on the left), shown with John Frederick Miller's painting, derived from Parkinson's unfinished drawing; see Pl. 78, p. 169. The genus, named in Banks' honour, comprises around 170 species endemic to Australia (only one occurs more widely, in New Guinea, with some fossils in New Zealand). Banksia serrata is naturally adapted to withstand bushfires.

remains but to refine those Drawings which are not quite complete, and to add synonyms from books which we did not take with us to sea, or which have since then been published. In a few months such minor additions should be made, if only the engravers can put the final touches to it.'[9] The less sentimental business of costs may have played a major part: Banks was contemplating an enormous expense in the printing and binding, and his own finances had been badly affected by the economic consequences of the American War of Independence, arrears in rent from his estates and the trading effects of a general depression.

In all this time, Banks had also become increasingly burdened by public duties, including onerous responsibilities for the King at Kew, his at times embattled Presidency of the Royal Society, his trusteeship of the British Museum and his critical contributions (often financial) to countless scientific ventures. He was heavily engaged, of course, in the running of his estates in Lincolnshire, which involved ambitious programmes of agricultural improvement and experimentation, and in his horticultural activities at his house, Spring Grove, at Isleworth. And he led a vigorous

private life, animated by energetic appetites, a love of company and a taste for good food and wine.

He knew, moreover, that the practical aim of publication – the dissemination of original information – had to some extent been achieved: scholars in natural philosophy from all over Europe had been welcome to study at Soho Square, and there had been proofs taken from the plates which were available for scholarly inspection, and perhaps as many as three sets were printed. Banks might well have felt that he had already fulfilled his obligation to science. Many years after their accession to the British Museum in 1827, duplicate herbarium specimens in the Banksian collection were distributed to botanical institutions all over the world, including nearly 600 each to New Zealand and Australia.

The world, however, had been deprived of a major work of botanical art. The copper plates, boxed and wrapped in protective paper, passed, in accord with Banks' will, to the British Museum (later the British Museum (Natural History), which also acquired Banks' herbarium and library), where they were stored untouched for decades. Through the nineteenth century various proposals were made for possible publication or part publication, but the Museum procrastinated, deferred and postponed, and nothing was done. In 1905 James Britten, acting for the Trustees, edited a monochrome *Illustrations of Australian Plants*, in which the plates were lithographically transferred from a set of the original black proofs, and Solander's Latin descriptions brought up to date. Fine a volume as it might be, it could not properly represent the finesse and beauty of the originals. Nor could the high-quality gravure printing and de luxe binding of the inaccurately titled *Captain Cook's Florilegium*, projected as an anniversary volume in 1968, and published, after long delay, by the Royal College of Art in 1973.

It was not until 1990 that the definitive Alecto/British Museum (Natural History) *Banks' Florilegium* finally revealed the full splendour of Banks', Solander's and Parkinson's achievement, over two hundred years after its projected publication. What was initially intended to be a selection of the engravings became a definitive publication of the entire collection, and under Studholme's direction what might have been monochrome black was printed from the original plates, as described above, in full colour. Announced as being in 34 Parts, it finally comprised 35, each housed, with perfect appropriateness, in a Solander box. The Supplementary Part contained prints of the five plates that were lost during the protracted publication of *Captain Cook's Florilegium* and were recreated in perfect similitude by two banknote engravers at the Bank of England, working from the original eighteenth-century proofs.

Banks' Florilegium – a title not used by Banks, but adopted for its twentieth-century publication – was intended in the first place as a major contribution to science: a presentation of previously unknown flora from many locations, unprecedented in its scale; the authoritative historical basis of a new taxonomy; the initiation of the publication of Australasian botany. For the modern viewer, however, it constitutes, above all, a work of outstanding graphic achievement and a radiant revelation of natural beauty in its infinite variety and particularity. We are accustomed to the idea of Science as a collaborative endeavour over space and time. The *Florilegium* is itself just such an achievement in Art: it is a major work, in which Enlightenment science and art is fused with ambitious modern printmaking technique and high production values. At the centre of that achievement, remarkably, is the effective collaboration, over two hundred years, of three remarkable young men, each in their twenties at the crucial moment of their contribution: Joseph Banks, Sydney Parkinson, and, finally, Alecto's Edward Egerton-Williams.

1. Letter from Banks to Johan Alströmer, 16 November 1784 (Chambers: *Select Letters* 23, p. 78).
2. For an account of Solander's development of this system, see Isabelle Charmantier and Staffan Müller-Wille, 'Carl Linnaeus's botanical paper slips 1767–1773', *Intellectual History Review*, 24.2, 2014, pp. 215–38.
3. Letter from Banks to Johan Alströmer, 1784 (Chambers: *Select Letters* 23, p. 78).
4. Sydney Parkinson's *A Journal of a Voyage to the South Seas* was first published by his illiterate brother Stanfield, in 1773, after it was lent to him by Banks on the understanding that it would not be published. It contained an introduction traducing Banks on the grounds that he had, among other things, failed to honour Sydney's will. The matter was finally settled, and a corrected version published 1784. Stanfield died, soon after his altercation with Banks, in a lunatic asylum.
5. For an account of Georg Dionysius Ehret, and of other botanical artists of the period, see Blunt, 1950.
6. Quoted in Smith, 1960.
7. Banks' interest in collection, identification and taxonomy did not preclude, however, the occasional insight into a broader view of things botanical. Remarks in his journal (20 January 1769) after landing at St Vincent's Bay in Tierra del Fuego, hint at the crucial evolutionary concept of geobiology, theoretically developed a century later by Alfred Russel Wallace: 'Of Plants here are many species and those truly the most extrordinary I can imagine, in stature and appearance they agree a good deal with the Europaean ones only in general are less specious, white flowers being much more common among them than any other colours. But to speak of them botanicaly, probably No botanist has ever enjoyd more pleasure in the contemplation of his Favourite pursuit than Dr Solander and myself among these plants; we have not yet examind many of them, but what we have have turnd out in general so intirely different from any before describd that we are never tird with wondering at the infinite variety of Creation, and admiring the infinite care with which providence has multiplied his productions suiting them no doubt to the various climates for which they were designd.'
8. Sheffield's letter is quoted in full in O'Brian, 1987, p. 168.
9. Letter from Banks to Johan Alströmer, 1784 (*Select Letters* 23, pp. 79–80).

The Modern Printing of the Florilegium

JOE STUDHOLME

But for a chance visit by a young botanist during the early years of the Second World War, the plates for Banks' Florilegium might have been lost forever. Returning to his old haunts in the British Museum (Natural History) in South Kensington while on a short leave from the RAF, William Stearn, according to his own account – which he often repeated but is now strongly doubted – was horrified to find, nestling under a tarpaulin in one of the basement corridors, all 743 of the original eighteenth-century copper-plate engravings, destined, with other material from the Museum's collections, to be sent off the next day to support the war effort. It was only his urgent pleas, he said, that saved them from being smelted for their metal content.[1] In retrospect this story, although widely circulated, seems improbable.

Over twenty years later, in 1963, Stearn, by then a senior scientific officer in the Botany Department, decided to test the quality of the engravings and the state of the plates by having some proofs taken in the printmaking department at the Royal College of Art nearby. They were found to be in much better shape than had been expected, and 30 plates, chosen for artistic rather than botanical reasons, were selected to be printed in black at the College for publication, the first impressions taken from any of these plates since the printers' proofs taken by the engravers when they had completed the plates in the eighteenth century.[2]

The whole exercise took a long time, and it was not until 1973 that the elegantly produced but misleadingly named *Captain Cook's Florilegium* finally appeared from the College's Lion & Unicorn Press, with introductory texts by Stearn and Wilfrid Blunt. During the ten-year production process five of the plates were lost.[3]

A perfect colour print of Xylomelum pyriforme *(Pl. 79, p. 172) being pulled off the rolling press. The original copper plate has been chromium-plated to protect it.*

When Stearn first initiated his experiments, the fledgling Editions Alecto, which had been founded the previous year by a group of university friends to print and publish original prints by contemporary painters and sculptors, had close connections with tutors and students working at the Royal College of Art. We saw the early proofs and were immediately enthused with the idea of printing and publishing the eighteenth-century plates in colour for the first time. Perhaps unsurprisingly, considering our youth and inexperience, our proposal was politely turned down, and another fifteen years elapsed before the idea was revived in 1978.

By then Editions Alecto, in addition to their contemporary publications, had diversified into producing new editions from nineteenth-century historical plates under the Alecto Historical Editions imprint, and while we were on a visit to the Natural History Museum to research a new project, botanist Dr Chris Humphries, who subsequently became the Botanical Editor of the publication, suggested to us that we might look again at the plates for Banks' Florilegium. There they still were, nearly a ton of finest copper, stored on the bottom shelf of a cupboard in the Botany Library, still encased in their original eighteenth-century wrappers and – with the exception of a very limited number of proofs, taken by the engravers in the eighteenth century – still unpublished.[4] This time our initial proposal to the Museum, to publish perhaps 300 of the plates in black in an edition of 150, with a smaller edition hand-coloured, was received more sympathetically, and we were lent five plates to carry out some proofing experiments.

Almost immediately an event occurred that might have killed the project stone dead. On the night of 5/6 December 1978 the company's studios at 27 Kelso Place in South Kensington were burnt down and all production came to an abrupt halt. The plates, thankfully, were safely retrieved.

One of the people retained to sort out the mess from the fire was 23-year-old Edward Egerton-Williams, who had joined the company the previous year straight from the Winchester College of Art. Edward had gained some experience of printing from historical plates from a previous Alecto publication, and he was given some of the Florilegium plates to try out, working by himself in a temporary studio. Printing in black proved relatively easy, but hand-colouring was a failure. It took an age to colour each print and much of the fine detail in the plate was obliterated by the watercolour paint.

Undeterred, Egerton-Williams began experimenting with a variant of the *à la poupée* technique, invented in the seventeenth century by the Dutch printer Johannes Teyler (1648–*c*. 1709). In this process, the individual colours in the print are worked into the plate with a twist of cloth (the *poupée* or 'dolly'). When all the lines are filled, and the white areas wiped clean, the inked-up plate, with a sheet of dampened paper placed over it, is laid on the press and cushioned by tissue and blankets to even out the pressure on its passage through the rollers.

The giant wheel of the rolling press is turned and the pressure of the steel cylinders forces the damp paper into the plate. When it emerges on the other side of the press, the paper is peeled off like a transfer to reveal a perfect colour print. Any ink left in the plate is wiped clean and the whole process of inking up begins again for the next impression. It is a laborious process, but it produces beautifully sharp images and, importantly, ensures that every detail from the engraved plate is retained.

Egerton-Williams' first *à la poupée* prints were a revelation, and we took the proofs to the Prints and Drawings Department at the British Museum to seek the approval of the Deputy Keeper Paul Hulton, then the doyen of natural history illustration. Hulton's reaction was immediate: 'If Joseph Banks was looking at these proofs, this is the way he would have had them done.' And without at the time fully appreciating the commitment of time and money, the decision was taken to print all 738 of the surviving plates in full colour.

On 6 October 1979 an agreement was signed with the British Museum (Natural History) for an edition of 100, to be published in 34 Parts, with 10 sets *hors commerce* for the publishers and an additional 6 sets to be used for exhibition purposes and divided between the printers. Egerton-Willliams was appointed Master Printer, space for a stock room and studio, with a good north light, were taken at 15 Appold Street, opposite the railway lines leading out of Broad Street station in the City of London, and work started in earnest.

Copper-plate line-engraving is one of the most demanding and skilful of printmaking techniques. The engraver cuts directly into the polished metal with a set of burins, engraving tools of different sizes and thickness, building up a network of lines to create the finished image. It requires a steady hand and sharp eyes. The illustrations in the majority of eighteenth-century natural history books were usually coloured with water-based pigments, painted on to each sheet by hand after it was printed, and the knowledge that the plates were going to be hand-coloured later allowed the engraver to cut fewer lines. The Florilegium plates are unique because Banks insisted that every botanical detail

OPPOSITE Inks for each plate were made up from pure ground pigment and boiled linseed; often ten or more were applied to an individual print. The white twists are the poupées *(dollies), made of scrim (strong, coarse cotton), used for working the ink into the incised copper. ABOVE: Inking up a plate in the Alecto studio at 15 Appold Street. The specially mixed inks are in tubes and an offset print is used as a colour guide for the printer.*

should be cut into the plate, so that even when printed in black the impressions could be used for scientific study. Every turn of a leaf or twist of a stem is determined by the width and depth of the engraved line.[5]

Although the plates themselves were miraculously free from damage, they still needed careful preparation. Old ink from the engravers' eighteenth-century proofs had set rock hard in the incised lines and had to be brushed out with repeated applications of solvents, specially prepared by chemists at ICI. Damage by 'foul-biting', caused by acid absorbed over 200 years leaching out of the eighteenth-century paper wrappers, had to be carefully smoothed and burnished out with specially made chrome-coated tools to prevent 'foxing' in the white areas of the print. Once the perfect printing surface had been recovered, it had to be protected from the risk of damage caused by repeated inkings. Steel-plating was not strong enough, nor was commercial chrome-plating; pure chromium, the quality used in hydraulic presses (and for burnishing tools), had to be applied. Only then could proofing begin.

To ensure that each coloured print was botanically accurate, the colours were agreed by the Botanical Editor,

Chris Humphries, working with Egerton-Williams from the original watercolour paintings in the Botany Library at the Natural History Museum. Once the colours had been agreed, sometimes up to 17 for a particular plate, they were matched to one of the Royal Horticultural Society's colour charts, the standard reference for plant colours, so that the inks could be prepared in the studio in Appold Street. The inks for each plate were made up individually from boiled linseed oil and pure pigment, ground out with a 'muller' to achieve a smooth texture. Stage proofs were taken back and forth to South Kensington, a 10-mile (16-km) round trip for Egerton-Williams, until a finished image was agreed by Dr Humphries and signed and dated as the *bon à tirer* ('good to pull') master print, BAT for short.

To achieve colour consistency in each plate, enough ink for the run of 116 prints, with some extra to allow for spoilage, was made up for each colour and put in tubes, with the 'recipe' inscribed on its side. Printing *à la poupee* is in essence a very sophisticated exercise in 'printing by numbers' and, as a guide, the printer was provided with an offset print, marked up with the correct colour for each area of the plate. Depending on the range and complexity of the colours, the printing for

Master Printer Edward Egerton-Williams inking up a plate. The time taken to complete a single inking varied from thirty minutes to two hours. Once a print had been pulled, any remaining ink was cleaned from the plate, and the whole process of inking up the various colours started all over again.

each impression could take a mere thirty minutes, or go so slowly that only three prints could be made in one day. The average time per print was just under one hour. In the interests of absolute uniformity, each complete print run was handled by one printer.

Every evening, that day's production was stacked between boards and specially made 800gsm blotting paper, and weighed down with 25-kg (55-lb) weights to dry and flatten the prints, a process repeated for the next seven days. The prints were then inspected for quality and imperfect impressions were rejected. The spoilage rate was high, sometimes as much as 20 per cent.

Most plates required small botanical details – the tips of stamens or the gradation of colours on a flower, for example – to be painted in by hand afterwards by artists using sable brushes. Each sheet was then inspected again and embossed with the 'chops' (seals) of the two publishers, BM (NH) and

AHE, and the Welsh dragon of the Egerton-Williams Studio. The Alecto Plate and Edition number, together with the initials of the printer responsible for that particular print, were recorded in pencil and the prints were inserted in window mounts before being placed in one of the Solander boxes in which each of the Parts are presented.[6]

On the face of the mount, the names of the artist(s) and engraver, the modern and the unpublished manuscript (Banksian or Solanderian) name of the plant, and the place and date of collection of the specimen illustrated are printed in letterpress. The typography for the mounts, as well as for the title, index and colophon sheets, was designed by Ian Mortimer and set and printed on his hand presses at I. M. Imprimit in London. The typefaces are Founder's Caslon Old Face and Old Face Open.

Maintaining the standard of materials and workmanship during the long production period was fraught with difficulties. The 300gsm mould-made paper, specially made with an AHE watermark at St Cuthbert's Mill in Somerset, was ordered in 1-ton makings. In order to achieve absolute precision, the paper was only lightly damped and the ink left thick; this required very high pressure on the press-cylinders, which sometimes cracked under the strain and had to be replaced. The supply of sable from Kashmir for the brushes was interrupted by war, as was that of lapis lazuli from Afghanistan for the cerulean blue. The chrome-plating firm went bankrupt (mercifully to be restarted).

By November 1989 all 738 of the plates had been printed and sent out to subscribers, two Parts issued at a time, with each subscriber required to commit to pay for the succeeding Part to make sure that they continued their subscription. Over the ten years of the publication only a handful of the 100 subscribers dropped out.

But the publication was not yet finished. The five plates lost during the publication of *Captain Cook's Florilegium* were still missing, and to complete Banks' 'grand design' we commissioned two of the Bank of England banknote engravers to cut new plates, working from the black eighteenth-century proofs. The missing illustrations were printed and published as Part 35. As a final *bonne bouche* each subscriber received a comprehensive catalogue of the publication, including seven bound-in plates taken from one of four complete sets of 743 plates printed in sepia, so that each catalogue is unique, containing seven different images.

Over ten years, the twenty-strong team in the Egerton-Williams Studio produced over 86,000 perfect colour prints. It was an astonishing achievement and would not have been possible without the Master Printer's dedication, technical skill and attention to detail.

Looking back from today, when so many things are an uneasy compromise between what is desirable and what is affordable, we can only marvel at the almost obsessive pursuit of excellence which illuminates everything that Joseph Banks put his hand to. In particular the copper-plate line-engravings for his Florilegium are unequalled, both for the scientific detail of the plants which they portray and for the technical brilliance of the engravings themselves.

In the early stages of the publication a distinguished Professor Emeritus of Botany at a Dutch university, comparing *Banks' Florilegium* with the university's many acquisitions of treasures from the Orient, remarked that, for him, it represented a supreme example of eighteenth-century European civilization, a unique marriage of art and science from the Age of Enlightenment.[7] I can think of no higher compliment.

Stored in the Natural History Museum, where they were transferred after his death in Banks' own cabinets from

Soho Square, are the dried specimens of the plants from the *Endeavour* voyage, annotated by Joseph Banks and Daniel Solander and marked with the locations and dates of their collection – often to the actual day. In the library are the other eighteenth-century records: the watercolours drawn by Sydney Parkinson on the voyage and by the five artists employed by Banks to work up Parkinson's unfinished field sketches into finished plant portraits; the original copper plates together with the black proofs taken by the engravers; and, perhaps most immediate of all, the printed volumes of Banks' and Cook's journals in which one can read what the explorers were doing when each specimen was collected.[8] The colour prints from the Alecto edition complete the record.

It has been a great privilege for all of us who have been involved in the production of *Banks' Florilegium* to have had such a direct connection, through the eighteenth-century material, with one of the truly great men of the Enlightenment. We very much hope that the discriminating Sir Joseph Banks would have approved of the final publication, even though we missed his publishing deadline by over two hundred years.

1. Conversation with the author, October 1979.

2. It is known that the engravers took about three sets of black ink impressions in the eighteenth century and that proofs of particular plates were sent by Banks to other botanists for private use. A group of 28 plates has been recorded as forming a folio volume in the Akademie der Wissenschaften, Berlin. In the late nineteenth century the Trustees of the British Museum authorized the New Zealand Government to obtain proof sets of the engravings of the New Zealand plants. The intention was to reproduce them in a reduced form as illustrations to a botanical work by Thomas Kirk, but Kirk died in 1897 and the project was abandoned. Between 1900 and 1905 photolithographic reproductions of the Australian plants were published by order of the Trustees under the title *Illustrations of Australian Plants Collected in 1770, with determinations by James Britten FLS*.

3. The lost plates were:
Plate 739: *Melaleuca armillaris* (Solander ex Gaerlner), Smith, *Trans. Linn. Soc. Lond.* 33 : 277 (1797) [Banksian name: *Metrosideros armillaris*]
Plate 740: *Helichrysum bracteatum* (Ventenat), Andrews, *Bot. repos* 6: t. 428 (vide t. 375) (1805) [Banksian name: *Xeranthemum aureum*]
Plate 741: *Banksia ericifolia*, Linnaeus f., *Suppl. Pl.*: 127 (1782) [Banksian name: *Leucadendrum ericaefolium*]
Plate 742: *Elatostema rugosum*, Cunningham, *Ann. Nat. Hist.* 1: 215 (1838) [Banksian name: *Dorstenia rugosa*]
Plate 743: *Drosera uniflora*, Wildenow, *Enum. Pl.*: 340 (1809) [Banksian name: [*Drosera uniflora*]

4. See note 2 above.

5. Although it is known that Banks had contacts with French colour printers, we found no documentary evidence to indicate whether or not he intended to produce his Florilegium in monochrome or colour. It is possible that the greatly increased cost of printing in colour may have been one of the reasons he delayed publication, see p. 303.

6. Dustproof boxes designed by Daniel Solander to store prints and specimens. We found a contemporary pamphlet with construction details.

7. Personal communication.

8. Banks' original *Endeavour* journal is kept at the State Library of New South Wales, Sydney. James Cook's original *Endeavour* journal is kept at the National Library of Australia, Canberra. Editions are listed in the Bibliography.

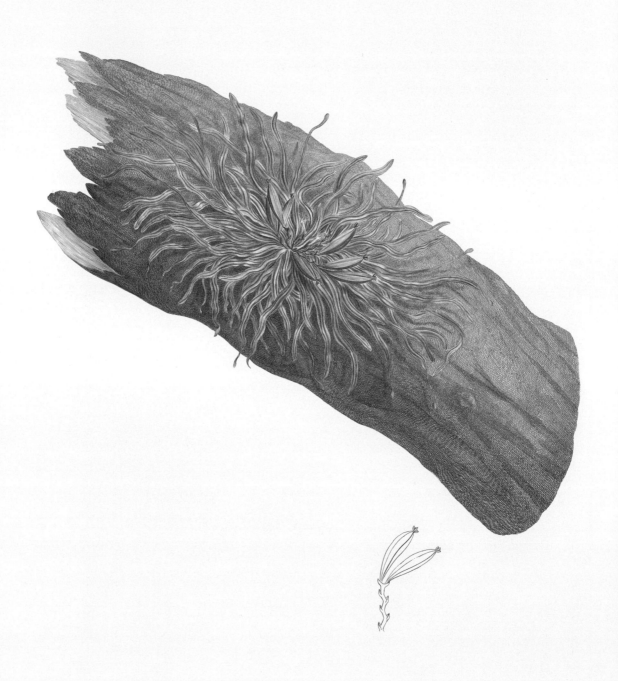

CONCORDANCE

This concordance indicates the numbering in the present edition (JBF), the Alecto Historical Editions set of prints, *Banks' Florilegium* (BF), and the catalogue compiled in 1984 and 1987 by Judith Diment et al. (see Bibliography), followed by the initials of artists and engravers listed here. Additional plates are indicated by page number (e.g., p. 312).

B	BANNERMAN
RB	ROBERT BLYTH
TB	THOMAS BURGIS
FC	FRANCIS CHESHAM
JC	JOHN CLEVELEY
D	VAN DRAZOWA
JG	JABEZ GOLDAR
JL	JOHN LEE
DM	DANIEL MACKENZIE
M	JEAN-BAPTISTE MICHELL
JM	JAMES MILLER
JFM	JOHN FREDERICK MILLER
TM	THOMAS MORRIS
FPN	FREDERICK POLYDORE NODDER
SP	SYDNEY PARKINSON
JR	JOHN ROBERTS
TS	THOMAS SCRATCHLEY
GS	GERARD SIBELIUS
GSM	GABRIEL SMITH
WS	WILLIAM SMITH
WT	WILLIAM TRINGHAM
EW	EDWARD WALKER
CW	CHARLES WHITE

JBF	BF	DIMENT	ARTIST	ENGRAVER
106	1	A1/1	FPN	GS
	2	A1/2	FPN	DM
89	3	A1/3	FPN	DM
	4	A1/4	FPN	GS
	5	A1/5	FPN	GS
140	6	A1/8	FPN	DM
	7	A1/9a	FPN	DM
	8	A1/9b	FPN	DM
	9	A1/10	FPN	DM
	10	A1/11	FPN	DM
	11	A1/12	FPN	DM
101	12	A1/13	FPN	GS
96	13	A1/14	JC	CW
	14	A1/15	JFM	GSM
	15	A1/16	FPN	RB
107	16	A1/17	FPN	GS
	17	A1/18	FPN	DM
109	18	A1/19	FPN	GS
	19	A1/20	FPN	GS
	20	A1/21	FPN	GS
	21	A1/22	?	CW
	22	A1/23	FPN	GSM
99	23	A1/24	FPN	GS
	24	A1/25	FPN	DM
	25	A1/27	JM	JG
	26	A1/28	FPN	GS
	27	A1/32	JFM	CW
	28	A1/33	JM	EW
	29	A1/34	JM	GSM
	30	A1/35	JC	GSM
	31	A1/36	FPN	GS
	32	A1/37	FPN	GS
	33	A1/38	FPN	GS
81	34	A1/39	JM	GSM
	35	A1/40	JFM	GSM
	36	A1/41	JC	GSM
	37	A1/42	FPN	GS
	38	A1/43	FPN	GS
82	39	A1/45	FPN	DM
	40	A1/46	FPN	GS
	41	A1/47	?	DM
	42	A1/48	JC	GS
	43	A1/49	JM	CW
110	44	A1/50	JFM	GS
	45	A1/51	JFM	CW
111	46	A1/52	JM	DM
112	47	A1/53	JFM	GSM
	48	A1/54	FPN	DM
113	49	A1/55	JC	GS
	50	A2/57	FPN	GS
114	51	A2/58	FPN	DM
	52	A2/59	FPN	DM
	53	A2/60	FPN	DM
83	54	A2/61	FPN	RB
115	55	A2/62	FPN	DM
116	56	A2/63	FPN	DM
	57	A2/64	FPN	RB
	58	A2/66	FPN	RB
	59	A2/67	FPN	GS
	60	A2/68	FPN	GS
117	61	A2/69	FPN	GS
	62	A2/70	FPN	GS
	63	A2/72	FPN	GS
	64	A2/73	FPN	DM
	65	A2/74	FPN	DM
	66	A2/74a	FPN	RB
	67	A2/75	FPN	RB
	68	A2/76	FPN	GS
	69	A2/77	FPN	RB
	70	A2/81	FPN	RB
	71	A2/82	FPN	RB
	72	A2/83	FPN	DM
118	73	A2/84	FPN	DM
	74	A2/85	FPN	DM
102	75	A2/86	FPN	GS
119	76	A2/87	FPN	GS
	77	A2/88	FPN	DM
	78	A2/89	FPN	GS
	79	A2/90	FPN	DM
120	80	A2/91	FPN	RB
	81	A2/92	FPN	RB
	82	A2/93	FPN	DM
124	83	A2/94	FPN	DM
103	84	A2/95	FPN	GS
	85	A2/96	?	GS
	86	A2/97	FPN	DM
	87	A2/99	FPN	FPN
	88	A2/100	FPN	DM
	89	A2/101	FPN	GS
	90	A2/102	FPN	GS
90	91	A2/103	FPN	DM
	92	A2/104	FPN	FPN
	93	A2/105	FPN	FPN
p. 1	94	A2/106	FPN	FPN
87	95	A2/107	FPN	FPN
125	96	A2/108	FPN	GS
126	97	A3/109	JC	GS
	98	A3/110	JFM	GS
	99	A3/111	JC	GS
88	100	A3/113	JC	GS
	101	A3/115	JFM	GS
	102	A3/117	?	DM
	103	A3/118	FPN	RB
	104	A3/120	FPN	GS
132	105	A3/121	?	DM
	106	A3/122	FPN	GS
	107	A3/123	JFM	JG
	108	A3/124	FPN	GS
	109	A3/125	FPN	GS
	110	A3/126	FPN	GS
	111	A3/127	FPN	DM
	112	A3/128	FPN	GS
	113	A3/129	FPN	GS
133	114	A3/130	FPN	GS
	115	A3/131	FPN	GS
134	116	A3/132	FPN	GS
	117	A3/133	FPN	GS
	118	A3/135	FPN	GS
	119	A3/137	FPN	DM
	120	A3/138	FPN	RB
95	121	A3/139	FPN	RB
	122	A3/140	FPN	DM
	123	A3/141	FPN	DM
	124	A3/142	FPN	DM
139	125	A3/143	FPN	GS
	126	A3/144	FPN	RB
138	127	A3/145	FPN	DM
100	128	A3/146	FPN	RB
	129	A3/148a	JM	WT
	130	A3/148b	JFM	WT
	131	A3/149	JFM	D
	132	A3/150	?	WT
	133	A3/151	FPN	GSM
93	134	A3/153	FPN	DM
	135	A3/156	FPN	DM
	136	A3/157	JM	DM
	137	A3/158	JC	GS
	138	A3/159	JFM	GS
	139	A3/160	JM	JG
	140	A3/161	JFM	DM
77	141	A3/162	JFM	GSM
	142	A3/163	JFM	DM
	143	A3/164	?	GSM
	144	A4/165	?	DM
	145	A4/166	JM	WT
	146	A4/167	JM	JL
135	147	A4/168	JM	GS
	148	A4/169	?	CW
	149	A4/170	JFM	CW
	150	A4/171	JM	CW
	151	A4/172	JM	D
	152	A4/173	JC	JG
	153	A4/175	JM	D
	154	A4/176	JM	GSM
	155	A4/177	JFM	GSM
	156	A4/178	?	GS
	157	A4/180	FPN	DM
	158	A4/181	FPN	GS
	159	A4/182	FPN	DM
	160	A4/183	FPN	DM
	161	A4/184	FPN	GS
	162	A4/186	FPN	DM
	163	A4/188	FPN	DM
	164	A4/189	FPN	DM
127	165	A4/190	FPN	DM
	166	A4/191	FPN	DM
92	167	A4/193	FPN	GS
	168	A4/194	FPN	GS
	169	A4/196	FPN	DM
	170	A4/197	FPN	DM
	171	A5/198	FPN	DM
	172	A5/199	FPN	DM
	173	A5/200a	FPN	DM
	174	A5/200b	FPN	DM
	175	A5/200c	FPN	DM
	176	A5/201	FPN	DM
	177	A5/202	FPN	DM
	178	A5/203	FPN	DM
	179	A5/204	FPN	GS
	180	A5/205	FPN	DM
	181	A5/206	FPN	GS
	182	A5/207a	FPN	GS
	183	A5/207b	FPN	DM
	184	A5/210	FPN	GS
	185	A5/211	FPN	GS
	186	A5/212	FPN	DM
84	187	A5/214	FPN	DM
	188	A5/216	FPN	DM
	189	A5/217	FPN	GS
	190	A5/218	JM	WT
	191	A5/219	JM	GSM
	192	A5/220	JFM	GSM
	193	A5/221	JFM	GSM
	194	A5/222	JM	DM
	195	A5/223	JC	JG
	196	A5/224	JC	DM
85	197	A5/225	JM	CW
	198	A5/226	JM	DM
	199	A5/227	JFM	JG
	200	A5/229	?	GSM
128	201	A5/232	JM	GSM
	202	A5/233	JFM	DM
	203	A5/234	JM	CW
	204	A5/235	JM	M
	205	A5/236	JFM	GS
	206	A5/237	JFM	D
	207	A5/238	JM	GSM
	208	A5/240	JM	GS
129	209	A5/241	?	FC
	210	A5/242	JFM	JG
	211	A5/243	JM	GSM
98	212	A5/244	JM	GS
	213	A5/245	JM	DM
	214	A5/246	?	GSM
	215	A5/247	?	DM
	216	A5/248	JM	GSM

JBF	BF	DIMENT	ARTIST	ENGRAVER
	217	A5/249a	JFM	GSM
	218	A5/249b	JFM	GSM
	219	A5/250	?	GSM
	220	A6/251	JFM	CW
	221	A6/252	JFM	D
	222	A6/253	JFM	GSM
104	223	A6/254	JFM	JL
	224	A6/256	JM	DM
	225	A6/257	JM	WT
97	226	A6/258	JM	DM
	227	A6/260	FPN	GS
	228	A6/261	FPN	DM
	229	A6/263	FPN	DM
	230	A6/264	FPN	DM
	231	A6/265	FPN	RB
	232	A6/268a	JFM	DM
	233	A6/268b	JFM	DM
	234	A6/268c	JFM	DM
	235	A6/269A	JFM	DM
	236	A6/269B	JFM	DM
	237	A6/270	JFM	DM
	238	A6/271a, b	JFM	DM
	239	A6/272a	JFM	DM
	240	16/272b	JFM	DM
	241	A6/273a	JFM	DM
	242	A6/273b	JFM	DM
94	243	A6/274	FPN	DM
105	244	A6/275	FPN	DM
137	245	A6/276	FPN	GS
	246	A6/277	JFM	GSM
	247	A6/278	FPN	GS
	248	A6/280	JFM	TS
	249	A6/281	JFM	TS
	250	A6/282	JFM	GSM
	251	A6/283	FPN	RB
	252	A6/284	?	WT
	253	A6/286	?	GS
136	254	A6/287	FPN	GS
	255	A6/292	FPN	RB
	256	A6/295	FPN	RB
	257	A6/296	JFM	GSM
	258	A6/297	FPN	GS
	259	A7/299a	FPN	GS
	260	A7/300	JFM	GSM
	261	A7/301	JM	GSM
	262	A7/302	JC	CW
	263	A7/303	JFM	DM
	264	A7/304	JC	GSM
	265	A7/305	JFM	EW
	266	A7/306	JFM	JL
	267	A7/307	FPN	DM
	268	A7/308	FPN	RB
	269	A7/309	JM	WS
	270	A7/310	?	WT
	271	A7/311	JFM	GS
130	272	A7/312	JFM	GSM
	273	A7/313	JM	CW
	274	A7/314	JM	GSM
79	275	A7/315	JFM	GSM
131	276	A7/316	JFM	DM
	277	A7/317	JFM	GS
	278	A7/318	?	WS
	279	A7/319	JM	WT
	280	A7/320	JFM	DM
	281	A7/321	?	DM
	282	A7/322	?	DM
	283	A7/323	JM	GSM
80	284	A7/325	?	CW
78	285	A7/326	JFM	GSM
	286	A7/327	JM	DM
	287	A7/329	JFM	TS
	288	A7/330	JM	DM
	289	A7/331	JFM	GSM
	290	A7/332	JM	GSM
121	291	A7/333	JC	DM
	292	A7/334	JM	GSM
	293	A7/335	FPN	GS
	294	A7/336	FPN	GS
	295	A7/337	FPN	DM
	296	A7/338	FPN	DM
	297	A7/339	FPN	DM
	298	A7/340	FPN	GS
	299	A7/341	FPN	DM
	300	A7/343	FPN	GS
	301	A7/344	FPN	GS
	302	A7/345	FPN	GS
	303	A7/346	FPN	GS
	304	A7/347	FPN	DM
	305	A7/348	FPN	GS
	306	A7/349	FPN	DM
	307	A7/350	FPN	DM
	308	A7/351	FPN	GS
	309	A7/352	FPN	GS
	310	A7/353	FPN	GS
	311	A7/355	FPN	DM
	312	A7/357	FPN	DM
	313	A7/363	FPN	DM
122	314	A8/366	FPN	GS
	315	A8/367	FPN	DM
	316	A8/368	FPN	GS
	317	A8/369a	FPN	DM
	318	A8/369b	FPN	GS
	319	A8/369c	SP	DM
123	320	A8/371	JFM	TS
	321	A8/371	JFM	TS
91	322	A8/372	JC	JG
	323	A8/373	JM	CW
	324	A8/374	JM	DM
86	325	A8/375	JM	EW
	326	A8/376	JFM	GS
	327	A8/377	JC	DM
	328	A8/378	JFM	GSM
	329	A8/382	JM	DM
	330	A8/385	FPN	DM
	331	A8/386	JC	DM
	332	A8/387	JFM	JG
	333	A8/388	JC	JG
108	334	A8/389	JM	GSM
	335	A8/390		JG
	336	A8/392	JFM	WT
	337	A8/393	FPN	GS
4	338	B1	SP	GS
	339	B2	SP	DM
	340	B4	SP	WT
5	341	B5	SP	GSM
6	342	B6/7	SP	CW
7	343	B8	SP	GS
	344	B11	SP	DM
	345	B12	SP	D
	346	B13	SP	GS
	347	B14	SP	GSM
	348	B15	SP	CW
	349	B16	SP	DM
	350	B17	SP	D
	351	B18	SP	D
	352	B19	SP	DM
	353	B22	SP	GSM
	354	B23	SP	GSM
8	355	B24	SP	GSM
9	356	B25	SP	GSM
10	357	B26	SP	DM
11	358	B27	SP	GSM
	359	B29	SP	D
	360	B33	SP	DM
	361	J1	FPN	GS
	362	J6	FPN	GS
	363	J13	JFM	JL
142	364	J15	JM	DM
	365	J18	JFM	DM
144	366	J21	FPN	DM
	367	J22	FPN	GS
	368	J24	JFM	GS
	369	J28	?	GSM
	370	J29	JC	DM
	371	J34	JFM	CW
146	372	J35	JFM	GSM
	373	J36	JFM	JG
143	374	J37	?	WS
145	375	J38	?	WS
	376	J40	FPN	DM
	377	J41	JM	CW
	378	J42	JFM	TM
	379	J46	JFM	GS
141	380	J47	FPN	DM
	381	J49	FPN	DM
	382	J50	FPN	GS
	383	J54	?	WS
	384	J56	JFM	GSM
	385	J57	JC	JG
	386	J58	JM	CW
	387	J59	FPN	GS
	388	J64	FPN	GS
147	389	J67	JFM	GSM
	390	J69	FPN	?
	391	M3	SP	DM
	392	M6	TB	DM
	393	M7	SP	GSM
1	394	M8	SP	GS
2	395	M9	SP	DM
	396	M11	SP	TS
	397	M12	SP	GS
3	398	M13	SP	GS
	399	M14	SP	TS
	400	M16	SP	DM
	401	M22	SP	DM
41	402	NZ1/1	FPN	GS
	403	NZ1/2	FPN	GS
	404	NZ1/3	FPN	DM
	405	NZ1/4	FPN	DM
57	406	NZ1/5	FPN	RB
	407	NZ1/6	?	DM
	408	NZ1/7	FPN	RB
	409	NZ1/8	FPN	RB
54	410	NZ1/9	FPN	GS
70	411	NZ1/10	SP	GS
	412	NZ1/11	?	DM
	413	NZ1/12	JM	CW
	414	NZ1/15	FPN	DM
	415	NZ1/16	FPN	GS
	416	NZ1/17	FPN	GS
	417	NZ1/18	FPN	RB
48	418	NZ1/19	FPN	GS
	419	NZ1/20	FPN	DM
	420	NZ1/21	FPN	DM
	421	NZ1/22	?	DM
65	422	NZ1/23	FPN	GS
43	423	NZ1/24	FPN	GS
	424	NZ1/28	JM	JG
	425	NZ1/29	JFM	WT
44	426	NZ1/31	JFM	GSM
	427	NZ1/35	JFM	GSM
	428	NZ1/36	?	GS
	429	NZ1/37	?	GS
39	430	NZ1/38	FPN	GS
	431	NZ1/39	FPN	FPN
45	432	NZ1/40	?	DM
	433	NZ1/41	FPN	GS
	434	NZ1/42	SP	GSM
	435	NZ1/43	JC	DM
	436	NZ1/44	JM	DM
	437	NZ1/45	SP	DM
	438	NZ1/46	JM	DM
	439	NZ1/47	JFM	GSM
	440	NZ1/48	FPN	GS
59	441	NZ1/49	?	GS
	442	NZ1/50	FPN	DM
	443	NZ1/51	FPN	GS
	444	NZ1/55	FPN	DM
56	445	NZ1/56	?	GSM
	446	NZ1/57	?	DM
	447	NZ1/58	?	GS
	448	NZ1/59	SP	WT
	449	NZ1/60	SP	GSM
	450	NZ1/61	SP	GSM
	451	NZ1/62	JC	JG
46	452	NZ1/63	JM	GSM
63	453	NZ2/64a	FPN	GS
	454	NZ2/67	SP	GS
	455	NZ2/68	SP	D
	456	NZ2/69	SP	D
67	457	NZ2/70	JFM	GS
	458	NZ2/71	JFM	GSM
	459	NZ2/72	JFM	JG
	460	NZ2/73	JM	JG
40	461	NZ2/74	JFM	GSM
	462	NZ2/75	JM	GSM
	463	NZ2/76	JM	D
	464	NZ2/77	FPN	FPN
	465	NZ2/78	JFM	GSM
53	466	NZ2/79	JFM	GSM
47	467	NZ2/80	FPN	DM
	468	NZ2/81	FPN	GS
68	469	NZ2/83	FPN	GS
	470	NZ2/84	FPN	DM
	471	NZ2/85	?	DM
	472	NZ2/86	FPN	DM
	473	NZ2/87	FPN	GS
	474	NZ2/88	FPN	DM
	475	NZ2/89	SP	WT
	476	NZ2/90	SP	GS
60	477	NZ2/91	FPN	DM
	478	NZ2/92	FPN	GS
58	479	NZ2/93	FPN	GS
	480	NZ2/94	FPN	GS

JBF	BF	DIMENT	ARTIST	ENGRAVER
	481	NZ2/95	FPN	DM
	482	NZ2/96	FPN	DM
	483	NZ2/97	FPN	GS
	484	NZ2/98	FPN	GS
	485	NZ2/101	FPN	GS
	486	NZ2/102	FPN	DM
42	487	NZ2/103	FPN	GS
49	488	NZ2/104	FPN	DM
	489	NZ2/105	FPN	GS
	490	NZ2/106	FPN	GS
	491	NZ2/107	FPN	DM
	492	NZ2/108	FPN	DM
	493	NZ2/109	FPN	DM
	494	NZ2/110	FPN	DM
72	495	NZ2/111	FPN	GS
	496	NZ3/112	FPN	DM
	497	NZ3/113b	FPN	DM
	498	NZ3/114	FPN	DM
	499	NZ3/115a	JM	WT
	500	NZ3/116	FPN	DM
	501	NZ3/117	JM	WT
	502	NZ3/118	JM	GSM
	503	NZ3/119	?	DM
	504	NZ3/120	JM	WT
	505	NZ3/121	JM	DM
	506	NZ3/122	FPN	FPN
	507	NZ3/123	SP	GS
	508	NZ3/124	JM	DM
	509	NZ3/126a	JFM	DM
	510	NZ3/125	JM	WS
	511	NZ3/126	?	DM
66	512	NZ3/128	JFM	WT
	513	NZ3/128a	JM	WT
	514	NZ3/129	?	TS
	515	NZ3/130	JM	CW
	516	NZ3/131	SP	GSM
69	517	NZ3/132	JFM	WT
	518	NZ3/134	SP	WT
	519	NZ3/135	SP	M
73	520	NZ3/136	SP	DM
	521	NZ3/137	SP	DM
	522	NZ3/138	?	DM
62	523	NZ3/139	FPN	GS
	524	NZ3/140	FPN	GS
51	525	NZ3/141	FPN	DM
	526	NZ/142a	SP	WT
74	527	NZ3/142b	SP	JL
	528	NZ3/143	SP	GSM
	529	NZ3/144	SP	B
	530	NZ3/145	JM	DM
	531	NZ3/146	FPN	GS
75	532	NZ3/147	FPN	GS
	533	NZ3/148	JFM	DM
	534	NZ/149	JC	EW
	535	NZ3/150	?	DM
	536	NZ3/151	SP	TS
	537	NZ3/152	?	DM
	538	NZ3/153	JM	GS
	539	NZ3/154	?	RB
52	540	NZ3/155	SP	GSM
	541	NZ3/156	SP	GSM
	542	NZ3/157	SP	GSM
	543	NZ3/158	SP	M
	544	NZ3/159	SP	M
	545	NZ3/160	JM	DM
	546	NZ3/162	JFM	DM
61	547	NZ3/163	FPN	DM
	548	NZ3/165	FPN	GS
	549	NZ3/166	?	DM
76	550	NZ3/168	FPN	GS
	551	NZ4/169	FPN	GS
	552	NZ4/172	FPN	DM
	553	NZ4/173	FPN	GS
	554	NZ4/174	FPN	DM
	555	NZ4/175	FPN	GS
	556	NZ4/178	FPN	DM
71	557	NZ4/180	?	FPN
	558	NZ4/184	JFM	GSM
	559	NZ4/185	JC	JG
	560	NZ4/188	JM	WT
	561	NZ4/189	FPN	DM
	562	NZ4/190	FPN	GS
55	563	NZ4/192	FPN	GS
	564	NZ4/194	JFM	GSM
	565	NZ4/199	JFM	GSM
	566	NZ4/195	JFM	GS
	567	NZ4/196	?	GS
	568	NZ4/197	JFM	GS

JBF	BF	DIMENT	ARTIST	ENGRAVER
	569	NZ4/198	JFM	GS
	570	NZ4/200	JFM	GSM
	571	NZ4/201	JFM	GS
	572	NZ4/202	JFM	DM
	573	NZ4/203	JFM	DM
	574	NZ4/204	JFM	GS
	575	NZ4/205	JFM	GS
	576	NZ4/206	JFM	GSM
	577	NZ4/208	JFM	GSM
64	578	NZ4/209	JFM	GS
	579	NZ4/210	JFM	DM
	580	NZ4/211	?	GSM
	581	NZ4/212	JFM	DM
	582	NZ4/213	JFM	GS
	583	NZ4/214	JFM	GS
	584	NZ4/215	JFM	GSM
	585	S11/2	SP	DM
22	586	S11/3	SP	GS
	587	S11/5	SP	GS
	588	S11/7	SP	DM
	589	S11/8	SP	GS
	590	S11/10	SP	GS
23	591	S11/12	SP	DM
	592	S11/13	SP	GSM
	593	S11/14	SP	GS
	594	S11/17	SP	GS
20	595	S11/18	SP	DM
	596	S11/20	SP	GSM
28	597	S11/21	SP	DM
24	598	S11/22	SP	DM
	599	S11/23	SP	CW
	600	S11/25	SP	DM
25	601	S11/26	SP	GS
	602	S11/27	SP	GSM
	603	S11/28	SP	DM
	604	S11/29	SP	GSM
	605	S11/30	SP	GS
26	606	S11/34	SP	DM
	607	S11/35	SP	DM
27	608	S11/36	SP	GSM
	609	S11/38	SP	CW
	610	S11/39	SP	WS
	611	S11/40	SP	JL
	612	S11/41	SP	JL
	613	S11/44	SP	GS
	614	S11/45	SP	WT
31	615	S11/46	SP	DM
	616	S11/47	SP	DM
	617	S11/48	SP	CW
	618	S11/49	SP	GS
	619	S11/50	SP	GSM
	620	S11/51	SP	GS
	621	S11/52	SP	CW
32	622	S11/53	SP	GS
	623	S11/56	SP	GS
33	624	S11/57	SP	GSM
	625	S12/1	SP	DM
	626	S12/2	SP	JL
34	627	S12/3	SP	GSM
	628	S12/4	SP	WT
	629	S12/5	SP	TS
	630	S12/6	SP	M
	631	S12/7b	SP	CW
	632	S12/8	SP	GSM
30	633	S12/9	SP	GSM
29	634	S12/10	SP	JR
	635	S12/11	SP	GSM
	636	S12/12	SP	GSM
	637	S12/13	SP	DM
	638	S12/14	SP	GS
	639	S12/15	SP	GS
	640	S12/16	SP	GSM
	641	S12/17	SP	DM
35	642	S12/18	SP	M
	643	S12/19	SP	M
	644	S12/20	SP	CW
	645	S12/21	SP	GSM
	646	S12/22	SP	DM
	647	S12/23	SP	DM
	648	S12/24	SP	GSM
	649	S12/26	SP	DM
	650	S12/27	SP	DM
	651	S12/28	SP	GSM
	652	S12/29	SP	GSM
	653	S12/30	SP	GS
36	654	S12/31	SP	GS
	655	S12/32	SP	GSM
	656	S12/33b	SP	GSM

JBF	BF	DIMENT	ARTIST	ENGRAVER
	657	S12/34	SP	GSM
	658	S12/35	SP	DM
	659	S12/36	SP	DM
	660	S12/39	SP	GSM
	661	S12/40	SP	DM
	662	S12/41	SP	CW
37	663	S12/42	SP	GSM
	664	S12/43	SP	DM
	665	S12/44	SP	DM
	666	S12/45	SP	GSM
	667	S12/46	SP	DM
p. 312	668	S12/47	SP	GSM
21	669	S12/48	SP	WT
	670	S12/49	SP	GS
38	671	S12/49a	SP	GS
	672	S12/52	SP	GSM
	673	S12/53	SP	DM
	674	TF1	SP	JG
16	675	TF3	SP	DM
18	676	TF5	SP	DM
	677	TF6	SP	DM
	678	TF7	SP	CW
	679	TF8	SP	JG
	680	TF9, 10, 11	SP	GSM
	681	TF13	SP	GS
	682	TF14	SP	GS
	683	TF15	SP	DM
	684	TF16	SP	GSM
	685	TF17	SP	DM
12	686	TF18	SP	CW
	687	TF19	SP	CW
	688	TF20	SP	GS
	689	TF22	SP	WT
17	690	TF24	SP	DM
	691	TF24a	SP	DM
	692	TF25	SP	GS
	693	TF26	SP	DM
	694	TF27	SP	DM
	695	TF28	SP	GS
	696	TF29	SP	GS
	697	TF30	SP	DM
14	698	TF31	SP	WT
	699	TF32	SP	WT
	700	TF34	SP	GS
	701	TF36	SP	CW
	702	TF37	SP	JG
	703	TF38	SP	DM
	704	TF39	SP	CW
	705	TF40	SP	DM
	706	TF41	SP	DM
	707	TF43	SP	GSM
	708	TF44	SP	GS
	709	TF45	SP	GSM
	710	TF46	SP	GSM
	711	TF47	SP	DM
	712	TF48	SP	JG
	713	TF49	SP	DM
	714	TF50	SP	DM
	715	TF51	SP	DM
	716	TF53	SP	DM
	717	TF54	SP	EW
	718	TF55, 56	SP	DM
	719	TF57	SP	WT
	720	TF58	SP	TS
	721	TF60	SP	DM
	722	TF61	SP	DM
	723	TF62	SP	DM
	724	TF63	SP	GSM
	725	TF64	SP	GSM
	726	TF65	SP	DM
13	727	TF66	SP	GS
	728	TF67	SP	DM
	729	TF68	SP	DM
15	730	TF69	SP	GSM
	731	TF70	SP	D
	732	TF71	SP	DM
	733	TF72	SP	DM
	734	TF73	SP	DM
19	735	TF74	SP	DM
	736	TF75	SP	WT
	737	TF76	SP	DM
	738	TF77	SP	GS
	739	A3/136	FPN	R. TALBOT AFTER GSM
p. 317	740	A4/192	FPN	R. HUGHES AFTER DM
	741	A7/324	FPN	R. HUGHES AFTER TS/DM
	742	NZ3/167	FPN	R. HUGHES AFTER GS
	743	TF23	SP	R. HUGHES AFTER DM

BIBLIOGRAPHY

Adams, B. 1986. *The Flowering of the Pacific* (London: Collins/British Museum Natural History)

Alecto Historical Editions. 1980–90. *Banks' Florilegium* (743 plates in 35 parts) (www.alecto-historical-editions.com)

Allan, H. H. 1982 [1961]. *Flora of New Zealand*. Vol. 1 (reprint) (Wellington, New Zealand: Government Printer)

Beaglehole, J. C. (ed.). 1955–69. *The Journals of Captain James Cook on his Voyages of Discovery*, 3 vols (Cambridge: Published for the Hakluyt Society)

—— 1963. *The Endeavour Journal of Joseph Banks 1768–1771*. 2 vols, 2nd ed. (Sydney: Public Library of New South Wales with Angus & Robertson)

Blunt, W. 1950. *The Art of Botanical Illustration* (London: Collins New Naturalist Series 14); rev. ed. 1994, W. T. Stearn (Woodbridge: Antique Collectors' Club)

—— and W. T. Stearn. 1973. *Captain Cook's Florilegium. A selection of engravings from the drawings of plants collected by Sir Joseph Banks and Daniel Solander on Captain Cook's first voyage to the islands of the Pacific* (London: Lion & Unicorn Press)

Britten, J. 1900. 'Robert Morgan', *Journal of Botany, British and Foreign* 38, 489–92

—— 1913. 'Bibliographical notes. LIII. John Frederick Miller and his 'Icones'', *Journal of Botany, British and Foreign* 51, 255–57

—— 1919. 'Bibliographical notes. LXXVIII. "John Frederick Miller and his Icones"', *Journal of Botany, British and Foreign* 57, 353

—— (ed.). 1905. *Illustrations of the Australian Plants Collected in 1770 during Captain Cook's Voyage round the World in H.M.S. Endeavour in 1768–71 by the Right Hon. Sir Joseph Banks and Daniel Solander* (London: British Museum (Natural History))

Carr, D. J. (ed.). 1983. *Sydney Parkinson. Artist of Cook's Endeavour Voyage* (London and Canberra: British Museum (Natural History) in association with Croom Helm)

Carter, H. B. 1988. *Sir Joseph Banks 1743–1820* (London: British Museum (Natural History))

Chambers, N. 2007. *Joseph Banks and the British Museum: The World of Collecting, 1770–1830* (London: Pickering & Chatto)

—— (ed.). 2000. *The Letters of Sir Joseph Banks: A Selection, 1768–1820* (London: Imperial College Press)

—— (ed.). 2007. *The Scientific Correspondence of Sir Joseph Banks, 1765–1820*, 6 vols (London: Pickering & Chatto)

—— (ed.). 2008. *The Indian and Pacific Correspondence of Sir Joseph Banks, 1768–1820. Volume 1. Letters 1768–1782* (London: Pickering & Chatto)

—— et al. 2016. *Endeavouring Banks: Exploring Collections from the Endeavour Voyage 1768–1771* (London: Paul Holberton Publishing; Seattle: University of Washington Press)

Chittenden, F. J. (ed.). 1951. *The Royal Horticultural Society Dictionary of Gardening*. 4 vols (Oxford: Clarendon Press)

Collingridge, V. 2002. *Captain Cook* (London: Ebury Press)

Cooper, W. (illustrated by W. T. Cooper). 2004. *Fruits of the Australian Tropical Rainforest* (Melbourne: Nokomis Editions)

Diment, J. A., C. J. Humphries, L. Newington and E. Shaughnessy. 1984. 'Catalogue of the natural history drawings commissioned by Joseph Banks on the *Endeavour* voyage 1768–1771 held in the British Museum (Natural History). Part I: Botany: Australia', *Bulletin of the British Museum (Natural History) Historical Series*, 11, 1–183

—— — J. R. Press, E. Shaughnessy and L. Newington. 1987. 'Catalogue of the natural history drawings commissioned by Joseph Banks on the *Endeavour* voyage 1768–1771 held in the British Museum (Natural History). Part 2: Botany: Brazil, Java, Madeira, New Zealand, Society Islands and Tierra Del Fuego', *Bulletin of the British Museum (Natural History) Historical Series*, 12, 1–200

Duyker, E. and P. Tingbrand (eds). 1995. *Daniel Solander. Collected Correspondence 1753–1782* (Melbourne: Melbourne University Press)

Flora of Australia. 1981–. (Melbourne: ABRS/CSIRO Australia), from 2016 online only

Gascoigne, J. 1994. *Joseph Banks and the English Enlightenment* (Cambridge: Cambridge University Press)

Harden, G. J. (ed.). 1990. *Flora of New South Wales*. Vol. 1 (Kensington NSW: New South Wales University Press)

—— 1992. *Flora of New South Wales*. Vol. 3 (Kensington NSW: New South Wales University Press)

—— 2002. *Flora of New South Wales*. Rev. ed., vol. 2 (Sydney: University of New South Wales Press)

Hawkesworth, J. 1773. *An Account of the Voyages Undertaken by the Order of His Present Majesty for Making Discoveries in the Southern Hemisphere…by Commodore Byron, Captain Carteret, Captain Wallis and Captain Cook…* 3 vols (London: W. Strahan and T. Cadell)

Henrey, B. 1975. *British Botanical and Horticultural Literature Before 1800*. 3 vols (London: Oxford University Press)

Hoare, M. E. 1982. *The Resolution Journal of Johann Reinhold Forster 1772–1775*. 4 vols (London: Hakluyt Society)

Huxley, A. (ed. in chief). 1992. *The New Royal Horticultural Dictionary of Gardening*. 4 vols (London: Macmillan; New York: Stockton Press)

Joppien, R. & B. Smith. 1985–87. *The Art of Captain Cook's Voyages*, 3 vols (New Haven and London: Yale University Press)

Mabberley, D. J. 1985. *Jupiter Botanicus: Robert Brown of the British Museum* (Braunschweig: J. Cramer; London: British Museum (Natural History))

—— 1992. *Tropical Rain Forest Ecology*. 2nd ed. (Glasgow and London: Blackie)

—— 1998. *Paradisus. Hawaiian Plant Watercolors by Geraldine King Tam* (Honolulu: Honolulu Academy of Arts)

—— 2013. 'Meliaceae'. *Flora of Australia* 26: 1–42 (Melbourne: ABRS/CSIRO Australia)

—— 2014. *Mabberley's Plant-book*. 3rd ed., 2nd reprint with corrections (Cambridge: Cambridge University Press); 4th ed., 2017, forthcoming

Moore, D. M. 1983. *Flora of Tierra del Fuego* (Oswestry: A. Nelson; St Louis: Missouri Botanical Garden)

Moorehead, A. 1966. *The Fatal Impact* (London: Hamish Hamilton; New York: Harper & Row)

O'Brian, P. 1987. *Joseph Banks: A Life* (Chicago: University of Chicago Press; London: Harvill)

Parkinson, S. 1783. *A Journal of a Voyage to the South Seas in His Majesty's Ship The Endeavour* (London: Stanfield Parkinson)

—— 1784. *A Journal of a Voyage to the South Seas in His Majesty's Ship The Endeavour* (London: Dilly, Phillips)

Press, J. R. and M. J. Short. 1994. *Flora of Madeira* (London: HMSO)

Smith, A. W. 1971. *A Gardener's Dictionary of Plant Names. A Handbook on the Origin and Meaning of Some Plant Names*. Rev. and enlarged by William T. Stearn, Isadore Leighton Lucie-Smith (London: Cassell)

Smith, B. 1960. *European Vision and the South Pacific 1768–1850* (Oxford: Oxford University Press)

Staples, G. W. and D. Herbst. 2005. *A Tropical Garden Flora: Plants Cultivated in the Hawaiian Islands and Other Tropical Places* (Honolulu: Bishop Museum)

Wheeler, J. R. (ed.), B. L. Rye, B. L. Koch and A. J. G. Wilson. 1992. *Flora of the Kimberley Region* (Como, Western Australia: Department of Conservation and Land Management)

Wilkins, G. L. 1955. 'A Catalogue and Historical Account of the Banks Shell Collection', *Bulletin of the British Museum (Natural History) Historical Series*, 1, no. 3, 69–119

Captions to plates on pages 312 and 317:

Page 312: *Taeniophyllum fasciola*: copper plate by Gabriel Smith, based on a finished watercolour by Sydney Parkinson dated 1769 of a specimen collected in the Society Islands (French Polynesia); BF 668; Diment SI2/47.

Page 317 (OPPOSITE): Five of the original Banks copper plates were lost. Alecto Historical Editions commissioned new plates from two banknote engravers at the Bank of England, who copied directly from black proofs made in the eighteenth century from the original plates. One of the modern engravings, by R. Hughes (1989), is shown here: *Xerochrysum bracteatum* (formerly *Helichrysum bracteatum*): modern line engraving after the lost original copper plate by Daniel Mackenzie, based on Frederick Nodder's 1779 watercolour, derived from Sydney Parkinson's drawing; BF 740; Diment A4/192. For a commentary on this plant, shown in another plate, see Pl. 92, p. 194.

ACKNOWLEDGMENTS

For help with identifications and finding germane literature, David Mabberley wishes to thank many people, in particular Greg Bourke (Mount Tomah, NSW), John Clarkson (Mariba, Queensland), Miguel Garcia (Sydney), Philip Garnock-Jones (Wellington, New Zealand), Mark Large (Auckland), Anthony Mitchell (Christchurch, New Zealand), Dhahara Ranatunga (Auckland War Memorial Museum) and Clarence Slockee (Sydney), but especially Andrew Drummond, who cheerfully endured yet another all-consuming project in our household.

The first edition of all 743 plants in Joseph Banks' Florilegium, printed from the original eighteenth-century engraved copper plates, was published in 35 Parts between 1980 and 1990 by Alecto Historical Editions, in association with the British Museum (Natural History).

www.alecto-historical-editions.com

Master printer: Edward Egerton-Williams

Proofing editors: Michael Barratt, Paul Brason

Handcolouring editors: Tussi Dunstall, Thomas Milne, Lisa Whelan

Printers and handcolourists: Carl Ansari, Russell Baker, Steve Barraclough, Michael Barrett, Carol Baxendale, Jon Berkeley, Aileen Beeston, Bridget Board, David Bowyer, Walter Bremner, Kenneth Bryce, Carmel Buckley, Gregory Burnet, Sue Callinan, Jonathan Cassidy, Paul Chamberlain, Sheila Christofides, David Costello, Paul Cyr, Adrian Davidson, Pierre Degryse, Tussi Dunstall, Karen Fiss, Judith Frost, Peter Goddard, Ramona Goodsall, Susan Harlock, Malcolm Humble, Vanessa Hunt, Delavar Karaien, Elizabeth Keyworth, Stefan Lenartowicz, Heather Libson, Karen Lightfoot, Michael Linfield, Isobel Loxton Knight, Kevin Malloy, Peter Mant, Carol Marshall, Catherine Naylor, Kenneth Oliver, Felicity O'Sullivan, Sarah Roberts, Gordon Robertson, Joanna Ryan, Martin Saull, Adrian Short, Richard Spare, Catherine Tirr, Jackie Wagg, Heather Walker, Brian Webb, Helen Wellard, Lisa Whelan, Debbie Williams

Plate restorers: Brian Baldwin, Harvey Brown, Delavar Karaien, Kevin Malloy

The botanical information was compiled with the cooperation of the British Museum (Natural History).

Editors: Judith Diment, Christopher Humphries

Nomenclature:* H. K. Airy Shaw, C. & W. Anderson, Patrick Brownsey, J. Camus, F. Raymond Fosberg, R. M. Harley, M. J. Huft, Charles Jarvis, A. C. Jermy, P. J. M. Maas, Donald McGillivray, David M. Moore, A. Paul, D. Philcox, John Robert Press, H. E. Robinson, Marie-Hélène Sachet, G. G. G. J. van Steenis, P. Stevens, J. Wurdack

Research: Elaine Shaughnessy

* For Alecto Historical Editions. Some botanical names have been updated in the present edition.

SOURCES OF ILLUSTRATIONS

A CHART of the WORLD

Exhibiting the Discoveries made by Captn. JAMES COOK